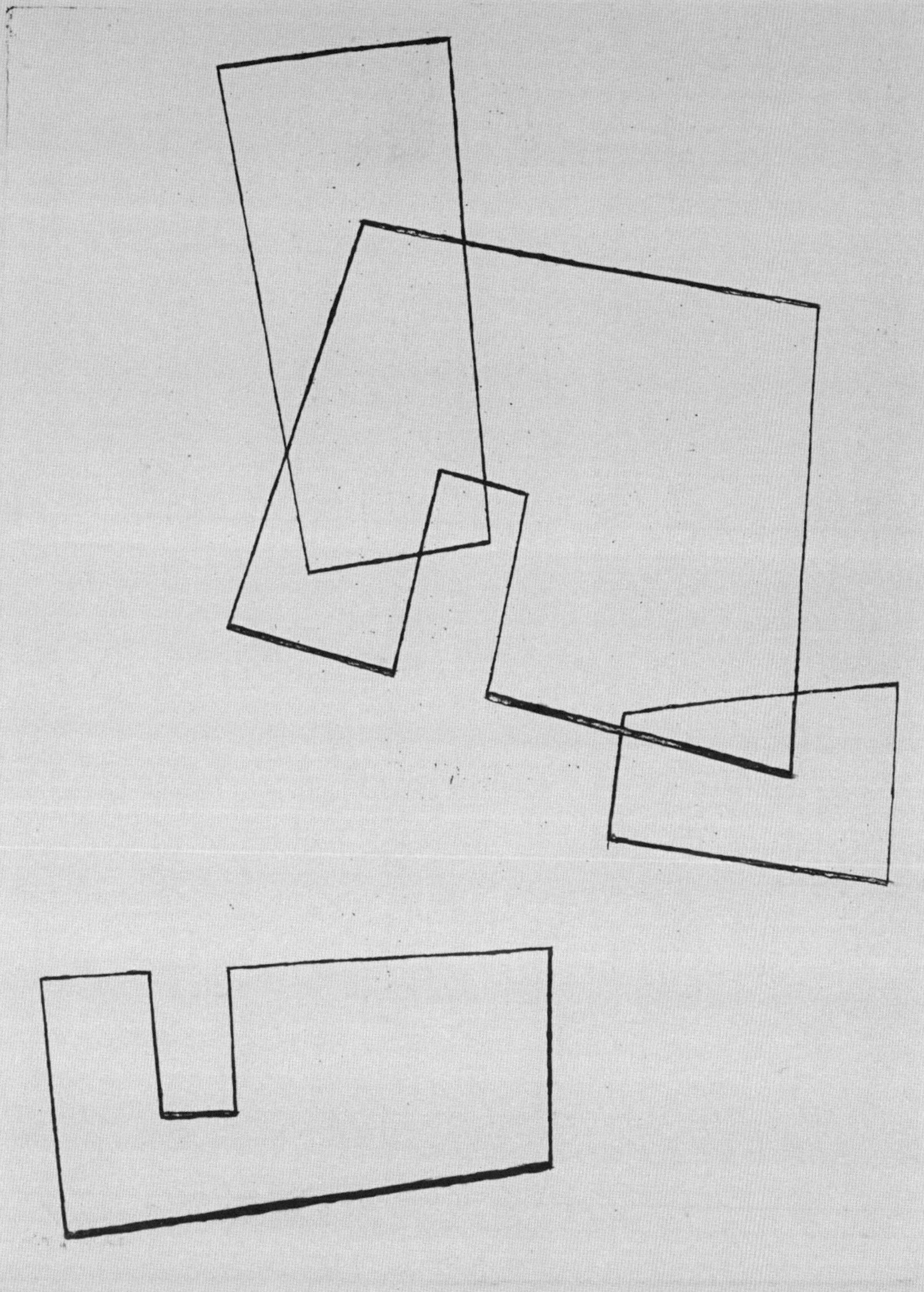

R Adams.

Artists Proof

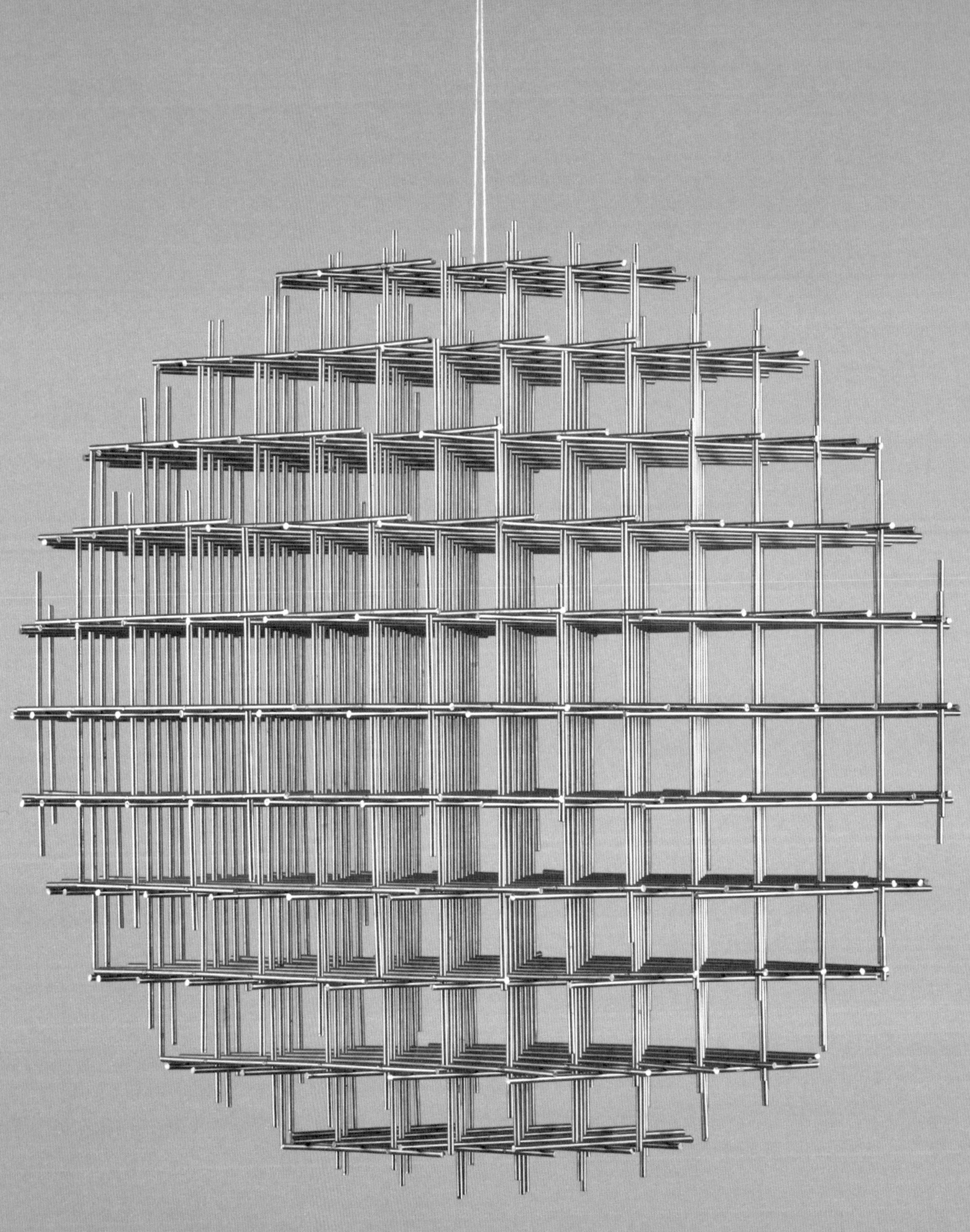

rhythm & geometry

constructivist art in Britain since 1951

EDITED BY **TANIA MOORE** & **CALVIN WINNER**

This publication accompanies the exhibition:
Rhythm & Geometry: Constructivist art in Britain since 1951
Sainsbury Centre, 2021–2022

First published in Great Britain by
Sainsbury Centre for Visual Arts
Norwich Research Park
University of East Anglia
Norwich, NR4 7TJ
sainsburycentre.ac.uk

British Library Cataloguing-in-Publication Data.
A catalogue record is available from the British Library.

ISBN 978-1-9161336-8-6

Editors: Tania Moore & Calvin Winner
Book Design: Johnson Design
Copyeditor and index: Brenda Stones
Printed and bound in the UK by Page Bros Group Ltd., Norwich

First edition

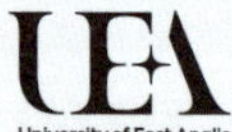

SAINSBURY CENTRE   **UEA** University of East Anglia

ILLUSTRATIONS
Front cover: **Mary Webb**
Fritton
1971
Oil on canvas
Sainsbury Centre

Inside covers: **Lygia Clark**
LC2 and LC3
1969
Aluminium
Sainsbury Centre

Inside gatefold: **Rana Begum**
No. 670 Mesh Installation
2016
Powder-coated galvanised steel
Long loan from the artist

Page 1: **Robert Adams**
Rectangular Forms
1955
Engraving on paper
Sainsbury Centre

Page 2: **François Morellet**
Sphère-trame
1962
Stainless steel
Sainsbury Centre

constructivism at the sainsbury centre

Tania Moore

FROM THE TURN OF THE TWENTIETH CENTURY, there have been many strands and definitions of abstraction which morph and re-emerge over time. *Rhythm and Geometry* follows just one of these strands: that of Constructivist art. Constructivist art is a form of geometric abstraction, often built up through systematic processes or new approaches to materials. Rather than creating the illusion of space, Constructivist artists create physical objects that have a new relationship to space. The varied artworks presented in this exhibition and publication under this umbrella term span painting, sculpture, printmaking, mobiles, reliefs, kinetic and participatory art made since 1951.

Including over 120 objects, this is the first major exhibition on this subject since the Sainsbury Centre's exhibition *Constructed* in 2008 and *Elements of Abstraction: Space, line and interval in modern British art* at Southampton City Art Gallery in 2005. The Southampton exhibition spanned the years from the inter-war period to the 1960s, and a book was published alongside it.[1] *Rhythm and Geometry* starts and ends later, covering the years 1951 to 2021, and reconsiders the narrative to bring in contemporary works and new artists. This publication demonstrates how the dialogue between artists has allowed the thread of Constructivist art to continue and develop over these seven decades.

Constructivism emerged in Russia in 1915. Painter and architect Vladimir Tatlin (1885–1953) and artist and graphic designer Alexander Rodchenko (1891–1956) developed this new style of pure, abstract art that was appropriate for a modern industrial society. Along with artists such as Varvara Stepanova (1894–1958), Liubov Popova (1889–1924) and El Lissitzky (1890–1941), they aimed to design a new world for the masses. For them, their art was political and would further the Communist revolution: art was to be part of everyday experience and useful to society. In this, their practice may at times be closer to a contemporary definition of design, as they worked variously in the spheres of architecture, graphic design, fashion and product design.

A parallel movement emerged in the Netherlands between 1917 and 1931. De Stijl, meaning 'The Style', was named after a magazine first published by Theo van Doesburg (1883–1931) in 1917. Founded by painter Piet Mondrian (1872–1944) and artist and architect van Doesburgh, De Stijl denoted painting and architecture with pared back grid-like geometries based on vertical and horizontal lines and a reduced palette of black, white and the primary colours. In 1925 van Doesburg introduced the diagonal line to his work, causing Mondrian to break from the movement. The influence of Constructivism and De Stijl was felt internationally, with active pockets of artists emerging in Germany – particularly surrounding the Bauhaus School – and France, Brazil and America.

As a result of the Second World War, widespread displacement across Europe led to the arrival of many important artists in Britain, who helped to disseminate theories about abstract art. Naum Gabo (1890–1977) introduced Constructivism to Britain when he arrived in London in 1936. In Russia, Gabo had developed his version of Constructivism, which was less political than that of Tatlin and Rodckenko. Rather than focusing on art as utilitarian, Gabo produced sculpture which enclosed space, considering its relationship to the environment. Along with Gabo, Piet Mondrian lived in London for a few crucial years between 1938 and 1941. German architect Walter Gropius (1883–1969), who had founded the Bauhaus School, was in London between 1934 and 1937. Hungarian artist László Moholy-Nagy (1895–1946) and Hungarian artist and designer Marcel Breuer (1902–1981), both of whom had taught at the Bauhaus, spent a period in London from 1935 to 1937. At the outbreak of the Second World War, when many left Britain, Gabo moved to St Ives where he lived alongside abstract artists including Barbara Hepworth (1903–1975), Ben Nicholson (1894–1982) and Margaret Mellis (1914–2009). Hepworth and Nicholson were engaged in Constructivist ideas alongside other interests, but in St Ives Mellis was rare in working in a Constructivist idiom throughout her career.

Due to its long international legacy, Constructivist art does not have a clear definition, and different terminology has been employed to denote various groups or distinctions.

← Jean Spencer
Square Relief 4 (detail)
1968
Wood with PVA
Sainsbury Centre

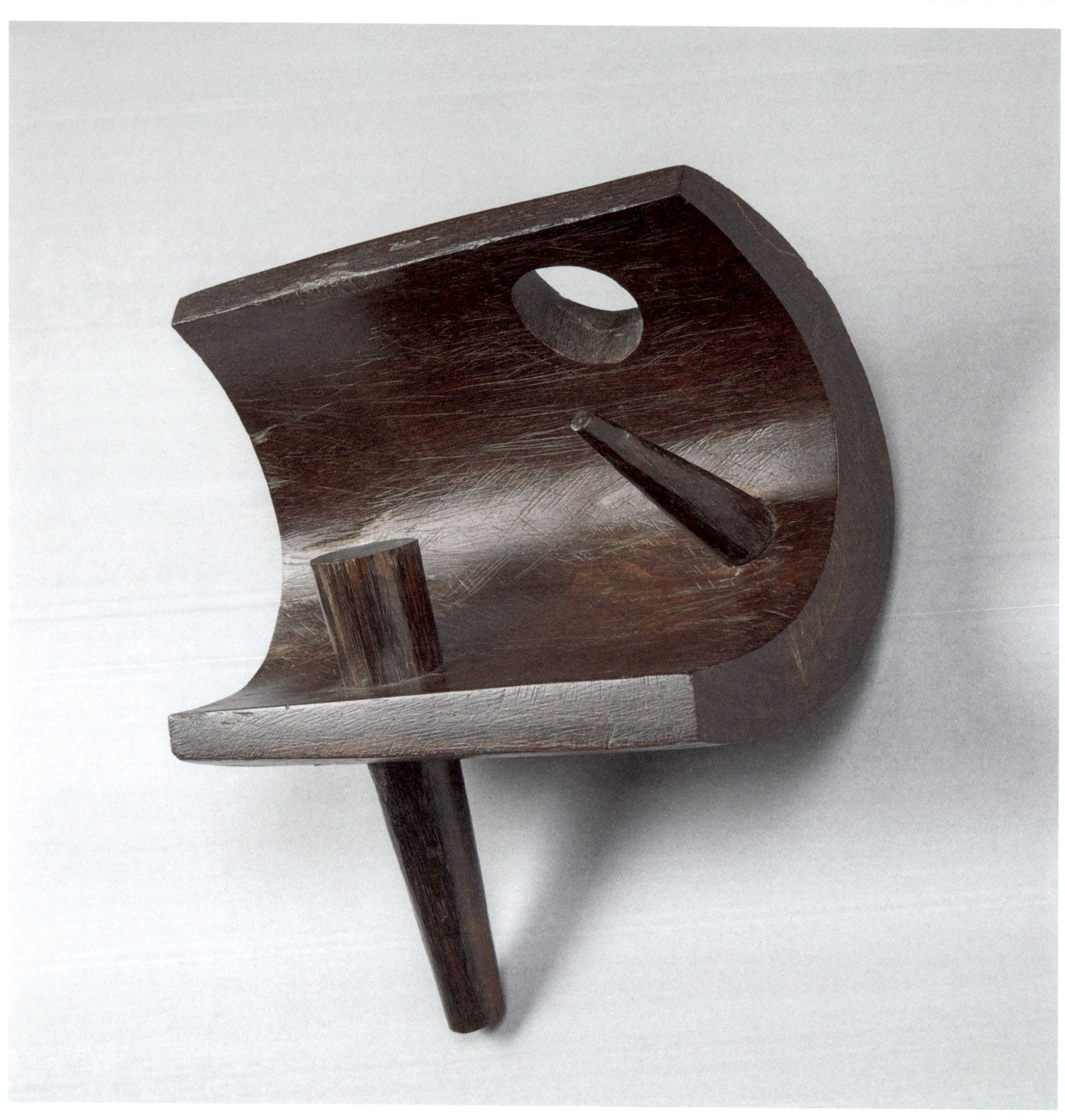

↑ Robert Adams
Pierced Relief
1952
Mahogany
Sainsbury Centre

The term Concrete art was coined by Theo van Doesburg in his 1930 *Manifesto of Concrete Art*, which is examined by Andrew Bick later in this publication. The term has since been used to encompass some Constructivist traditions internationally, particularly in Switzerland with regard to the work of artist Max Bill (1908–1994). In this exhibition and book, we use the term Constructivist to encompass numerous artistic traditions, opening up the definition to invite new artists into the narrative.

A number of artists have formed groups to demonstrate a shared commitment to geometric abstract art. Between the 1950s and 1990s in Britain were the Constructionists, the Systems Group and Countervail. The Constructionists worked in London in the 1950s making predominantly three-dimensional constructed work. The Systems group worked from the 1960s, primarily in painting. Following this, Countervail were an all-woman group working in the early 1990s. Although these terms are not used universally, we use Constructionist and Systems throughout this book for clarity and to distinguish these particular threads. Despite these factions, there was much collaboration amongst artists and across generations, as explored by Jon Wood in his chapter on Construction and Collaboration. Some artists also worked with architects. A pivotal moment for this was the groundbreaking exhibition *This is Tomorrow* at the Whitechapel Gallery in 1956, in which groups of artists and architects collaborated to make dynamic work together. Calvin Winner's chapter focuses on the Constructivist artists that were part of this exhibition. Finally, Andrew Bick demonstrates how much of the legacy of Constructivism has been passed on via teaching, demonstrating how the Constructivist art of the 1950s still impacts on some artists working today. Together, these chapters aim to explore the dynamic and enduring legacy of Constructivist art in Britain, bringing together various strands that have formerly been considered independently, such as the Constructionist and Systems groups.

The international activities of artists working in the Constructivist tradition were brought together in the collection of the University of East Anglia, amassed from 1968 and absorbed into the Sainsbury Centre when it opened a decade later. UEA collected abstract art and modernist design, including furniture and architectural models. Geometric abstraction was considered to be an appropriate theme for the collection of a young university, housed in a new modernist campus.[2] The first curator of the collection was Peter Lasko, Professor of History of Art at UEA. He was supported by Alastair Grieve, who later took over as the collection's curator. Grieve published some of the most important texts about Constructivism in Britain, including the first in-depth study of a tight-knit group of artists. *Constructed Abstract Art in England: A Neglected Avant-Garde* focuses on Robert Adams (1917–1984), Stephen Gilbert (1910–2007), Adrian Heath (1920–1992), Anthony Hill (1930–2020), Kenneth Martin (1905–1984), Mary Martin (1907–1969), Victor Pasmore (1908–1998), Gillian Wise (1936–2020) and John Ernest (1922–1994).[3] These artists comprise the core of the group self-termed the Constructionists.

In 1968, to mark the beginnings of the new collection, Alastair Grieve curated the exhibition *Art and the Machine* in the UEA Library. This wide-reaching exhibition demonstrated the effect of industry and technology on art and design from the time of the Great Exhibition in 1851 to the contemporary. Almost the entire collection was exhibited at the Museum of Modern Art, Oxford in 1975. The exhibition was retrospectively described by Grieve:

> The Collection was favourably received there and its homogeneity was very striking. The individual parts came together. One work led to another. There was a shared concern among all the artists represented for harmonious proportions, for real rather than illusionist space, for simple shapes and basic colours held in balance.[4]

Alastair Grieve was in close contact with the artists of the period, often buying work directly from them. He formed enduring relationships with the artists working in Britain, resulting in close studies of their work;

he published monographs on Victor Pasmore and Anthony Hill and compiled the catalogue raisonné of Robert Adams as well as survey books on Constructivism.[5] Grieve also had close contact with Joyce and Michael Morris, two private collectors who were themselves building an impressive collection of art in the Constructivist tradition. They were alumni of UEA and bequeathed their collection to the university in 1984. This was coordinated by former Head of Learning at the Sainsbury Centre, Veronica Sekules, who fostered the relationship with the Morrises and who also acquired many other important works for the collection. Joyce Morris was an educationalist who pioneered the teaching of phonics, which she disseminated through influential books and BBC television series.[6] It was Michael Morris who studied abstract art intently and engaged in correspondence with many of the artists.

The Morris bequest, consisting of over 200 works, was a major collection of post-war art by British and international artists working in the field of abstract and Constructed art. The acquisition was overseen by Calvin Winner, who led the project to retrieve the collection and associated archive. The bequest includes numerous works by the aforementioned Constructionists. These are John Ernest (five works), Stephen Gilbert (one work), Anthony Hill and his alias Achill Redo (twenty-three), Kenneth Martin (eleven), Mary Martin (six) and Gillian Wise (five). Significantly, it includes an important and unrivalled group of works by Robert Adams of twenty-eight sculptures and reliefs, seven works on paper and a textile. In addition to these were works by their international contemporaries working in abstraction, including Yaacov Agam (b.1928), Charles Biederman (1906–2004), Eduardo Chillida (1924–2002) and Sonia Delaunay (1885–1979).

Since 2020, an extensive conservation project has taken place to repair, clean and preserve many of the artworks. The project was undertaken and managed by Conservator Maria Ledinskaya, who has prepared the works of art for exhibition and publication. Along with the Morris bequest came approximately 400 books largely focused on abstraction, and thousands of archival items including journals, cuttings and photographs. The archive demonstrates Michael Morris's unwavering commitment to the study of abstract art. Many of the books are filled with intricate annotations demonstrating how closely he was studying them and deducing his own theories. He was in direct correspondence with many artists; in particular, numerous letters from Anthony Hill demonstrate their friendship. The different aliases Hill used to address letters to Joyce and Michael Morris included: 'Drs Rhoas 'n' Jaspa Morrie' at 'Jingelbells Court'; 'Docs Florent Mike Morri and Georg Wallys-Mgoo' at 'The Society for Ascriptics'; and 'Prof Dok. Fritz Moritz, Ethnoaesthetitian'. The curious letters are filled with sketches and signed by variations on Hill's own alias, Achill Redo, which he used for the Dadaist strand of his work.

Michael Morris extended his meticulous theoretical thinking on abstraction to his PhD in Experimental Aesthetics that he completed in 1957.[7] He wanted to inquire into the theory that there are universal rules for composition, which would suggest that the most 'pleasing' composition is the most artistic. He bought a 1953 print by Kenneth Martin titled *Lino Print (Red and Black)* and made a facsimile of it in order to separate the compositional elements of the four black rectangles and two red rectangles. He asked participants to position them into their preferred composition. The variations in results within the experiment and from the original work of art meant that Michael Morris deduced that there are no overriding compositional rules that relate to perception.[8] *Lino Print (Red and Black)* was one of the works of art that were given to the Sainsbury Centre as part of the Morris bequest.

The scope of *Rhythm and Geometry* – to focus on Constructivist art in Britain since 1951 – has been defined predominantly due to the strength of this area in the bequest from Joyce and Michael Morris. This is the first time

→ Michael Morris' PhD experiment based on a facsimile of Kenneth Martin's *Lino Print (Red and Black)*.

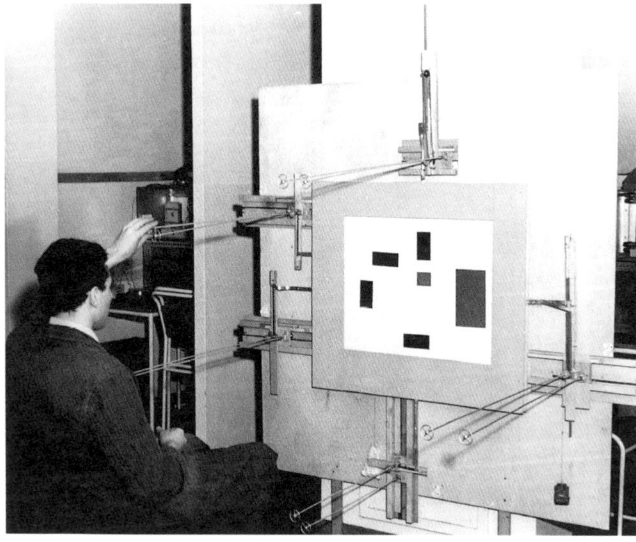

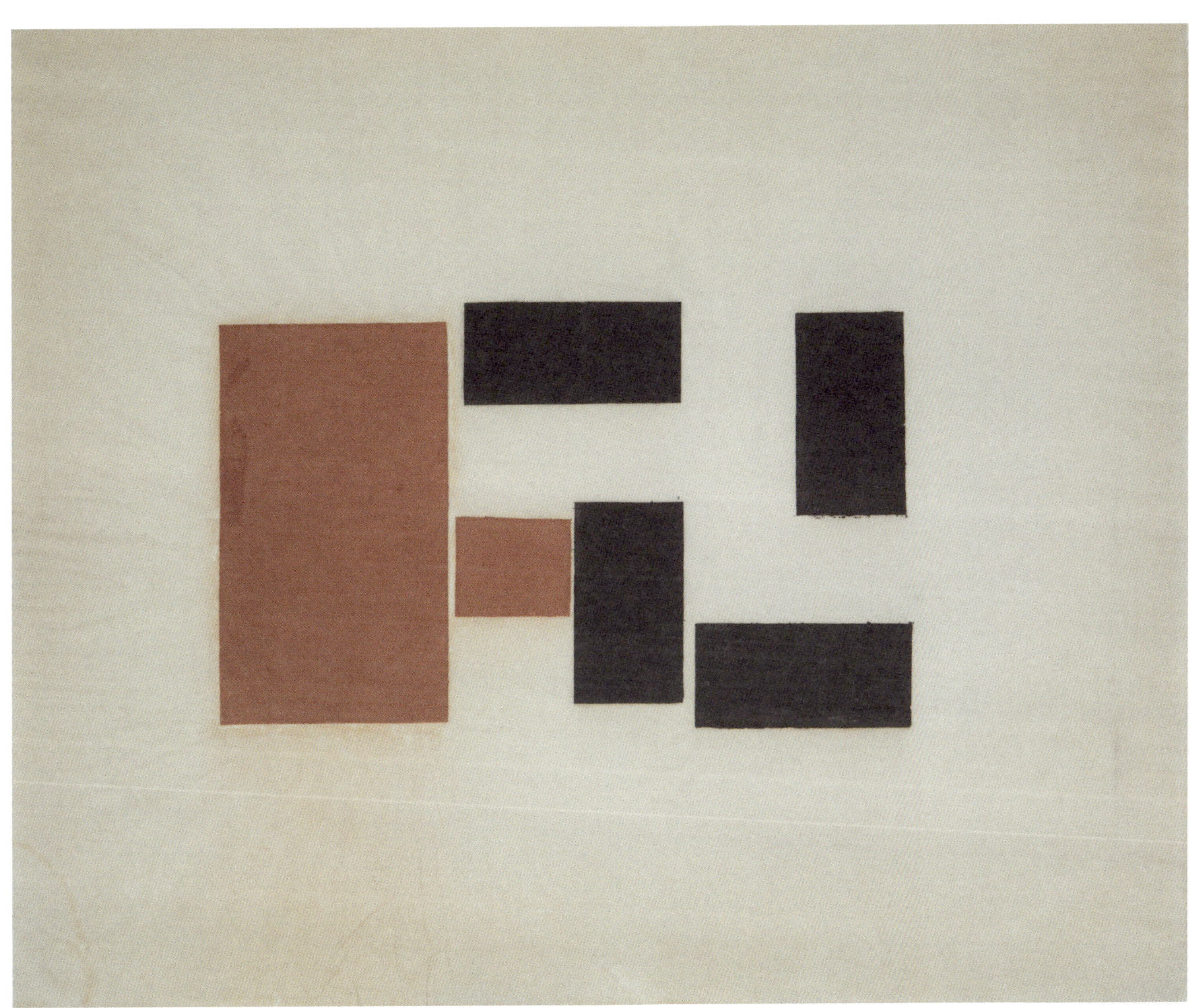

↑ Kenneth Martin
Lino Print (Red and Black)
1953
Lino print on paper
Sainsbury Centre

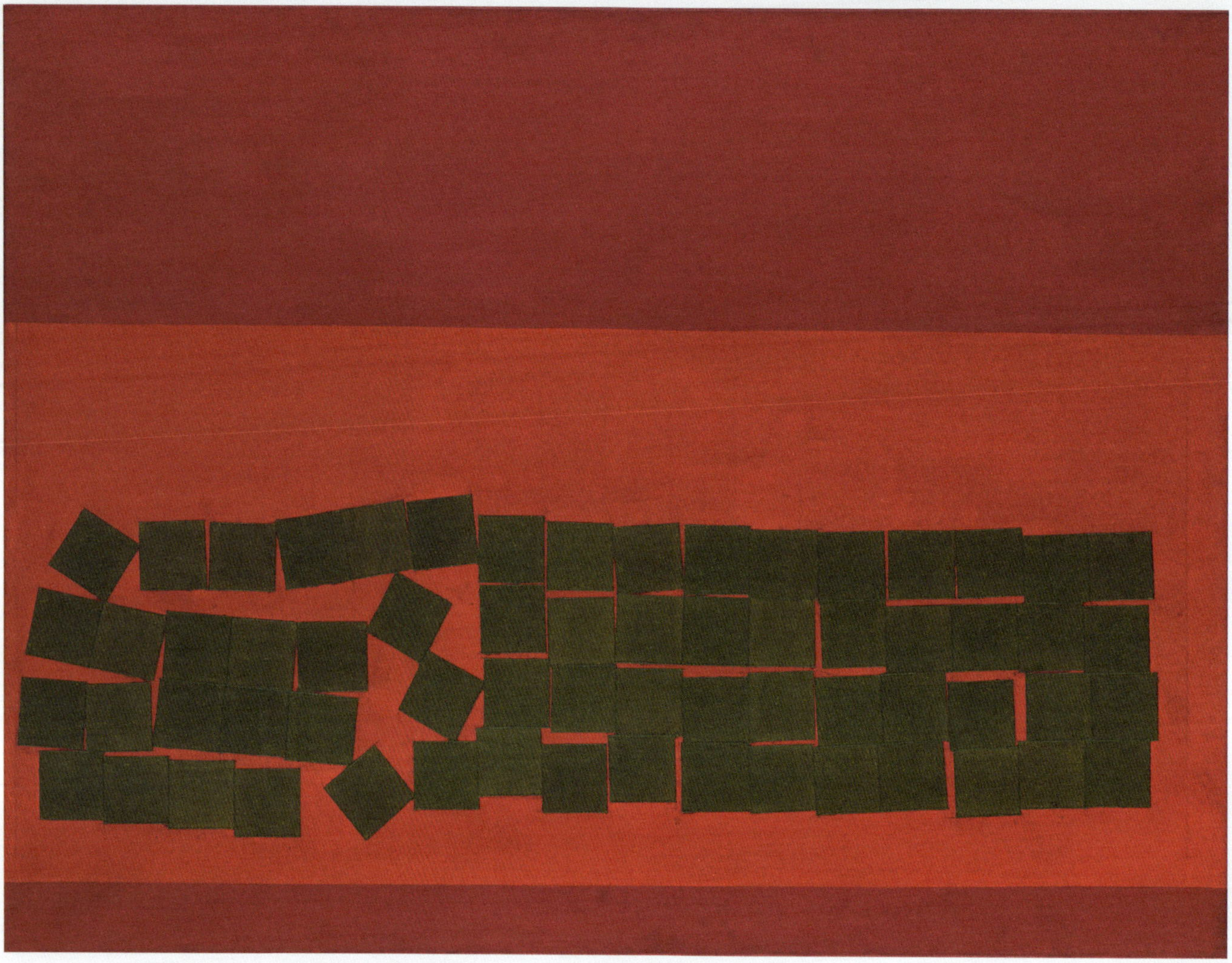

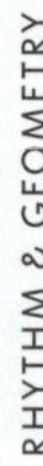

↑ **Wilhelmina Barns-Graham**
Olive Green Squares on Vermillion
1968
Oil on canvas
Sainsbury Centre

some of the artworks have been exhibited and published as part of the Sainsbury Centre collection: about half of the exhibition is from this bequest. The other half are the works that were acquired by the UEA from the 1960s or works that have subsequently been acquired by the Sainsbury Centre. The UEA had a small acquisitions fund of £10,000 in 1968, which had been spent by 1973. Soon after, in 1975, Robert and Lisa Sainsbury gave £3,000 to the university to acquire work in this area. Acquisitions have continued to come in since, via gifts or grants. Thanks to all these acquisitions, the Sainsbury Centre now has the most significant collection of Constructivist art in the country.

Natalie Dower (b.1931) gave three important works in 2020: a painting, a relief and a sculpture. The three works together demonstrate her range, as she was unique amongst her Systems peers in working across sculpture and painting. Some of the most contemporary works to come into the collection are by Rana Begum (b.1977) and Lubna Chowdhary (b.1964). The Sainsbury Centre purchased a 2016 relief by Begum in 2019, *No. 684 L Fold*, with support from the Art Fund, the V&A Purchase Grant Fund and the Sainsbury Centre Founding Friends. Two works by Chowdhary from her *Switch* series, *Series 2: Number 2* and *Series 2: Number 4*, were purchased in 2021 thanks to the Art Fund New Collecting Award. Also in 2021 we received an important painting from the Wilhelmina Barns-Graham Trust, *Olive Green Squares on Vermillion* (1968). Scottish artist Barns-Graham (1912–2004) moved to St Ives in 1940 where she worked alongside what has become known as the St Ives School, a strand of abstraction rooted in landscape. The addition of her work to the Sainsbury Centre collection allows us to celebrate her important place in abstraction in Britain. By acquiring work by more women artists into the collection, we can now represent a wider breadth of abstraction.

All exhibitions and books have to be selective, and there will always be artists who could (and probably should) have been included – all the more so when working with a single collection. However, the consistent thread running through *Rhythm and Geometry* demonstrates the interconnected thinking when building these collections: one at a university and museum, and the other a private collection. It is rare to be able to produce such a consistent exhibition from a single collection, and it is to the credit of such pioneering and dedicated curators and collectors that we are able to do so. We believe that *Rhythm and Geometry* celebrates the major makers of Constructivist art in Britain over the last seventy years and demonstrates its living legacy to the present day. Moreover, we firmly believe that the Constructivist ethos will continue into the future and be a continuing area for growth in the collection at the Sainsbury Centre. This exhibition and publication are just one combined element of a sustained area of research, and there will be more to follow. ◻

ENDNOTES

1   Alan Fowler and Brandon Taylor, *Elements of Abstraction: space, line and interval in modern British art* (Southampton: Southampton City Art Gallery, 2005).

2   Alastair Grieve, 'A Retrospective View of the University Art Collection', in *The University of East Anglia Collection of Abstract and Constructivist Art, Architecture and Design* (Norwich: University of East Anglia, 1994), p.7.

3   Alastair Grieve, *Constructed Abstract Art in England: A Neglected Avant-Garde* (New Haven and London: Yale University Press, 2005).

4   Alastair Grieve, 'A Retrospective View of the University Art Collection', in *The University of East Anglia Collection of Abstract and Constructivist Art, Architecture and Design* (Norwich: University of East Anglia, 1994), p.7.

5   Alastair Grieve, *Victor Pasmore: Writings and Interviews* (London: Tate Publishing, 2010); Alastair Grieve, *Anthony Hill: A Retrospective Exhibition* (London: Arts Council of Great Britain, 1983); Alastair Grieve, *The Sculpture of Robert Adams* (London: Lund Humphries, 1992) and Grieve (2005).

6   BBC *Look and Read* from 1967, BBC *Words and Pictures* from 1970, and the *Language in Action* series (1974–83).

7   Michael Morris, 'A Study of Some Hypothesis in Experimental Aesthetics: A thesis submitted for the degree of doctor of philosophy in the University of London, Birkbeck College', June 1957.

8   The experiment is summarised in R.W. Pickford, *Psychology and Visual Aesthetics* (London: Hutchinson Education Ltd, 1972), pp.34–35.

geometry

rhythm &

constructivist art in Britain since 1951

Tania Moore

IN 1951, A NEW GROUP of artists emerged who took on the Constructivist tradition more than anyone in Britain before. Their new style came at a vibrant time for the arts and culture in Britain, during a period of rebuilding and celebration after the Second World War. In the summer of 1951, the Festival of Britain was staged across the country, pitched as 'a tonic to the nation' and to promote British arts and industry. In the same year, Victor Pasmore (1908–1998) and Mary Martin (1907–1969) made their first reliefs, Kenneth Martin (1905–1984) his first mobile, and the first exhibition dedicated purely to abstract art since before the war was staged at the Artists' International Association.

With this moment came debate about the fundamental principles of abstraction, as artists asked not only what abstract art is, but also what it can be. On 14 March 1950, 'the strange case of abstract art' was debated by a group of artists, art historians and architects at the Institute of Contemporary Arts.[1] First of all, they grappled with the term itself, as it had been used both for art that is abstracted from reality and for art that is entirely non-representational. Two of the participants in the debate were Kenneth Martin and Victor Pasmore, who were at the forefront of Constructivist art as it was developing in Britain. The Constructivist tradition comes under the 'non-representational' definition, and it was this that was at the cusp of a resurgence in Britain. Martin's and Pasmore's comments demonstrate the fundamental aims of their art, which differed from the views of some they were debating. Martin believed that 'abstract art was one of the ways in which artists were at present trying to get down to the basis of the human imagination', and echoing this sentiment was Pasmore who explained that 'contemporary art was trying to get down to fundamental principles, both spiritual and material'.[2]

1951 therefore marked not only a shift in the way in which artists were making but also in which they were thinking. This essay presents this shift and the subsequent evolution of Constructivist art up to the present day. Three thematic sections mark distinct strands encompassed by the term. Presented chronologically, they indicate the ways in which Constructivist art has evolved and changed. Chance and Order looks at the artists from the 1950s working with systematic processes or with rigid geometries, including the artists studied by Alastair Grieve as set out in the introduction to this book.[3] Movement and Participation charts the development of participatory and kinetic art practice in the 1960s. Finally, Colour and Rhythm explores the painting and printmaking in geometric abstract styles from the late 1960s onwards when colour was embraced. This moment of colour in the 1960s has been presented recently in the Arts Council exhibition and publication *Kaleidoscope: Colour and Sequence in 1960s British Art*.[4] Often these aspects of Constructivist art have been considered independently; by exploring them together here, this essay aims to demonstrate the consistent thread running across these art forms and decades.

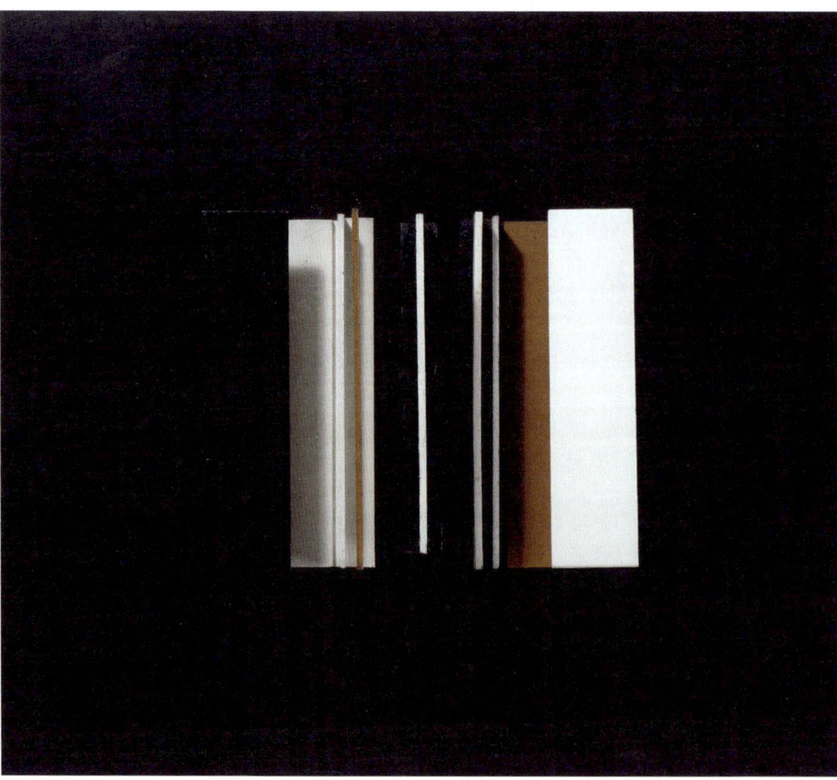

← John Ernest
Mosaic Relief III (detail)
1964
Aluminium and Formica on
cellulose-sprayed board
Sainsbury Centre

→ Victor Pasmore
Transparent Relief Construction
in Black, White and Ochre
1956–57
Plywood, paint and PMMA
Sainsbury Centre

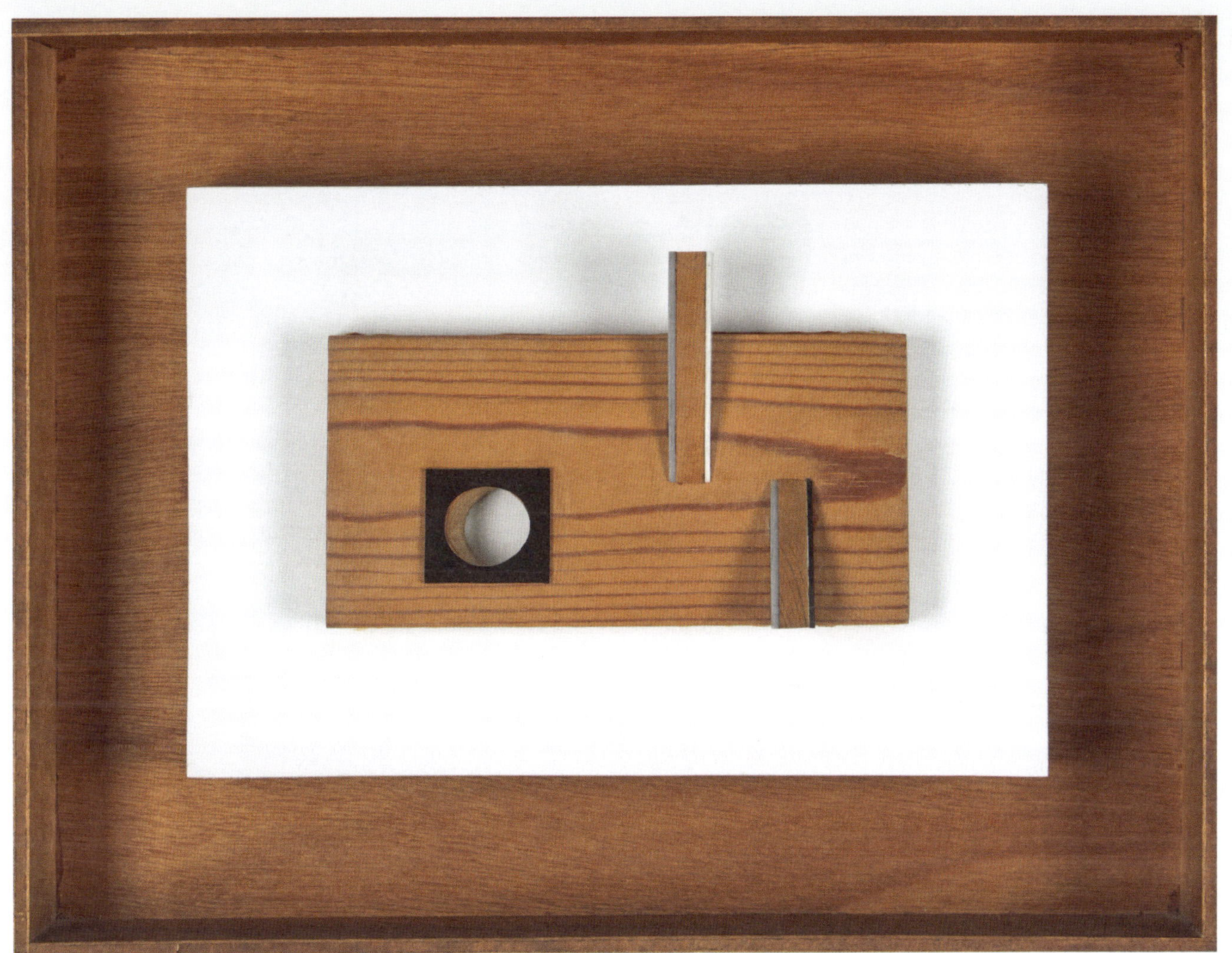

↑ **Mary Martin**
Pierced Relief
1959
Wood and Perspex
Sainsbury Centre

1951 in Britain was a period of austerity and rebuilding after the war. Whilst rationing stayed in place until 1954, the late 1950s and '60s saw an increase in optimism and prosperity. At face value, the austere and monochrome Constructivist work of the 1950s in contrast with the colourful abstract work of the 1960s presented in the following pages may seem to be reflective of this social situation. Lynda Nead argues in *The Tiger in the Smoke* that the relevance of colour in art and popular culture was tied to the politics of the post-war context. She describes the Festival of Britain as an 'infusion of colour into a gloomy and shabby landscape'.[5] However, that is not to say that the artists working in monochrome in the 1950s were doing so without optimism. They had ambitious aims for the place of their work in the rebuilding of Britain. Some went on to work with architects or to carry out large-scale commissions, but on any scale they were conceiving how their work could relate to daily life. These overt political associations may have dropped off into the 1960s, but there remained consistent threads running across generations, as is made clear by Lisa Tickner in her study of the 1960s, *London's New Scene*.[6]

The shift in Victor Pasmore's art from the figurative to the abstract in the years around 1947 marked a moment of change for art in Britain. In 1948, Pasmore had an exhibition at the Redfern Gallery, London: *Abstract and other paintings* spanning 1928 to 1948, in which seven of the twenty paintings were abstract. The following year, his exhibition at the same gallery, *Recent Paintings 1948–1949*, included all abstract paintings. Pasmore's 1950 exhibition, *New Paintings*, included all abstract works, although some had titles that suggested natural phenomena, which were later changed. For example, *Square Motif, Red and Mustard. Moonrise* (1950) became *Rectangular Motif in Red and Mustard*. After seeing the exhibition catalogue for his 1950 exhibition, artist Ben Nicholson (1894–1982) wrote to Pasmore from St Ives and they met in London soon after. Nicholson had been at the centre of abstraction since before the War, first in London then in St Ives, and his influence can be seen in some of Pasmore's early abstract

works. In 1951 Pasmore made his first constructed relief. These first reliefs were in wood and collage, before he moved on to glass and Perspex with wood, which offered variations in translucency. He exhibited eight reliefs in plywood, plastic and aluminium at the Redfern in 1952.

Also in 1951, Mary Martin made her first abstract relief and her husband, Kenneth Martin, made his first mobile. Both these artists had also formerly been figurative painters, and had arrived at abstraction in the late 1940s. Pasmore and the Martins developed their form of abstraction through close dialogue with each other. Whilst Pasmore used an informal geometry, Kenneth and Mary Martin tended towards the grid; however, their reliefs and mobiles have a number of characteristics in common. They were constructed – through the assembling of material – but also in the way they built up form through repetitions of rectangles, squares and lines. Moreover, they related to the environment in a way their paintings had not: the artists were now considering how their work interacts with space.

Thus gathered a small but active number of artists who began to work in these new ways. Alongside Pasmore, Mary and Kenneth Martin were Robert Adams (1917–1984), Adrian Heath (1920–1992), Anthony Hill (1930–2020) and Gillian Wise (1936–2020). These artists exhibited and published together and collectively described themselves as 'Constructionists'. In this, they gave themselves an identity that was closely tied to, but distinct from, the Russian Constructivist artists that had preceded them. Constructivism had its origins in Russia in 1915 with the utopian and pioneering work of Vladimir Tatlin (1885–1953) and Alexander Rodchenko (1891–1956), who wanted their art to reflect the modern industrial world. The Constructionists found the term they chose as their moniker in Charles Biederman's (1906–2004) *Art as the Evolution of Visual Knowledge*, an expansive book covering art from the palaeolithic age to contemporary forms of abstraction at its publication in 1948.[7] Biederman used the term Constructionist throughout his book when describing the Constructivist styles associated with the Russians Tatlin and Rodchenko

→ **Kenneth Martin** (1905–1984)
Screw Mobile
1953
Brass and mild steel
Sainsbury Centre

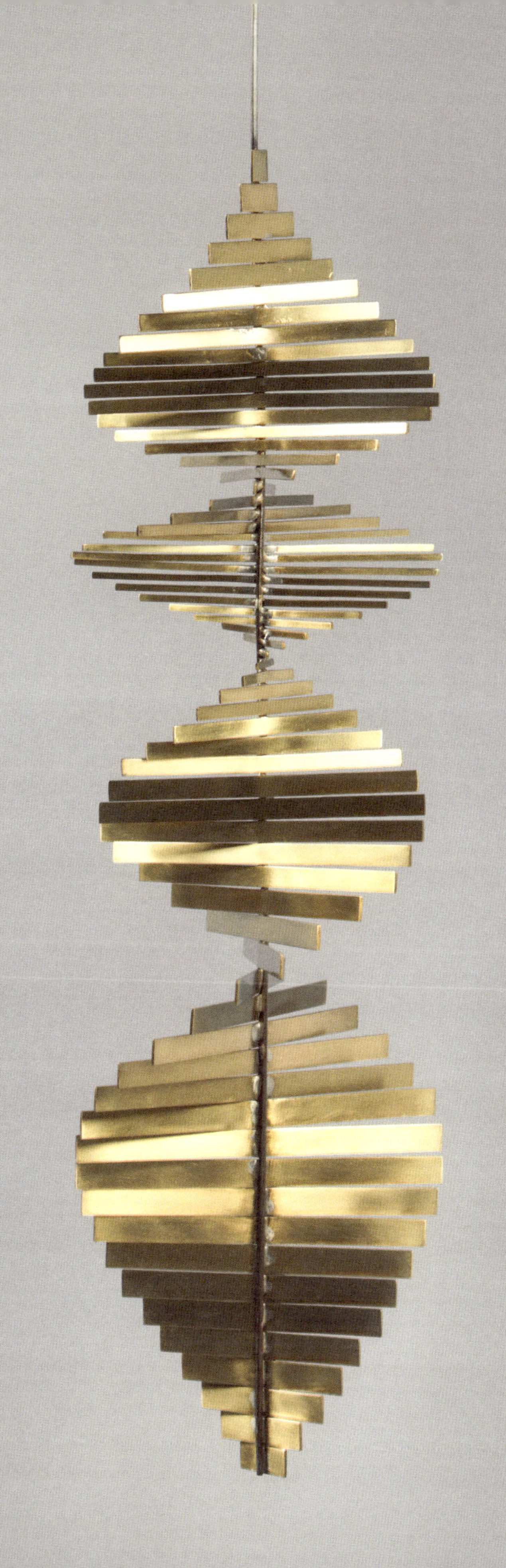

and the artists that continued their legacy including Naum Gabo (1890–1977) and Antoine Pevsner (1884–1962) who had brought the style from Russia to Britain.

American Constructivist artist Biederman was of great influence on the Constructionists. They looked to Biederman's work and writings as a guide more than the British abstractionists before them. In the interwar period, a group of artists had gathered their writings and works in a single publication devoted to abstraction. *Circle: International Survey of Constructive Art* (1937) was edited by Naum Gabo, Ben Nicholson and architect Leslie Martin (1908–1999), and designed by Barbara Hepworth (1903–1975).[8] The book included texts by these and other artists working in abstract styles, including László Moholy-Nagy (1895–1946), Henry Moore (1898–1986) and Piet Mondrian (1872–1944), and modernist architects such as Le Corbusier (1887–1965) and Walter Gropius (1883–1969). Although published in Britain, the book included only a handful of British artists. Naum Gabo was the driver of Constructivism in Britain before the Second World War. He had emigrated from Russia where he had written 'The Realistic Manifesto', which was co-signed by his brother Antoine Pevsner in 1920. Their Manifesto differed from that of Vladimir Tatlin, pioneer of Constructivism, for whom art was political. Instead of reinventing society, Gabo and Pevsner wanted to reconceive the art object:

> Space and time are re-born to us today.
> Space and time are the only forms on which life is built and hence art must be constructed.[9]

Whilst Gabo's works were consistently constructed from rods, enclosing and defining space, the work of the few British artists involved in *Circle* remained closer to representation: still lifes in the case of Nicholson, and the human or organic with Hepworth. Most of the artists associated with *Circle* left London during the Second World War. Many left the UK altogether, and Nicholson, Hepworth and Gabo relocated to St Ives, Cornwall, to join artist Margaret Mellis (1914–2009). St Ives thus became a

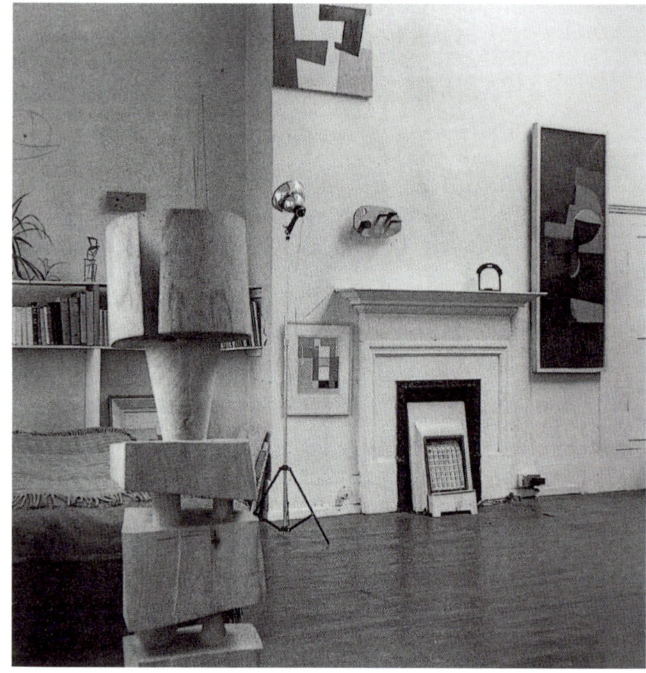

centre for abstraction. *Circle* remains a lasting document of the interwar style and the attempts to define a movement directly from its protagonists. However, many of the artists and architects soon dispersed and their styles changed. Indeed, the book has been described as the 'swansong' for this moment in Britain.[10]

Instead, Constructivist art in Britain had a resurgence in the artists who turned to abstraction after the War. 1951 was key, not only in the first reliefs and mobiles by a new generation, as described above, but it was also the year they began to exhibit abstract art exclusive from other art forms. In February 1951, a section of the London Group exhibition was dedicated to abstract art, and in May later that year an exhibition opened at the Artists' International Association (AIA) entirely dedicated to abstract art, the first group exhibition since before the War to be so. The exhibition titled *Abstract Paintings, Sculptures, Mobiles* was organised by artist Adrian Heath and included the

↑ First exhibition at Adrian Heath's studio, March 1952.

work of twenty-two artists spanning various styles. The exhibition was staged as a contribution to the Festival of Britain. Coinciding with the exhibition, many of the artists contributed to a publication, *Broadsheet No. 1: Devoted to Abstract Art*, which was followed by a second a year later. Soon after, in August, Anthony Hill organised an exhibition *British Abstract Art* at Gimpel Fils. In 1952 Adrian Heath went on to organise three weekend-long exhibitions in his London studio.[11] Abstract works of art were presented in dialogue with each other to create a complete environment. The artists worked with architects on the design. Trevor Dannatt (1920–2021) designed the first two and John Weeks (1921–2005) the next. This paved the way for more ambitious collaborations such as the *This Is Tomorrow* exhibition at the Whitechapel Gallery in 1956.

Through their self-organised exhibitions, these artists were offering a radical vision that was antithetical to the established styles. The art that was accepted in Britain institutionally was either figurative or a less austere gestural abstraction. The prominent styles had been showcased at the Festival of Britain with exhibitions across the United Kingdom in the summer of 1951. Architects and artists were selected to create new buildings and artworks for the 'centrepiece' of the Festival on the South Bank in London. These artists included major names of the day

including Jacob Epstein (1880–1959), Henry Moore and Barbara Hepworth, all of whom had been announced as creating new commissions for the Festival by *The Times* as early as January 1950.[12] If not entirely figurative, like Epstein's *Youth Advances* or Moore's *Reclining Figure: Festival*, artworks tended to be highly suggestive of the figure, such as Hepworth's *Contrapuntal Forms* (1950–51). In a rarely constructivist form, both for Hepworth and the Festival of Britain, her other commission *Turning Forms* (1950–51) was decidedly abstract and revolved every two minutes, using kineticism reminiscent of some of the ambitions of the early Russian Constructivists.

Some of the few abstract works for the Festival came from Victor Pasmore who created three spiral paintings for different elements of the Festival. His oil on canvas, *The Snowstorm: Spiral Motif in Black and White* (1950), was created for *60 Paintings for '51*. With sixty artists, the exhibition was intended to exhibit a cross-section of work being made at the time, although Pasmore's painting was one of only two abstract works, along with William Gear's (1915–1997) *Autumn Landscape* (1950). This exhibition was celebrated in the Arts Council's Annual Report as the most important of their London exhibitions in 1951 'in terms of popularity and significance'.[13] Pasmore also made a street banner for the Peace Congress in Sheffield, and his

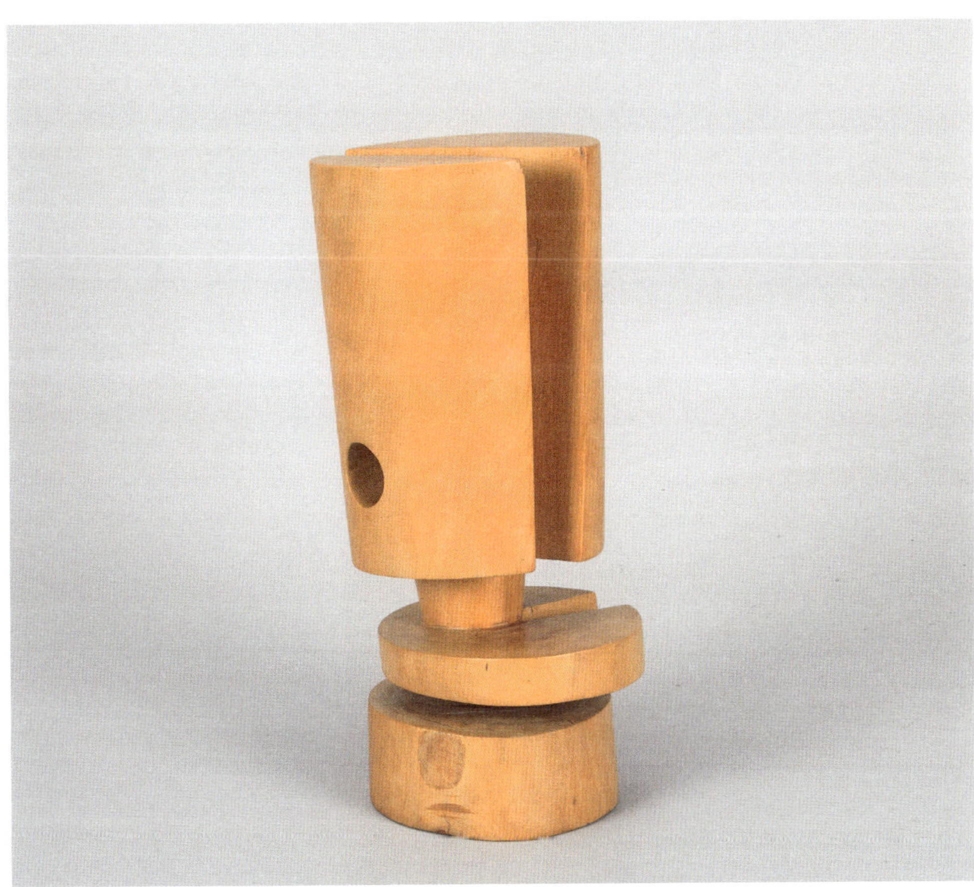

→ Robert Adams
Divided Column
1952
Holly (wood)
Sainsbury Centre

largest work was a mural, *The Waterfall* (1950), which was hand-painted on tiles. The mural was commissioned by architects Misha Black (1910–1977) and Alexander Gibson (1906–1977) for an exterior wall at the Restaurant on the South Bank site.

Pasmore wrote, 'The Regatta Restaurant was an elegant building designed in the best tradition of modern architecture by Design Research Unit and so provided an excellent ally to the purely abstract style in painting which I myself had come to adopt in response to the new situation'.[14] He explained that he decided to 'transform [the architecture] by means of contrast', which explains his lyrical approach to form.[15] Though decidedly abstract, the titles of these paintings suggest subjects from nature. The spiral motif for Pasmore did emerge in representative works, such as in *The Gardens of Hammersmith* (1947–49), *Spiral Development: The Fiery Sky* (1948) and *Spiral Motif: The Wave* (1949–50), which gradually became more abstract over the years. His purely abstract spiral paintings had first been exhibited at his 1950 Redfern exhibition. Alastair Grieve has described his works for the Festival of Britain as 'the apogee' of Pasmore's spirals.[16]

Lynn Chadwick's (1914–2003) sculpture *Cypress* (1951) was placed outside the Regatta Restaurant. Its elegant, elongated ovoid shape suggests the tree of its title, but in its context resembles the Skylon, the iconic structure that became symbolic of the Festival of Britain. The Skylon seemed futuristic in its engineering and style, but almost harked back to Russian Constructivism. Its long, slender form represented the achievements of new engineering techniques and were echoed in the contemporary design across the Festival site. The Antelope and Springbok

chairs designed by Ernest Race (1913–1964) used new manufacturing techniques, with curved, slender metal frames and legs. They were positioned on the Restaurant terrace, near Chadwick's *Cypress*. Disregarding its title, *Cypress* appears abstract, but a related work from later in the same year implies human connotations in its title *Hollow Men*, taken from a poem by T. S. Eliot (1888–1965).[17]

Robert Adams also created an ambiguously figurative work for the Festival in *Apocalyptic Figure* (1951), now in the Arts Council Collection. It was shown at the RBA Galleries in the exhibition *60 Paintings for '51*, one of a handful of sculptures presented alongside the sixty paintings. The wooden sculpture was constructed from a furniture-making technique involving woodworking joints and is aesthetically reminiscent of furniture parts. Adams held an ambiguous place amongst the Constructionist artists. Like the artists discussed above, his work was once figurative and became more and more abstract. Through his abstract work, he continued to work in a range of techniques including carving, which was antithetical to many definitions of constructivism, in its being a reductive rather than constructive form of creation. He exhibited in many of the exhibitions with the Constructionist artists, including in the exhibitions at Heath's studio and Heath's *Abstract Paintings, Sculptures, Mobiles* exhibition at the AIA.

In 1954 a group of artists organised an exhibition and publication, *Nine Abstract Artists*. The artists were Robert Adams, Adrian Heath, Anthony Hill, Kenneth Martin, Mary Martin and Victor Pasmore, as well as the artists working in a more gestural style of abstraction, Terry Frost (1915–2005), Roger Hilton (1911–1975) and William Scott (1913–1989). The latter group tended to abstract from nature, whilst the former made purely abstract forms. The text was written by critic Lawrence Alloway (1926–1990) who described these differing styles, designating the former artists the 'Pasmore Group'. He associated them with the Swiss artists Max Bill (1908–1994) and Richard Paul Lohse (1902–1988) and American artists Burgoyne Diller (1906–1965), Fritz Glarner (1899–1972) and Richard Lippold (1915–2002).[18] In doing so, Alloway indicates the

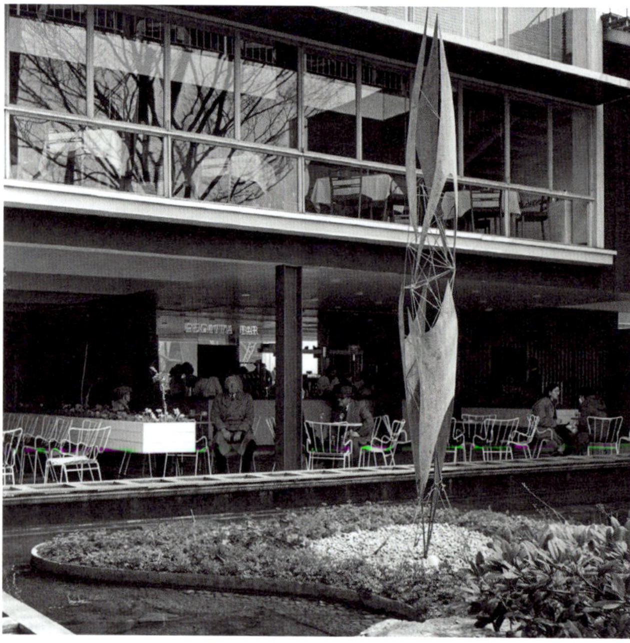

← Lynn Chadwick, *Cypress*, 1951 at the Festival of Britain with Ernest Race Antelope chairs on the terrace.

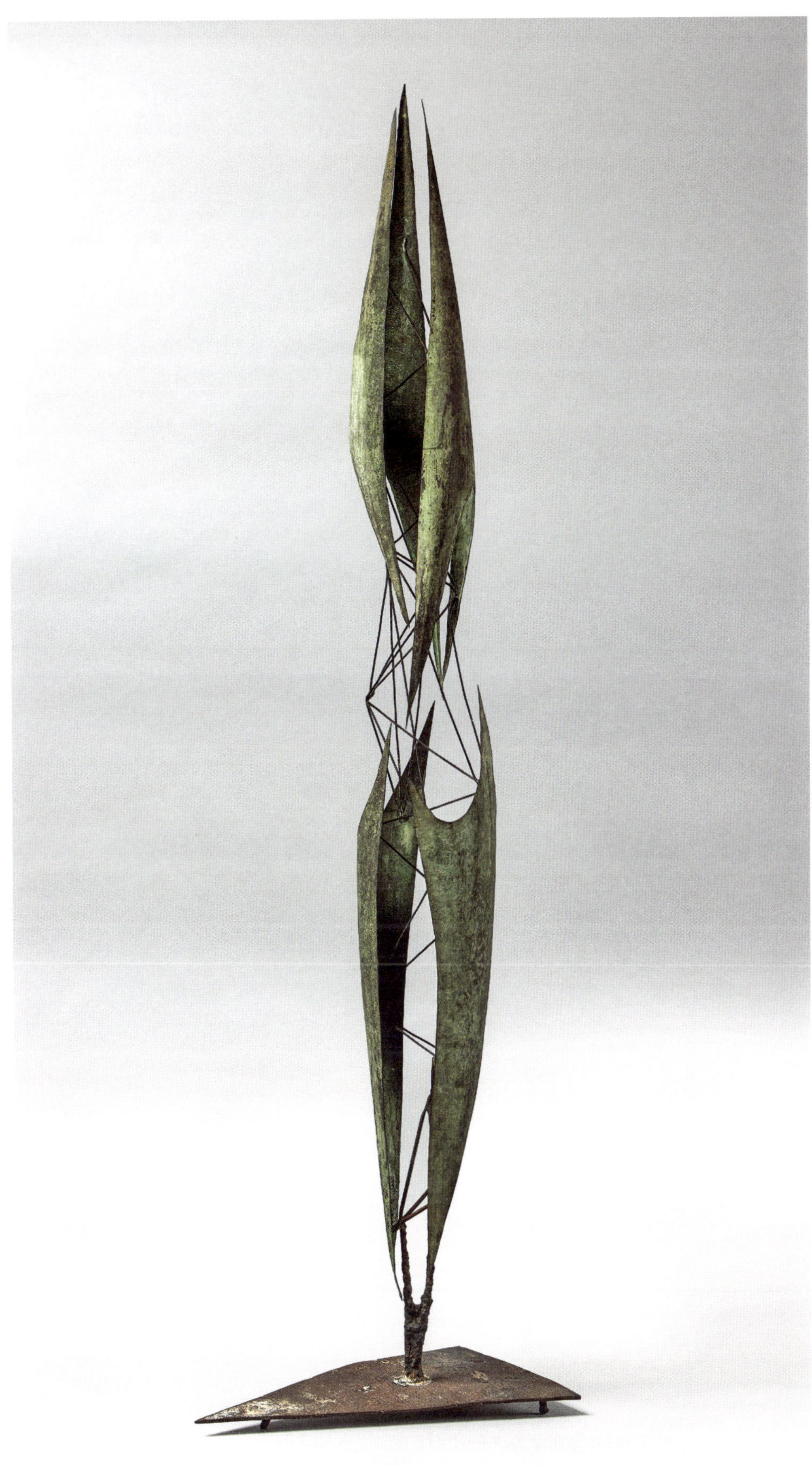

→ Lynn Chadwick
Hollow Men
1951
Copper, brass and iron
Sainsbury Centre

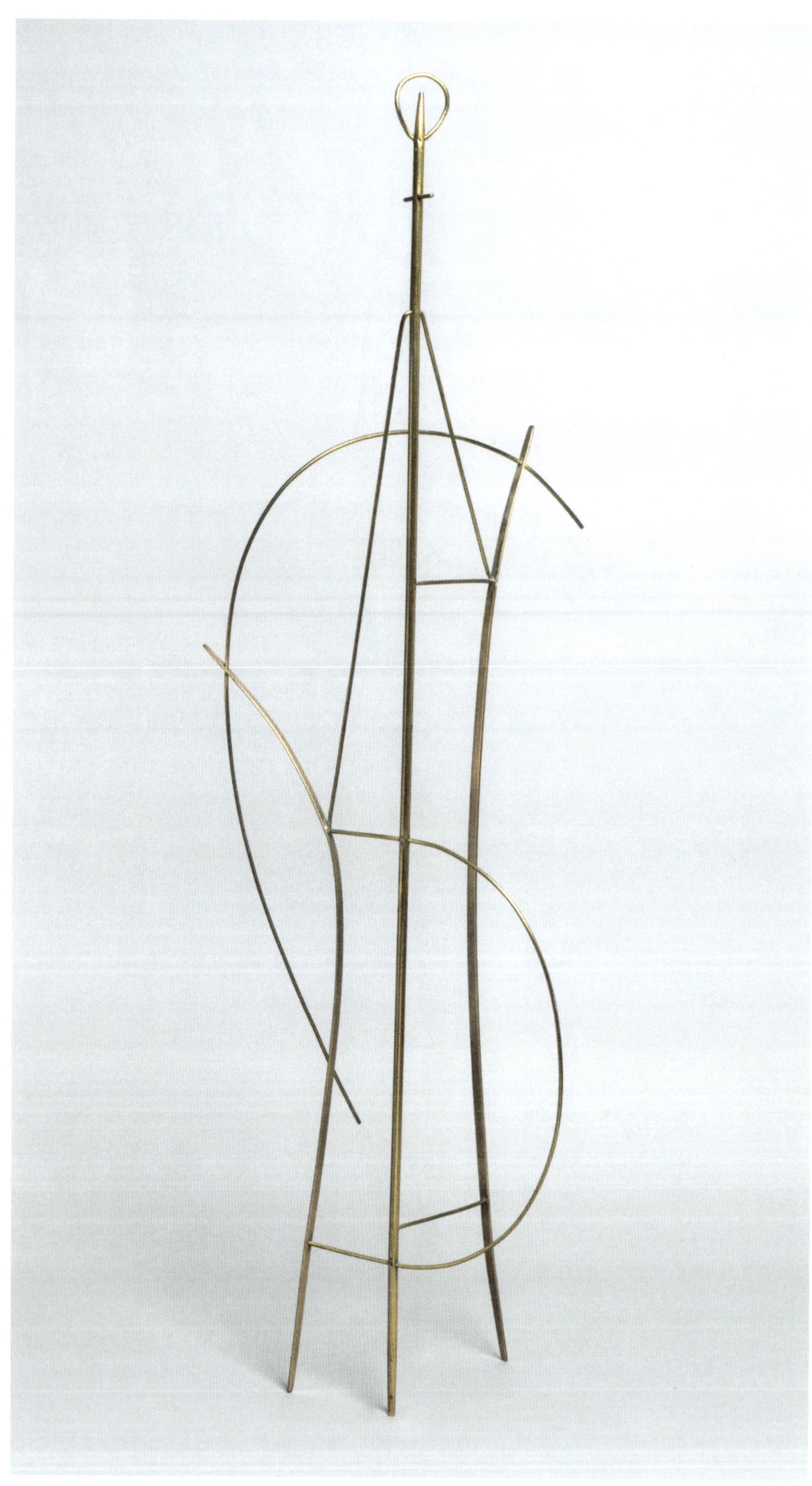

← **Robert Adams**
Standing Figure
1949
Brass
Sainsbury Centre

internationalism underpinning the style, which suggests the way in which these artists felt their work pointed towards a universal, global future.

CHANCE AND ORDER

Chance and Order was the title of a series of prints by Kenneth Martin from 1969. He conceived a set of rules that would dictate the placement of lines and colours when pulling out cards at random. The numbers on the cards corresponded to a numbered grid indicating where the lines would intersect. His process demonstrates his interest in unpredictability within a rigid system. Anthony Hill also used grids and mathematical systems in the production of his work. Hill was interested in graph theory, as was John Ernest (1922–1994), who came under the influence of the Constructionist artists as a student at St Martin's School of Art. Ernest worked methodically and mathematically to create intricate patterns of squares and triangles, describing them as 'Mosaics'. In Hill's series of *Five Regions Reliefs*, he divided a grid of twenty-five squares into five regions using eight cuts. He used mathematical processes to come up with the scenarios possible within this

structure, demonstrating the variety that could be achieved. By working in series, Hill and Martin could emphasise the possible variations offered by chance within their systems, and offer the suggestion of progression.

The idea of progression and evolution was fundamental to the book *On Growth and Form* by D'Arcy Wentworth Thompson (1860–1948), published in 1917 with a second edition in 1942.[19] Thompson pioneered mathematical biology, and the book became important well beyond his sector across generations and disciplines, being taught at both art and architecture schools.[20] From the second half of the twentieth century it was particularly influential on the Constructionist artists who admired the philosophy of growth and structure. The book was illustrated with images and diagrams that demonstrate how natural forms in vegetation and animals grow according to mathematical rules. Thompson showed how the spiral found in nature, such as in snail shells, followed the Fibonnaci sequence. Mary Martin used this sequence, or proportions based on the golden section, in her constructed spiral reliefs in works such as *Rotation* (1968). Martin repeats a single unit, as does in painting Adrian Heath in *Growth of Forms*

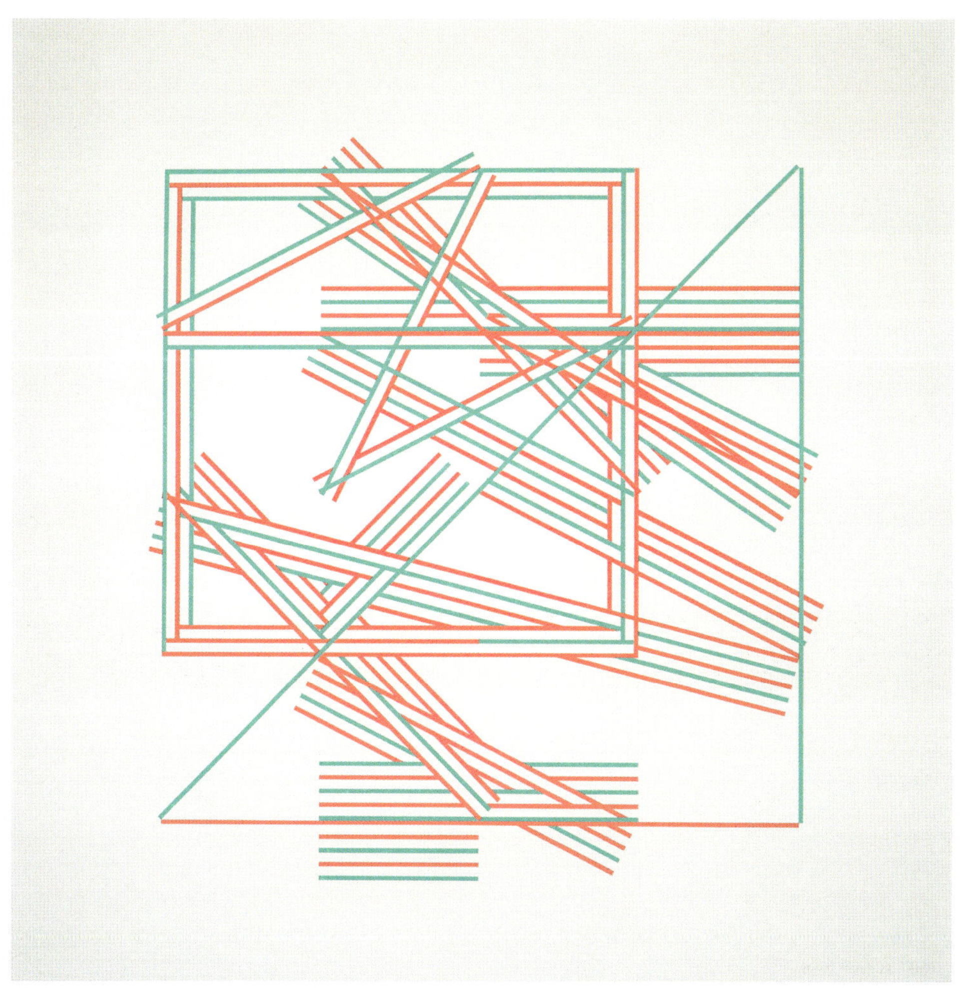

← Kenneth Martin
Chance and Order III
1972
Screenprint on paper
Sainsbury Centre

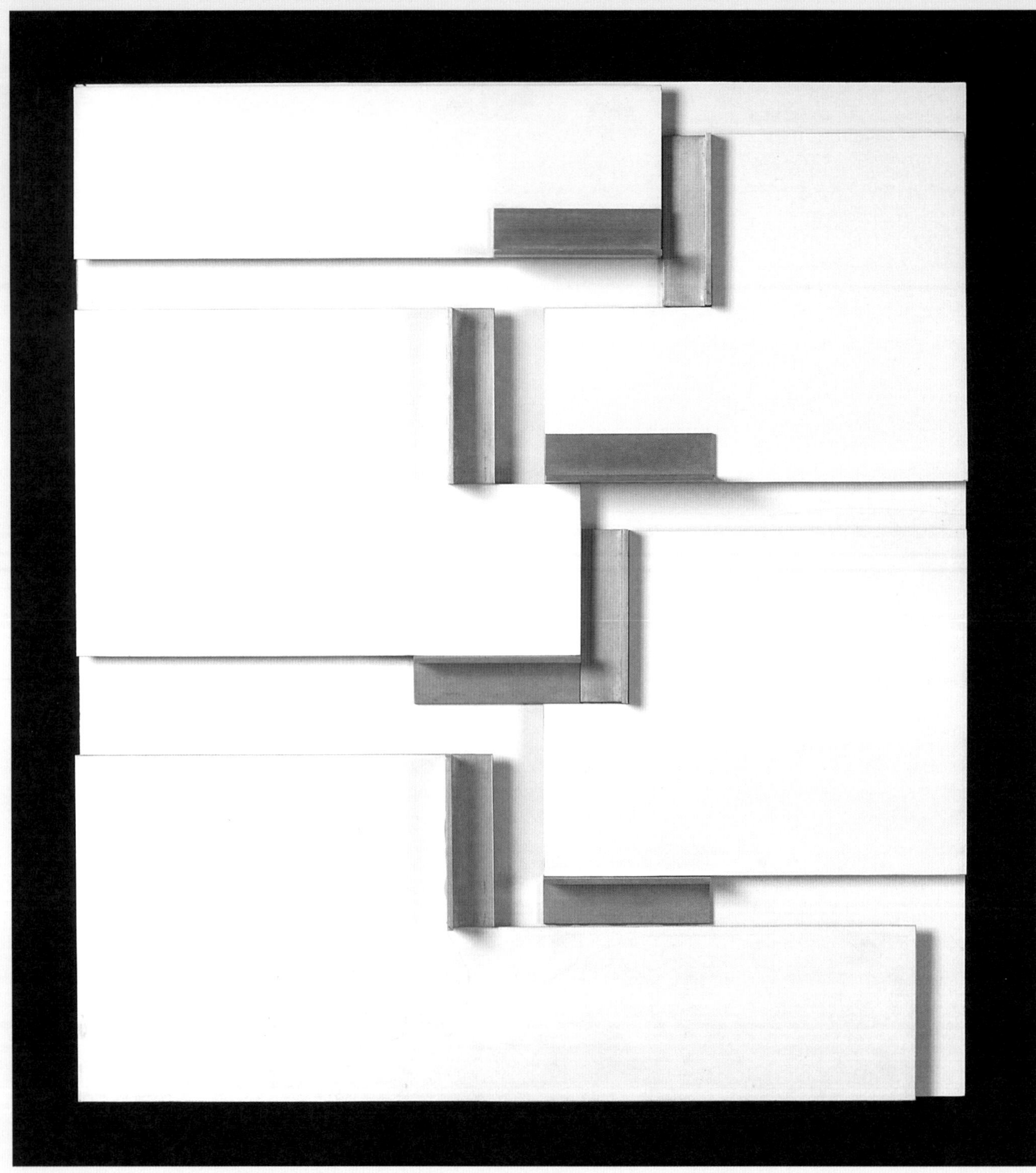

↑ Anthony Hill
Five Regions Relief
1960–62
Aluminium, plastic and hardboard
Sainsbury Centre

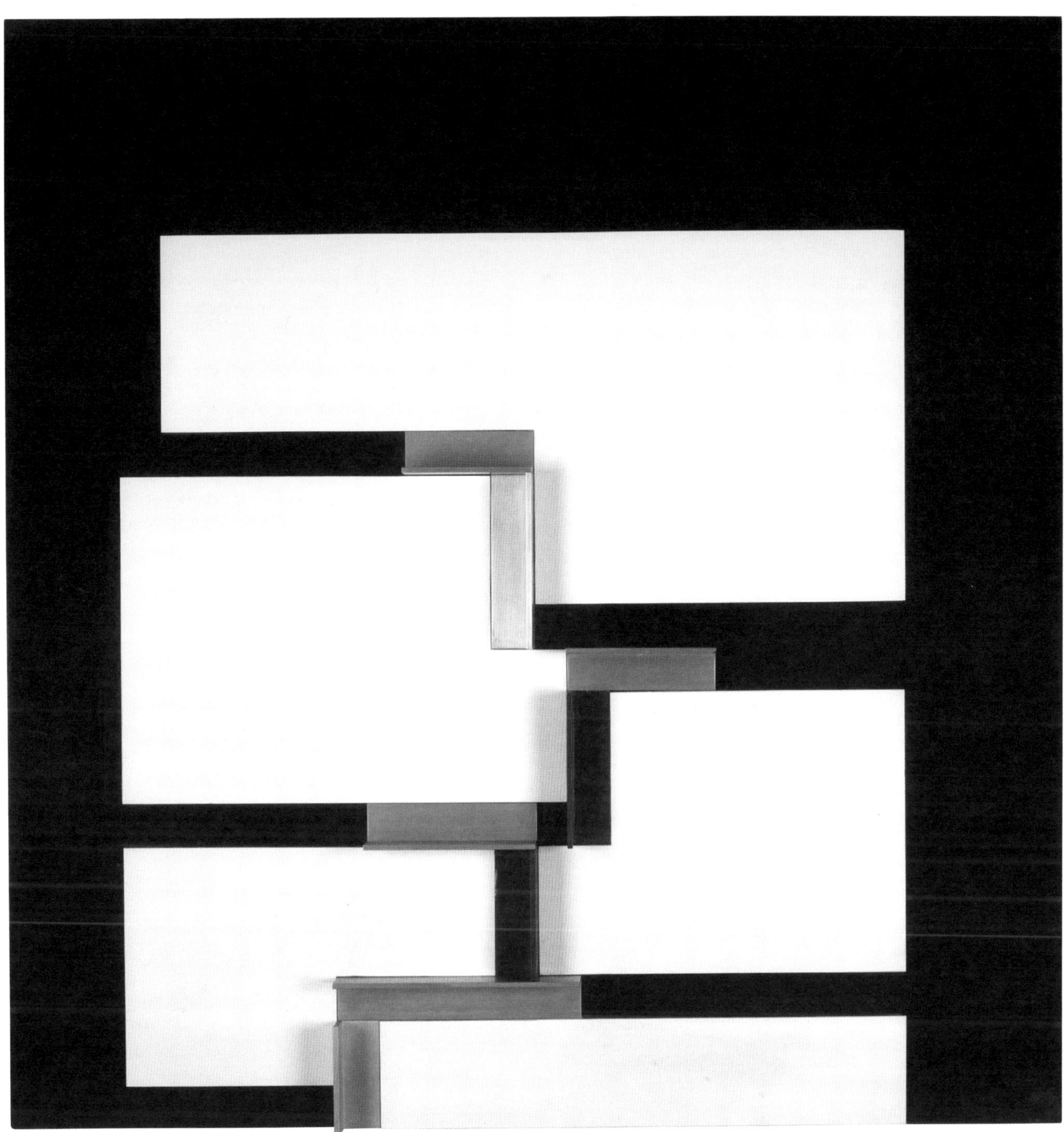

↑ Anthony Hill
Five Regions Relief
1960–62
Aluminium, wood and Perspex
Sainsbury Centre

(1951). These works are indicative of the way in which the Constructivists fundamentally work, in that they start with a single element and build it up.

The interest in biological structures was permeating the arts, and had been found in a number of the designs for the Festival of Britain, notably those of the Festival Pattern Group. At the suggestion of crystallographer Helen Megaw (1907–2002), this group of scientists, designers and manufacturers produced designs based on atomic structures for carpets, fabrics, wallpapers and ceramics. Discourse about the relationship between art and science was particularly rife at the ICA. Leading this discourse were a group of young artists, architects and critics, who have since become known as the Independent Group. They included Richard Hamilton (1922–2011), Eduardo Paolozzi (1924–2005), William Turnbull (1922–2012), Nigel Henderson (1917–1985) and Lawrence Alloway. Alloway had written *Nine Abstract Artists* and curated exhibitions with the Constructionist artists, and Paolozzi and Henderson had exhibited their abstract work alongside them. The Independent Group admired Dada art for how it absorbed its subjects from everyday life, and they are now known as being at the forefront of Pop Art in Britain. Like many Constructivist artists, they wanted art to be incorporated into daily life. Furthermore, they saw visual art as interconnected with science and technology and they looked to the latest developments in the latter for their own artistic activity.

The journal *The Structurist* was founded in 1960 to explore the relationship of art, design and architecture to science, technology and nature. In 1965, they published an issue dedicated to 'growth in art and nature'. The issue included photographs from nature, in particular showing the growth patterns like those found in *On Growth and Form*, such as the spiralling seeds in the head of a sunflower and a dandelion in seed. The issue includes a feature on Charles Biederman's *Structurist Reliefs*, in which images of his reliefs are captioned with quotes from the artist. One of them makes the link with the forms found in nature that are illustrated elsewhere in the publication: 'No longer confined to copying the RESULTS of nature's Structural Process, but actually using this process to create his own art-results, the new artist is incomparably less limited than in the past'.[21]

Biederman had shared this idea in his book *Art as the Evolution of Visual Knowledge*.[22] He had echoed the sentiment above in which he argues for replicating the structures underpinning forms rather than the image of nature.

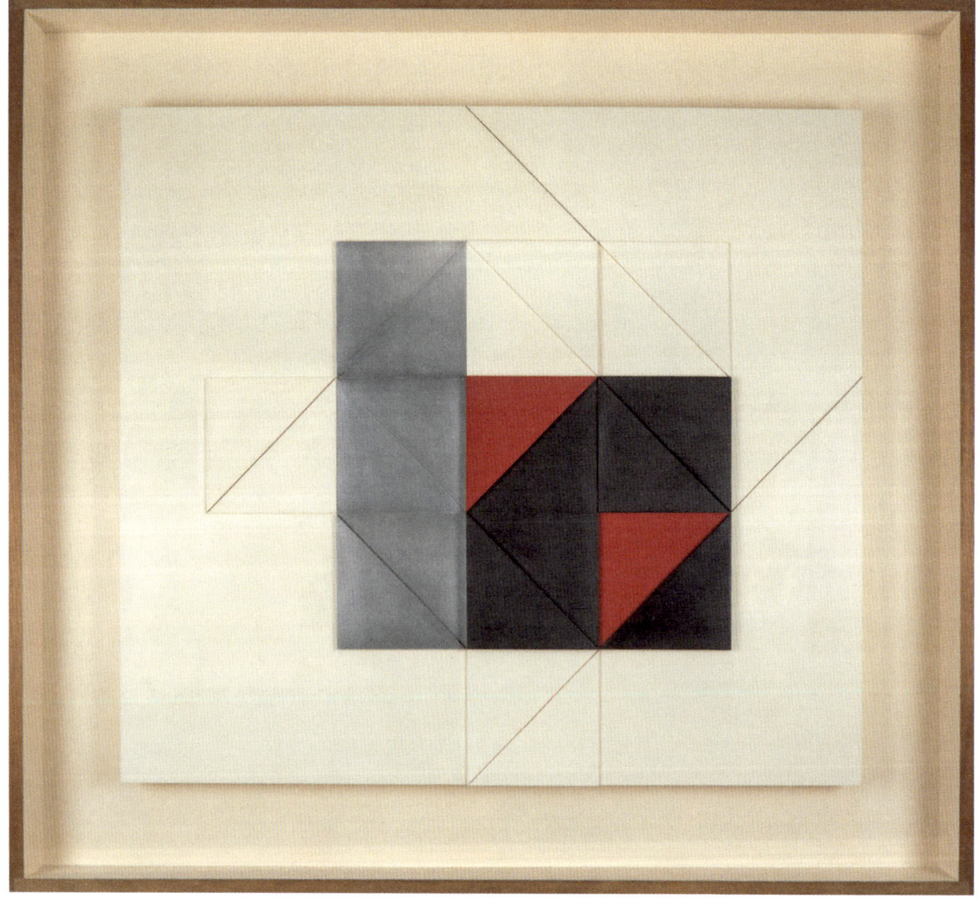

← John Ernest
Mosaic Relief III
1964
Aluminium and Formica on cellulose-sprayed board
Sainsbury Centre

As well as the theoretical aim to construct works – to build them up as the forms in nature are structured – Biederman influenced the group of British artists in their creation of the relief. Biederman's early works reflected the style of other artists, for example figurative paintings by Paul Cézanne (1839–1906), before he created work in the style of Fernand Léger (1881–1955), with whom he made friends when he was living in Paris from 1936 to 1937. *Untitled 3* (1936) in the Sainsbury Centre collection demonstrates this influence, wherein the blocks of colour are reminiscent of Léger's 'mechanical' period of *c.*1918–23, in which he composed figures and objects from tubular forms.

Where Biederman truly created his own style was in the reliefs he created from 1937. His earliest reliefs incorporated many geometries and materials, but from around 1950 they had become more simplified and powerful with planes of painted aluminium protruding from the backboard at a perpendicular angle. Biederman came to this form through his interest in Dutch De Stijl and Russian Constructivism, and it is these reliefs that came to influence some of the abstract artists working in Britain in the 1950s. Whereas Biederman's reliefs were highly colourful, the work of the British artists was largely monochromatic, having known Biederman's work from black and white reproductions. Anthony Hill worked solely in monochrome from 1953 to 1956, first in painting, then in his reliefs which used industrial materials – plastic and aluminium – in white, black and grey. His first relief was *Progression of Rectangles* (1954–55) in which rectangular pieces of black and white plastic gradually enlarge across the transparent plane that is parallel to the wall. Hill had wanted to exhibit *Progression of Rectangles* in the exhibition *Artist vs Machine* in 1954 at the Building Centre, London, but he had not finished it in time. The exhibition was organised by Victor Pasmore, Kenneth Martin, Robert Adams and the architect John Weeks. The exhibition promoted art that used industrial techniques, and demonstrated their interest in the intersection between art, science, technology and architecture. Despite this interest in the machine, the artists in this exhibition were making their works by hand, often

with irregular results. The concept of the machine stemmed from the materials they were using such as plastics, but also in the systematic way in which they were working. Furthermore, the aesthetic signified the possibilities the machine offered in the postwar period.

In 1958, Pasmore organised with his colleagues from Newcastle University an exhibition *Art, Machine and Environment* at the Laing Art Gallery. The premise of the exhibition argued that artists should engage with machine technologies. A decade later, *Cybernetic Serendipity* at the ICA in 1968 was the first exhibition to present works of

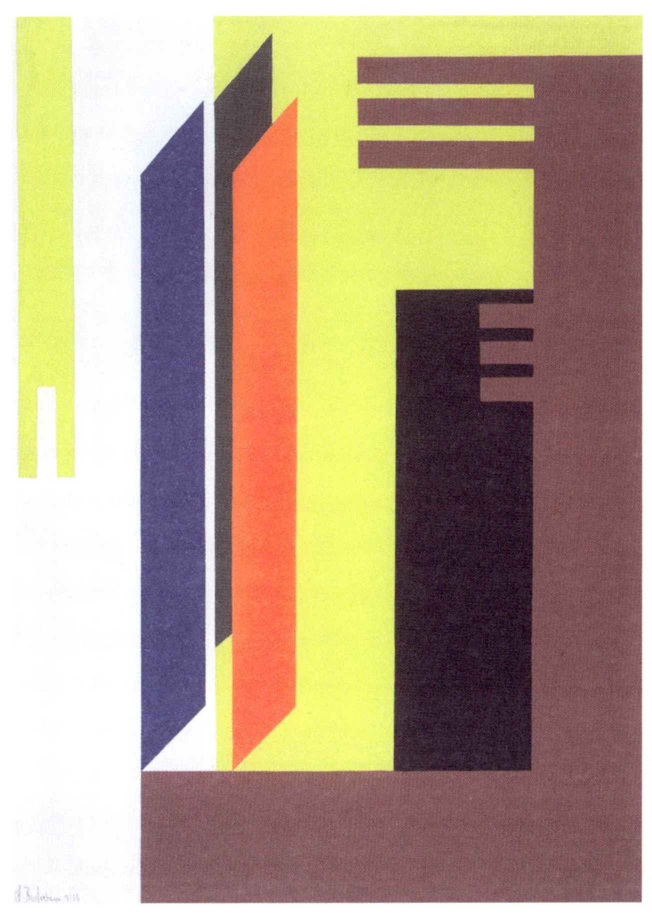

↑ Charles Biederman
Untitled 3
1936
Gouache on paper
Sainsbury Centre

art in relation to computer technologies. The catalogue illustrates an experiment with the work of abstract artist Jeffrey Steele (1931–2021) and Op Artist Bridget Riley (b.1931), demonstrating computer-generated variations of their paintings. Other illustrations of pixelated images or grid-based plotted drawings show the visual link with the repetition and gradation found in Op Art. The exhibition positioned computer experiments or computer-generated graphics alongside artworks. The exhibition's curator and Assistant Director of the ICA, Jasia Reichardt (b.1933), acknowledged the divergence between the two disciplines in the catalogue:

> The computer is only a tool which, at the moment, still seems far removed from those polemic preoccupations which concern art. However, even now seen with all the prejudices of tradition and time, one cannot deny that the computer demonstrates a radical extension in art media and techniques.[23]

One of the first abstract artists to use computer technology to make art was Hungarian artist Vera Molnár (b.1924). She had been creating abstract art since 1946, but in 1968 she used an algorithm to create drawings for the first time, and enjoyed the surprise afforded by the computer technology. Her series of computerised drawings, *Twenty-five Squares* (1989–90), demonstrate her interest in the grid combined with the randomness generated by the technology. Molnár described herself as 'between the three "cons": computers, constructivism and conceptualism'.[24] In 1973, artist Harold Cohen (1928–2016) wrote a computer program AARON, which could produce works of art autonomously. In his exhibition at Tate in 1983, the program controlled four 'drawing machines' made by the artist, each of which produced individual works of art throughout the exhibition.[25] Cohen continued to develop AARON, but found that the images did not become more complex, although later versions incorporated colour.

Dominic Boreham (b.1944) also produced art through computer programming, and this was his sole means

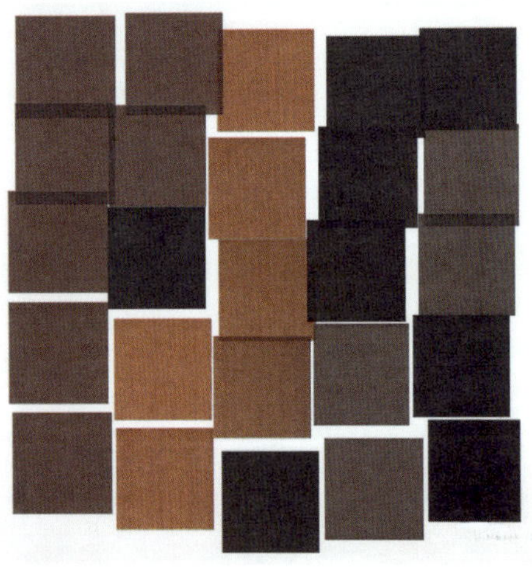

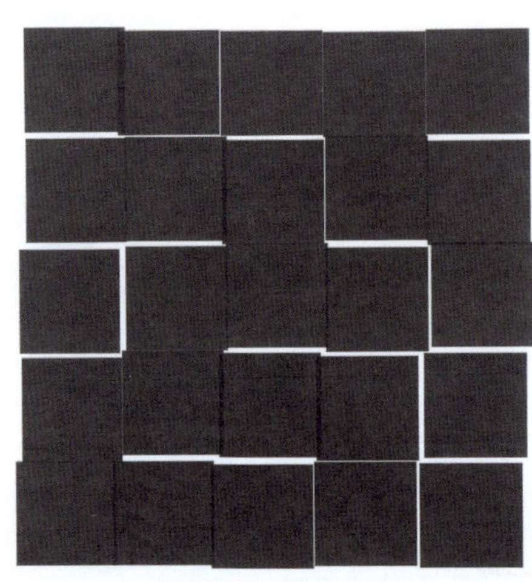

← Vera Molnár
Twenty-five Squares
1989
Ink on paper
Sainsbury Centre

← Vera Molnár
Twenty-five Squares
1989
Ink on paper
Sainsbury Centre

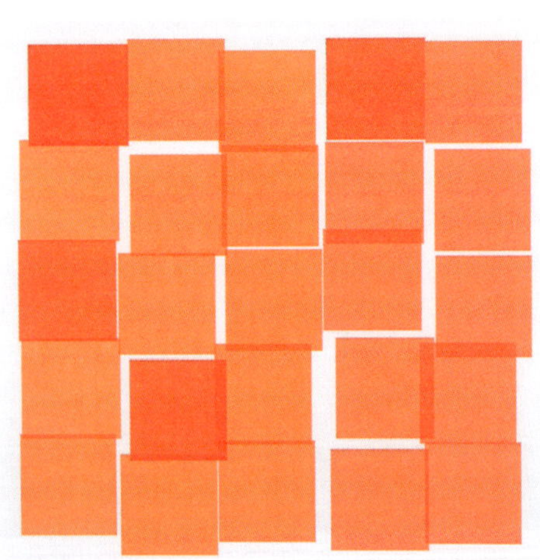

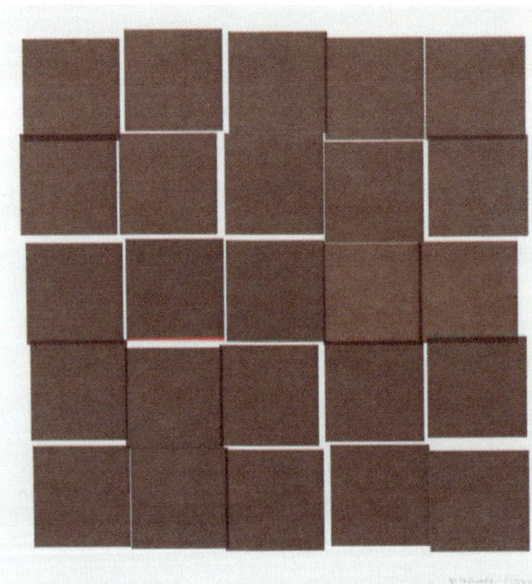

← Vera Molnár
Twenty-five Squares
1989
Ink on paper
Sainsbury Centre

← Vera Molnár
Twenty-five Squares
1989
Ink on paper
Sainsbury Centre

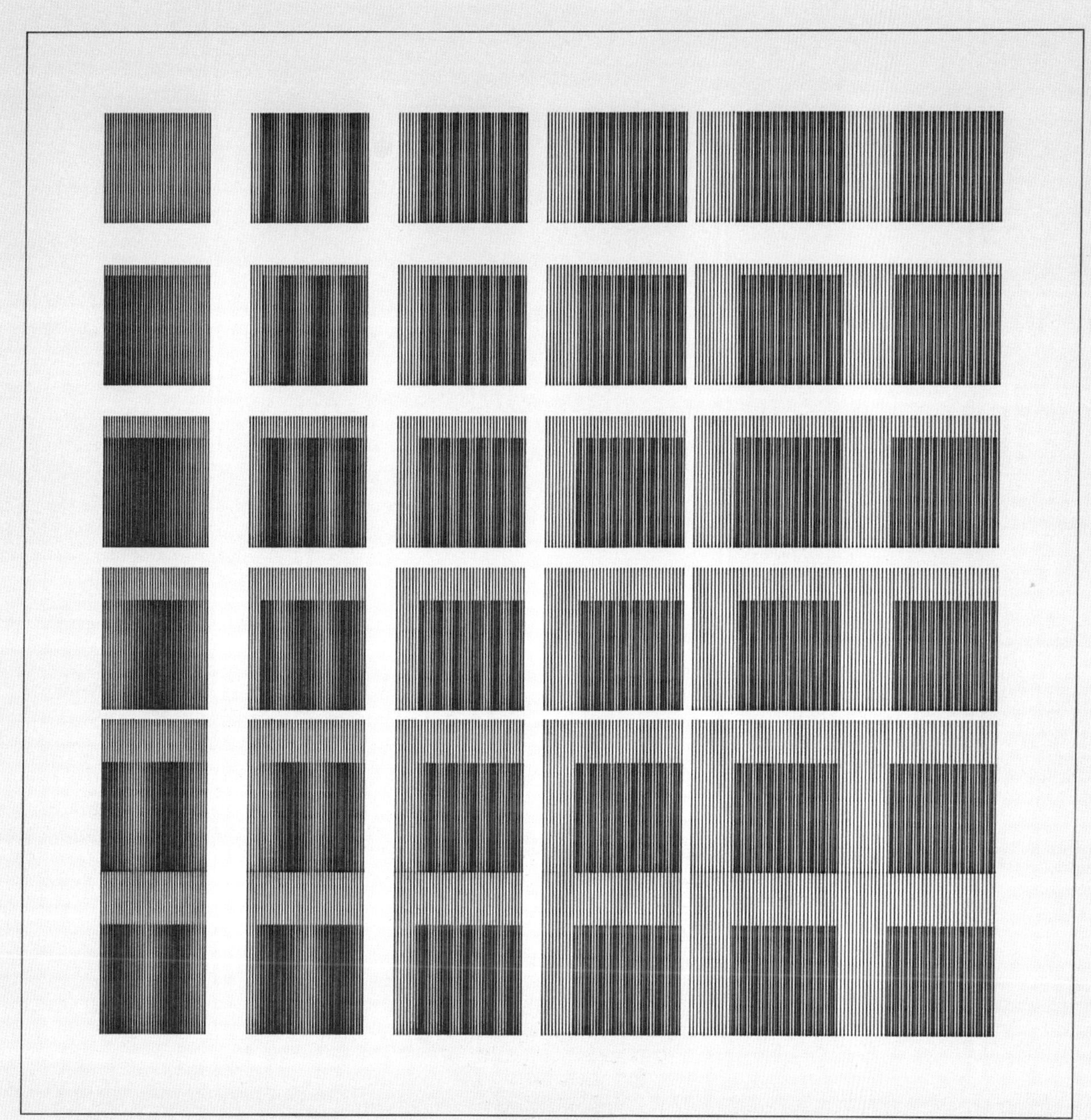

↑ Dominic Boreham
IM 36(2) P0.5, 16.VIII.78
(interference matrix)
1978
Ink on paper
Sainsbury Centre

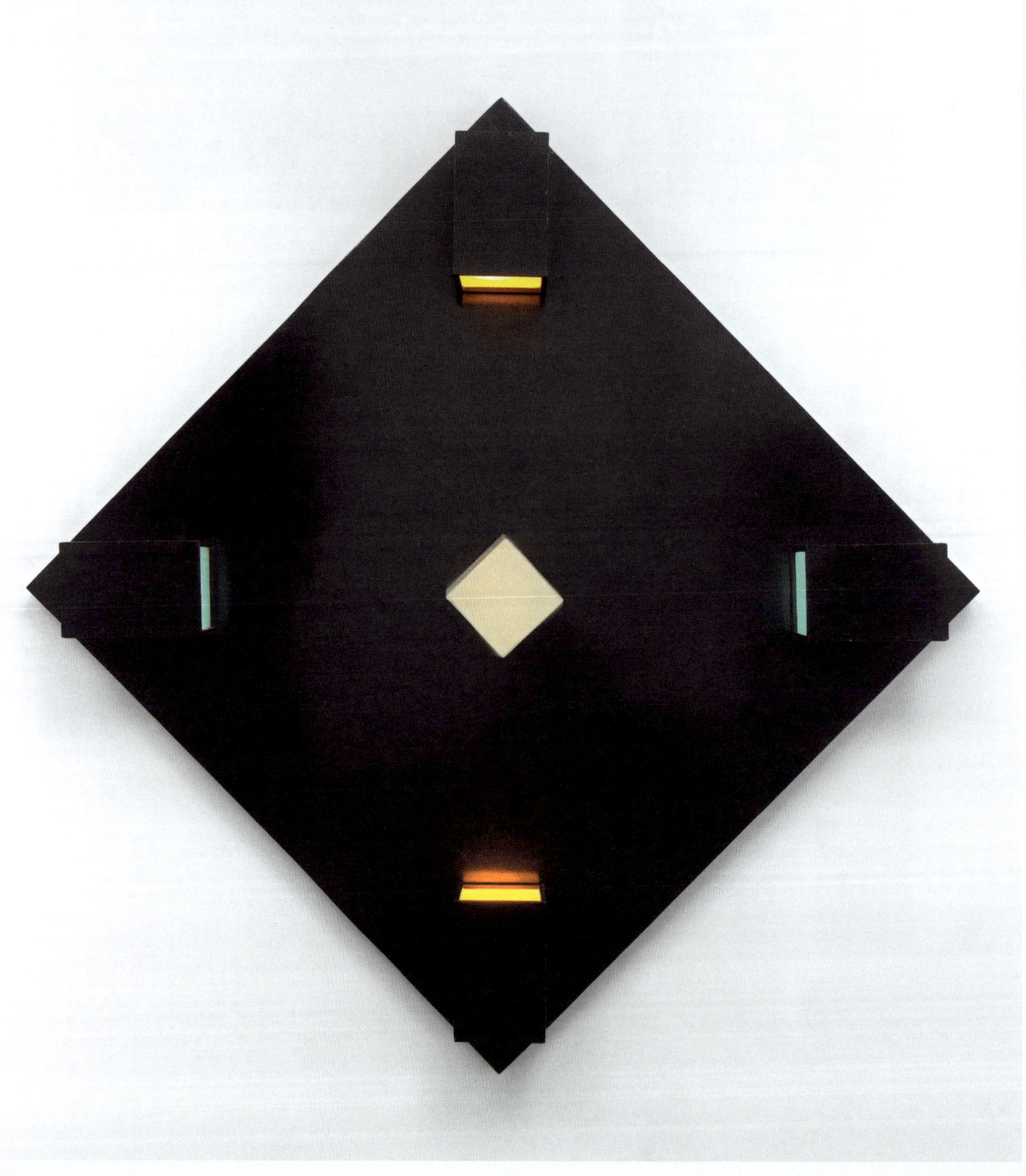

↑ Stephen Willats
Visual Automatic No. 1
1964–65
Wood, paint, Perspex, electrical
components and mixed media
Loan courtesy the artist and
Victoria Miro.

of creation between 1977 and 1983.[26] His *Interference Matrix* series was made in the Slade School of Fine Art's Experimental and Computing Department; it layered drawings produced from a flat-bed plotter driven by the program FORTRAN. Although Cohen had not produced work in the Constructivist style, Boreham had pushed Constructivist art firmly into the realm of the machine.

Whilst *Cybernetic Serendipity* paired the work of scientists and artists, the ICA presented another exhibition in 1971, *Electric Theatre: 25 artists working with light sound and space*, which included experimental artworks which had employed technology in their making. The exhibition featured twenty-five international artists, including Bruce Lacey (1927–2016), Gillian Wise and Stephen Willats (b.1943). In Willats' *Visual Automatic No. 1* (1964–65), the lights at the four corners turn on and off completely randomly. A central block rotates at the speed of the alpha rhythm, which alters perception. This block disrupts the light beamed from each corner. Willats is interested in how the viewer perceives order that isn't there in the pattern in which the lights turn on and off. *Visual Automatic No.1* was one of a number of light works included in Willats' 1968 solo exhibition at the Museum of Modern Art, Oxford (now Modern Art Oxford). Willats created a labyrinthine dark installation, which allowed for each of the works to be viewed individually, but together formed a total experience. Willats still works in the Constructivist tradition, creating what he describes as 'social constructivism', as opposed to the 'numerical constructivism' of the Constructionists.[27] He often creates work in which audience engagement adds to the construction, for example in asking the viewer to document their interaction, which becomes part of the work.

MOVEMENT AND PARTICIPATION

In the 1960s there emerged a growing interest in kinetic art, spanning art that itself moves, or suggests movement via optical effects. This required a new interaction from the viewer, and with it emerged new art forms that required active participation. Kineticism had been of interest to some of the founders of Constructivism. Vladimir Tatlin

had imagined his *Monument to the Third International* to be kinetic in that it had four internal structures that would rotate at different speeds. The tower, although never realised, was intended to reach a height of 400 metres in St Petersburg. A third taller than the Eiffel Tower, it was designed to be the symbol of modernity. A cube at the base would have taken a year to rotate; above this, a pyramid would rotate over a month; next, a cylinder would take a day to rotate. Each of these would have housed different functions. Naum Gabo, who brought his vision of Constructivism to Britain in the 1930s, considered kineticism fundamental to the new art that he was conceiving. Although he only made three kinetic works,[28] Gabo considered kineticism a fundamental aspect of art, as described in his manifesto:

> We *renounce* the thousand-year-old delusion in art that held the static rhythms as the only elements of the plastic and pictorial arts.
> We *affirm* in these arts a new element the kinetic rhythms as the basic forms of our perception of real time...[29]

The term kinetic art was coined in 1931 by artist Marcel Duchamp (1887–1968) to refer to Alexander Calder's

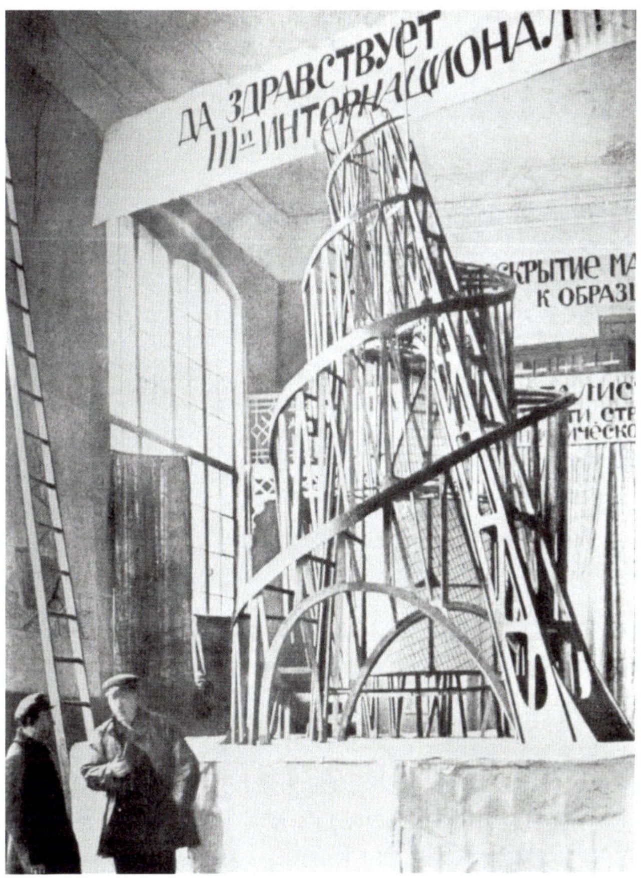

→ Vladimir Tatlin with the model of his Monument to the Third International, Moscow 1920.

(1898–1976) sculptures with parts operated by small motors. The following year Calder began making mobiles which, when hung from the ceiling, would move with the air currents. In 1934 his outdoor stabiles were activated by the wind. In Britain during the War, Lynn Chadwick had made some kinetic design objects as part of the display in trade exhibitions. In 1947, he created his first mobile, using balsa wood and small found objects. He displayed it in an exhibition stand designed for the Aluminium Development Association at the Building Exhibition. More mobiles followed for trade stands, and Gimpel Fils included one of his mobiles in the window of their gallery in 1949. Through this display, Chadwick transitioned from designer to artist. It was this mobile that brought Chadwick to the attention of the architects of the Festival of Britain's South Bank exhibition. He made a mobile for the Festival, as well as his large sculpture *Cypress* outside the Regatta Restaurant.

Constructionist artist Kenneth Martin's most iconic works are mobiles. His 'Screw Mobiles', begun in 1953, have straight or curved metal bars which spiral out from a central rod, ebbing and flowing as though twisting in movement. One of the earliest, *Screw Mobile* (1953), has slight gradations in the length of the metal bar, each separated by an equal distance, offering a gently undulating twist. His later *Variable Screw* (1967) introduces the additional element of variation as the rods can be rearranged. Martin was interested in how the light reflected from his mobiles when in movement, and the shadows they create. He was also interested in how the movement makes the viewer more aware of the environment, and in turn in their own position in that environment.[30]

Often the Constructivist interest in movement may have been via static forms. As Mary Martin described:

> I have related works to the wall and floor. The expressive content has been concerned with movement and change, being geometrically or mathematically based. Being concerned with movement and change, it has involved rest and constancy. I have not used actual movement.[31]

One of the primary ways in which the work of the Constructionist artists interacted with space and movement in static forms was via reliefs. The three-dimensionality of the wall-based works encouraged viewers to move in parallel to their surface, seeing the works from different angles. Working outside Constructivism but making

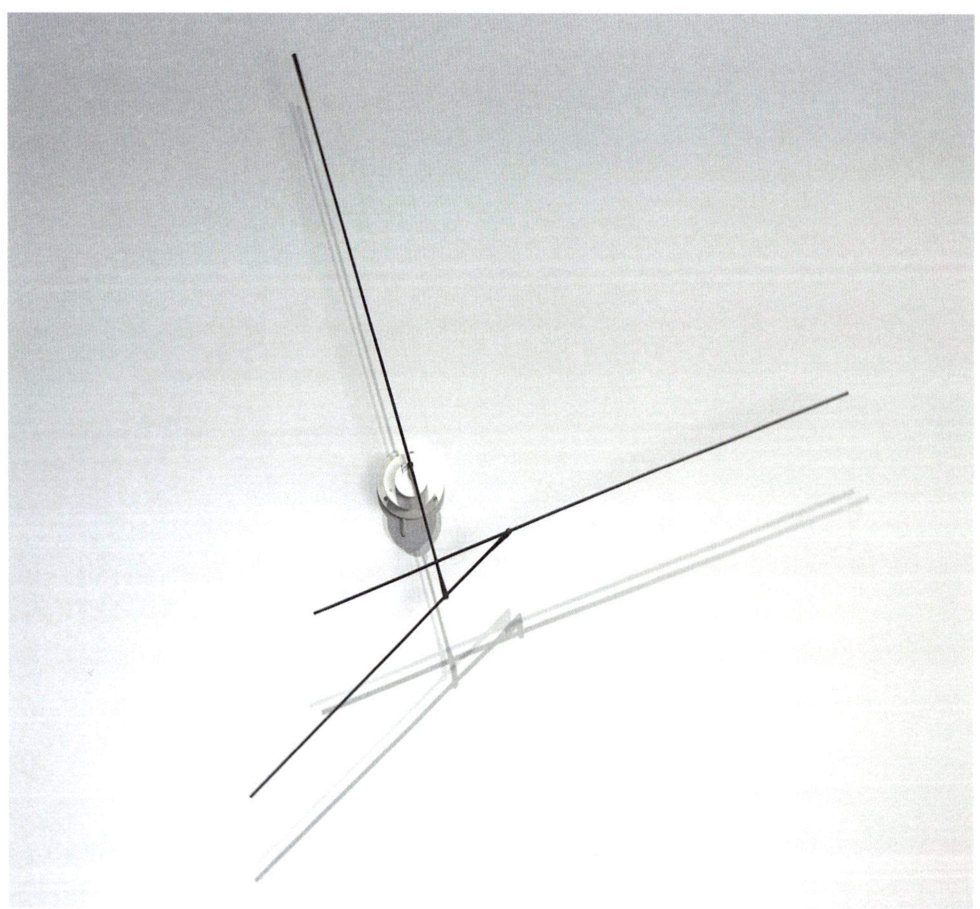

← Eric Snell
Cuneiform III
1978
Aluminium, paint, PVC, resin,
electrical motor and components
Sainsbury Centre

→ Kenneth Martin
Variable Screw
1967
Brass
Sainsbury Centre

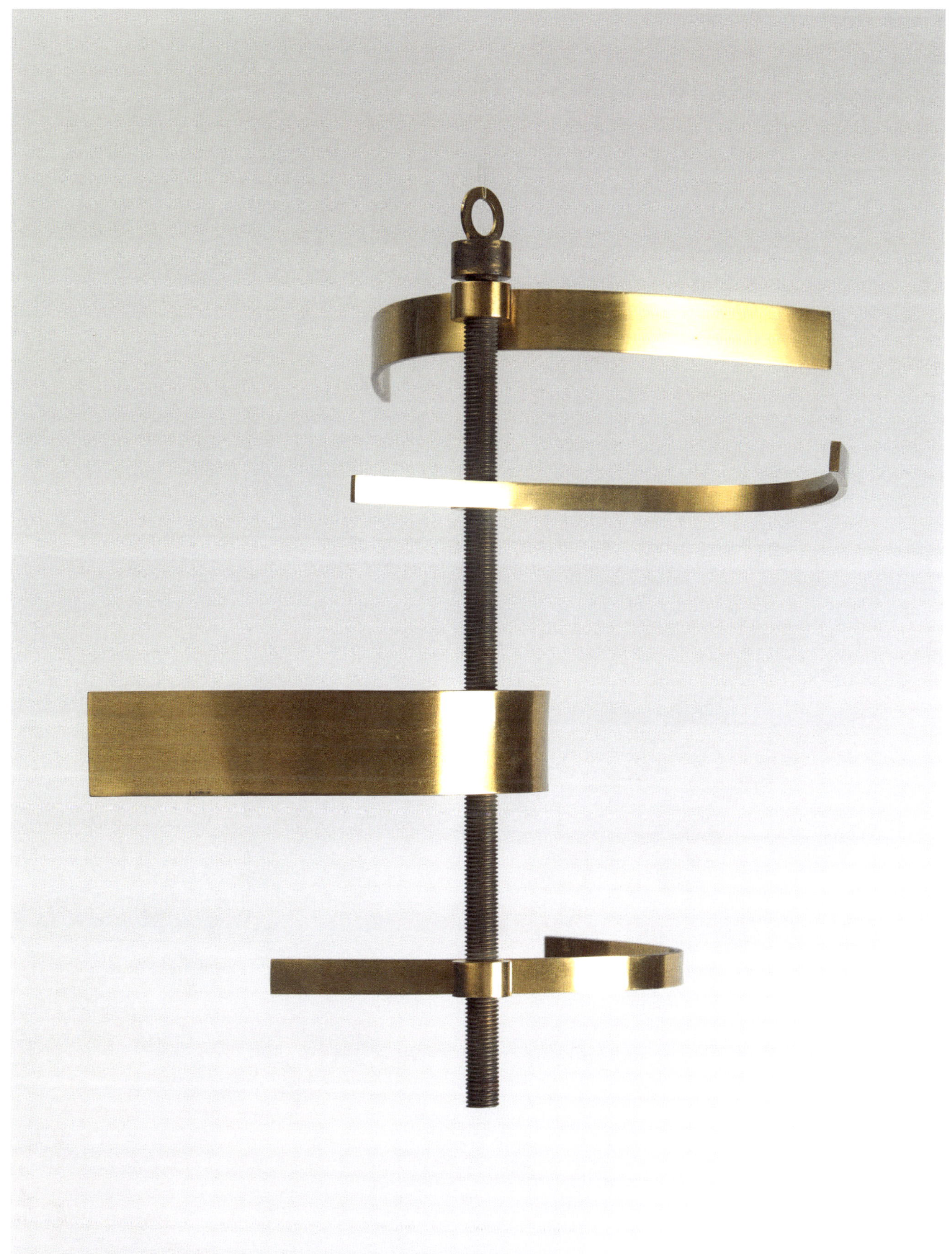

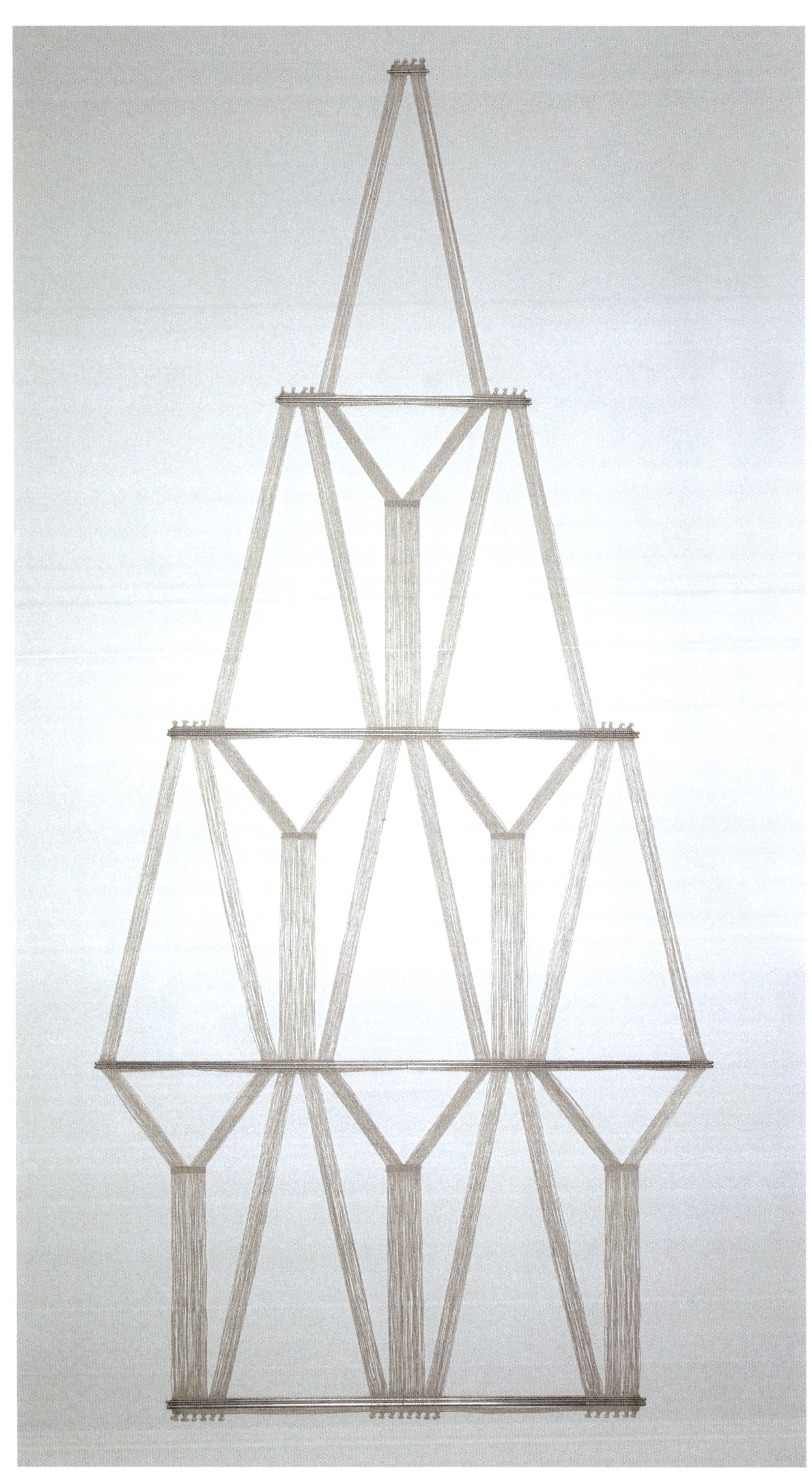

← **Peter Collingwood**
Macrogauze: EX4, M. 178
c.1978
Linen, steel and aluminium
Sainsbury Centre

→ **Stephen Gilbert**
Structure 12 B
1961
Aluminium
Sainsbury Centre

strikingly Constructivist works was Peter Collingwood (1922–2008), who was considered the most radical weaver of the twentieth century in Britain. He developed his wall hangings which he described as 'Macrogauzes' in the 1960s, with the warp threads crossing over rather than following vertical lines. They later developed into three-dimensional hanging structures, reminiscent of the reliefs of some of the Constructivist artists and engaging with space in dynamic ways.

The suggestion of flux and rapidity often occurs through asymmetrical, spiralling or curved forms. Stephen Gilbert (1910–2007) made a series of sculptures in streamlined, curved aluminium, suggestive of the potential of speed. Gilbert lived in Paris, where he joined the CoBrA group as one of two British artists, along with William Gear. Taking inspiration from children's art, folklore and surrealism, CoBrA worked within tachiste and European abstract expressionist idioms. Gilbert moved away from this style in the 1950s and created constructions that closely linked him to the British Constructionists. Robert Adams was also interested in the portrayal of movement in static sculpture. He explained, 'I am concerned with energy, a physical property inherent in metal. A major aim

I would say, is movement, which I seem to get through asymmetry'.[32] *Horizontal Movement No. 1* (1959) is composed of seven sheets of welded steel in an undulating curve. It is relatively two-dimensional, so it would be viewed from only two planes rather than in the round, and it t hus has a strong silhouette from one aspect. Its curved shape therefore suggests movement from left to right.

Adams' earliest works were figurative, before he progressively reduced his forms into a mode of abstraction. One of his earliest purely abstract sculptures was *Conic Form* (1952–53). Composed of two cones joined at the base so it sits on the diagonal edge, it looks as though it is on the brink of rolling. Adams pushed the balance of his carvings to their most extreme in *Counterbalance No. 2* (1955), in which he pieced together three sections of wood, with an almost horizontal section dramatically jutting from two tapering cones. It suggests an elegant swan or a ballerina, captured in a brief moment of pause. Adams was particularly inspired by the avant-garde ballet dancer and choreographer Kurt Jooss (1901–1979). His four *Counterbalance* sculptures were Adams' last carvings; Alastair Grieve, compiler of his catalogue raisonée, writes that he 'must have felt he had reached the limits of

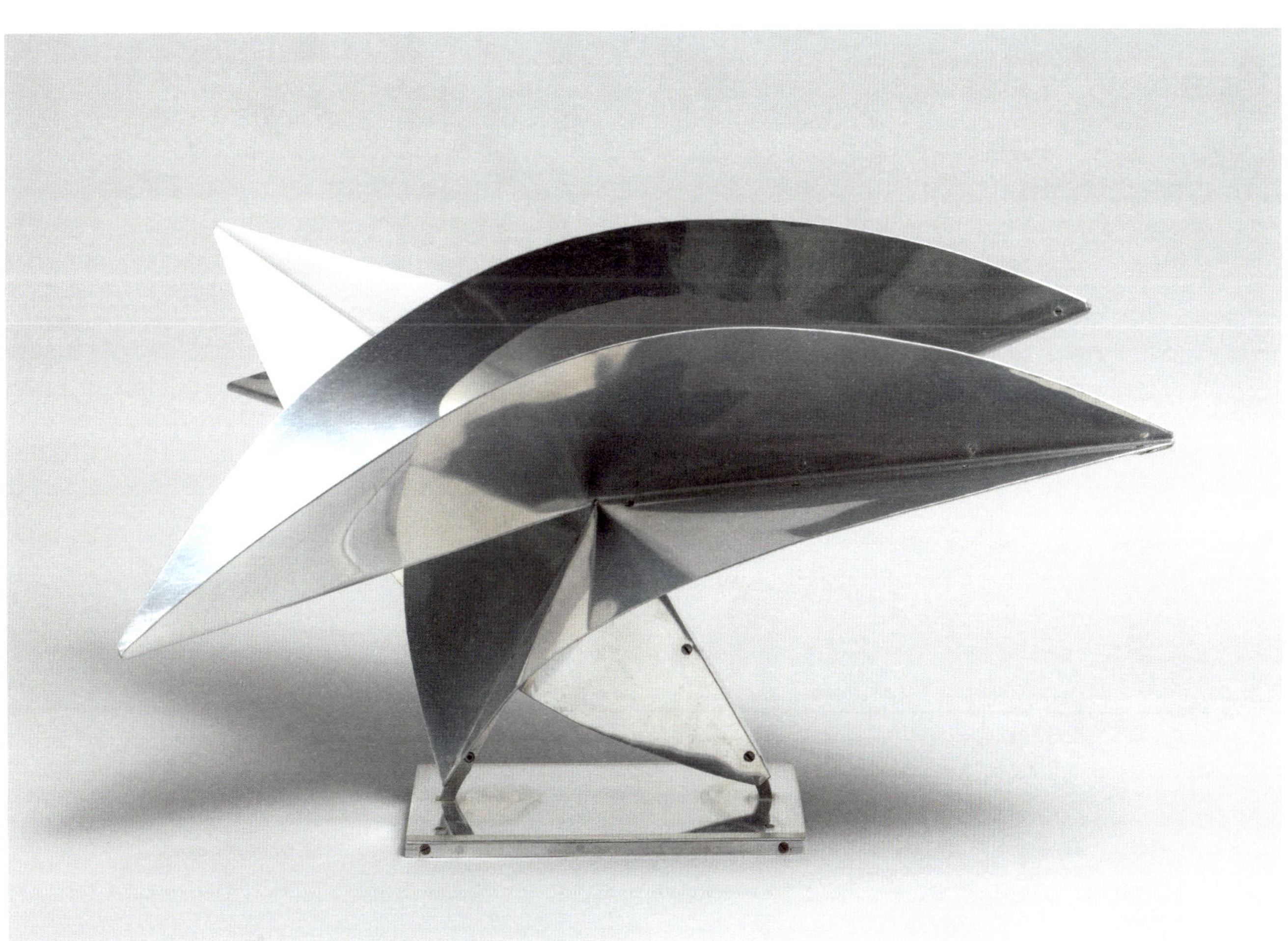

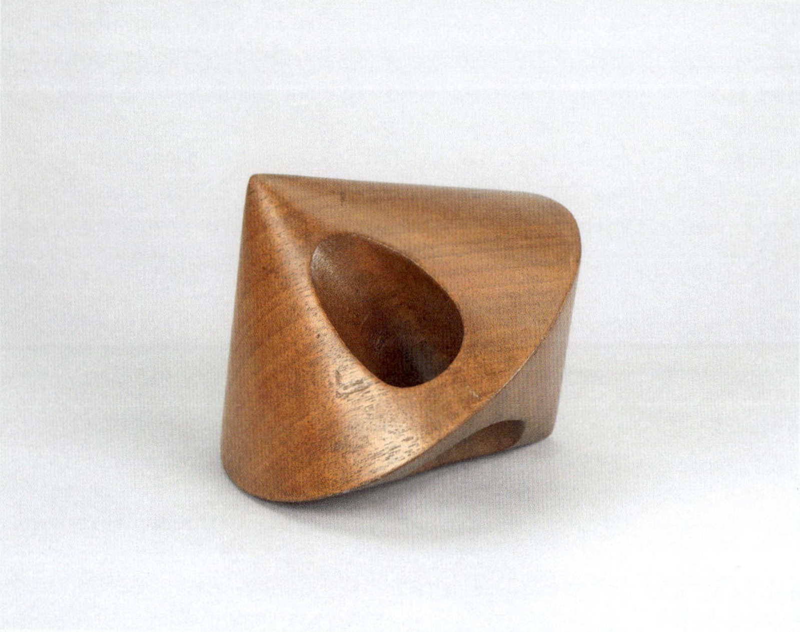

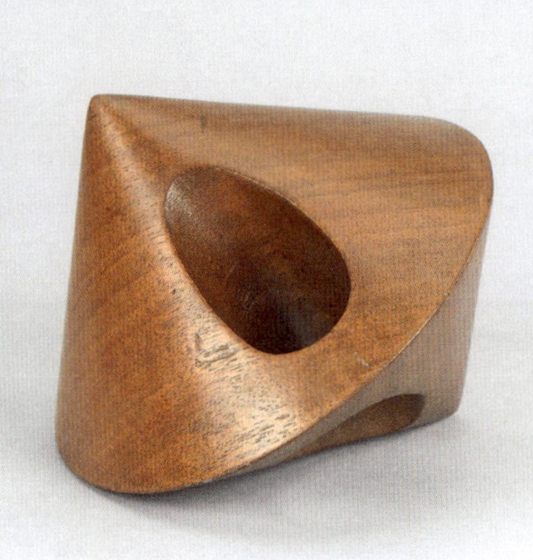

← **Robert Adams**
Conic Form
1952–53
Teak
Sainsbury Centre

↓ **Robert Adams**
Counterbalance No. 2
1955
Mahogany
Sainsbury Centre

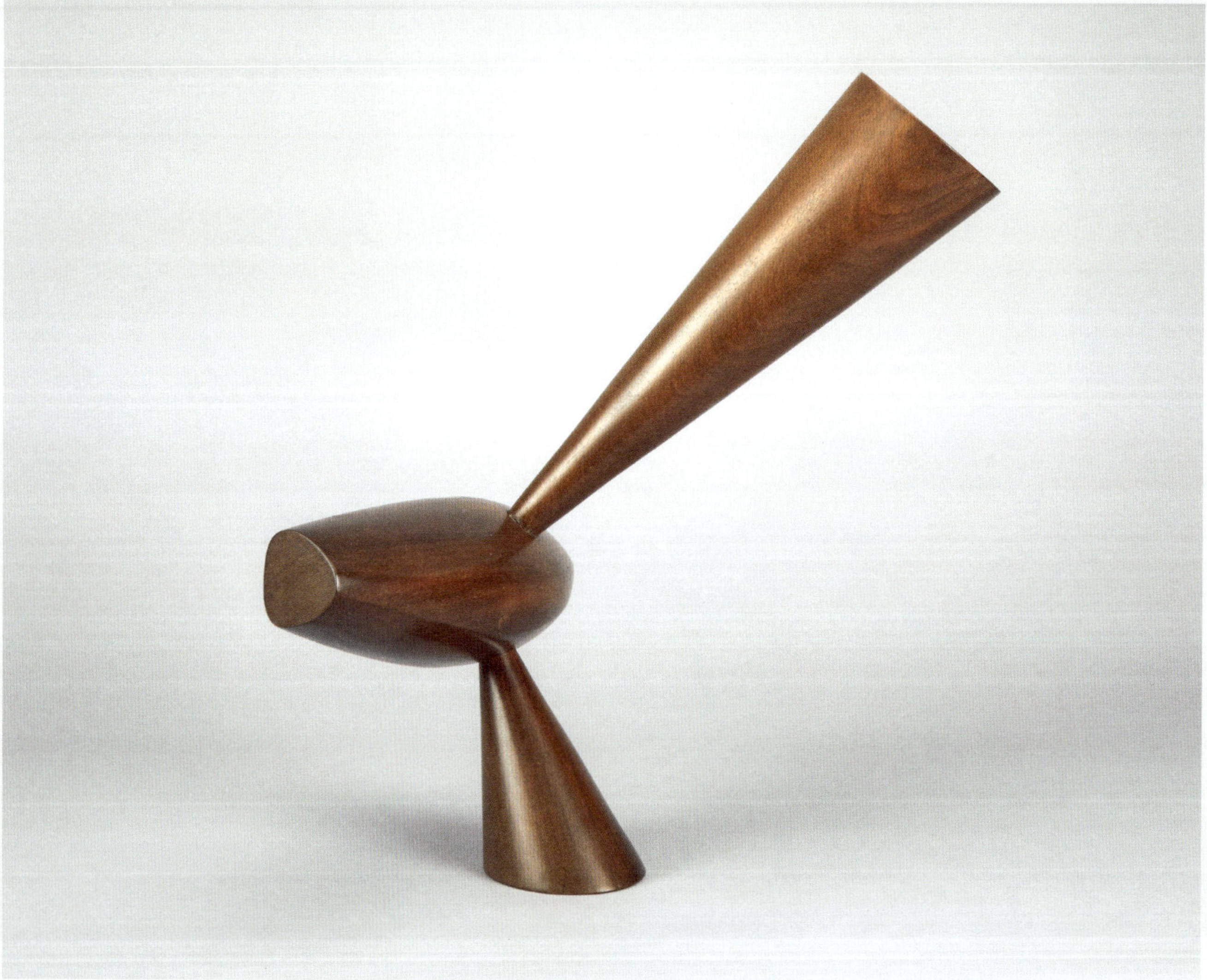

carving'.[33] Adams was unique amongst the Constructionist artists in that he explored abstraction through carving, although after the *Counterbalance* sculptures he began to construct then cast in metal. Jocelyn Chewett (1906–1979) on the other hand continued to carve geometrically abstract work throughout her career. Her carvings in stone and wood suggest blocks that have been built up – cubes and spheres pieced upon each other – but are in fact created through the reductive technique of carving.

Kinetic art was first showcased in a dedicated group exhibition at the Galerie Denise René in Paris in 1955, in the exhibition *Le Mouvement* [Movement]. The exhibition included work by Alexander Calder, Marcel Duchamp, Jesús Rafael Soto (1923–2005), Victor Vasarely (1906–1997), Jean Tinguely (1925–1991) and Yaacov Agam (b.1928). Israeli artist Agam had held an exhibition of his kinetic work in Paris two years earlier at the Galerie Craven. His work was often activated by the viewer, for example in his relief *Movement on White* (1955–56), the shapes can be exchanged between the holes on the base. The movement arises from the viewer spinning the circular board, visually disrupting these shapes. Denise René (1913–2012) brought her radical vision to London in 1968 in an exhibition at the Redfern Gallery. In the exhibition catalogue, she reminisced about the success of the 1955 Paris exhibition: 'Many people saw the potential of kinetic art as a successful synthesis of time and space. Others recognized that the future of modern art couldn't be limited to Tachism. We proved that fascinating experiments were possible outside its orbit'.[34]

Often a sense of movement was achieved through perceptual or optical effects. Of the artists René exhibited, Jesús Rafael Soto created optical sculptural works with repeated strands of almost vibrating nylon thread, dematerialising the form. François Morellet (1926–2016) also seems to break up form in his *Sphéres-Trames*, which are composed of intersecting metal rods, disrupting the totality of the sphere. The lines shift as the viewer traverses

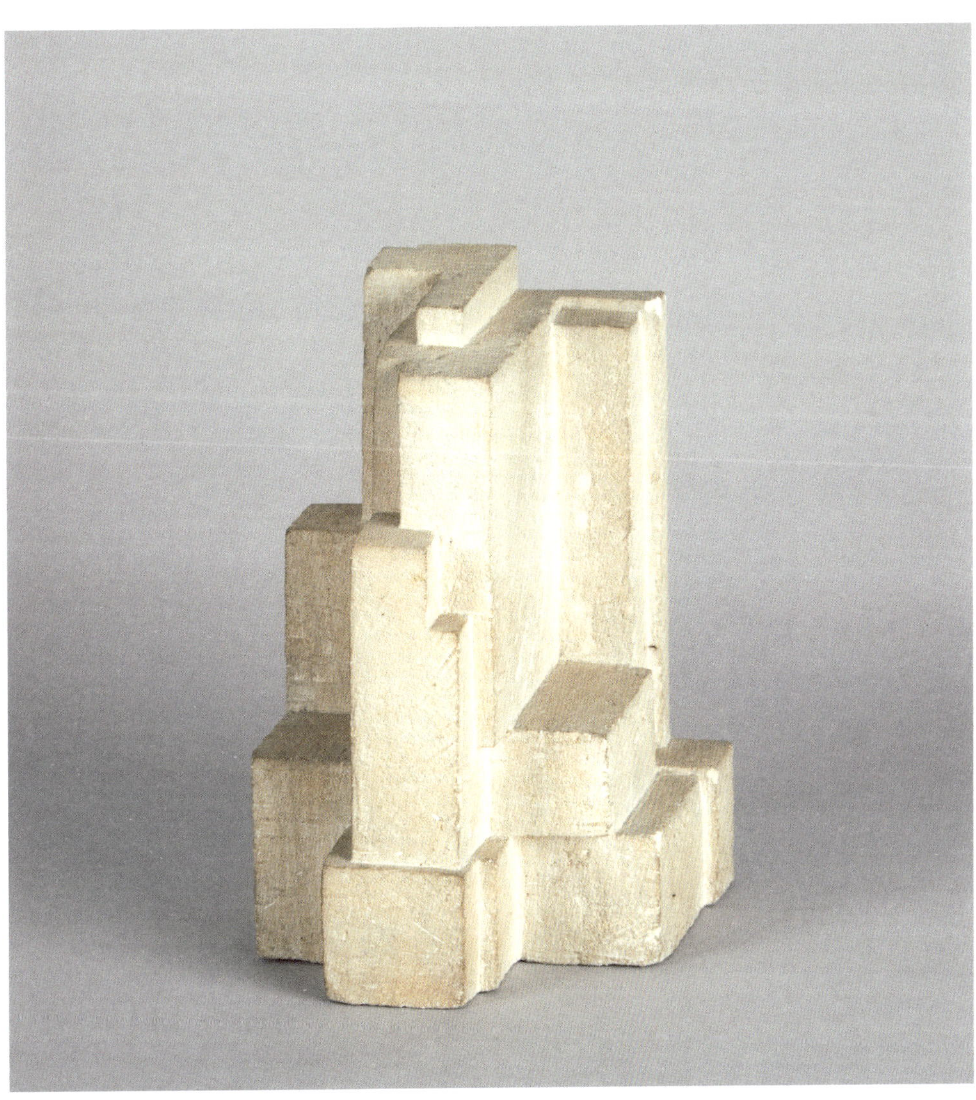

→ Jocelyn Chewett
Untitled
1949
Limestone
Sainsbury Centre

their form; and as mobiles, the objects themselves subtly move. A similar effect is achieved by Matthew Frère-Smith (1923–1999) in his sculptures which he builds up in a modular system. He likens the way in which he makes his sculptures to the way nature is structured, which is reminiscent of the Constructionist artists. Like them, he too had utopian views of how his work can engage with the environment.[35] These sculptures by Soto, Morellet and Frère-Smith are situated in the Op Art style, which is often more readily associated with painting.

Op Art was first showcased institutionally at the Museum of Modern Art, New York in 1965 in the exhibition *The Responsive Eye* which included both painting and sculpture. It was in reference to this exhibition that the term was coined.[36] Exhibition curator William Seitz (1914–1974) explained how 'perceptual constructions evolved out of the constructivist tradition', as 'perceptual painting evolved out of geometric abstraction'.[37] With many loans from Denise René, the exhibition included sculpture and painting by Constructivist, minimalist and Op Artists including Yaacov Agam, Josef Albers (1888–1976), Max Bill, Agnes Martin (1912–2004), François Morellet, Frank Stella (b.1936) and Victor Vasarely. With artists from America and Europe, the exhibition included five British artists: Michael Kidner

(1917–2009), Bridget Riley, Peter Sedgely (b.1930), Jeffrey Steele and Peter Stroud (1921–2012).

Today, Bridget Riley has become the most prominent Op Artist and it was the MoMA exhibition that brought her to international notice. Her painting *Current* (1964), in their collection, appeared on the front cover. In a work now typically associated with her style, fine black and white lines curve vertically and seem to vibrate across the picture plane. Riley used repeated shapes or lines, but subtle variations in width or angle make the canvas itself appear to warp and shift before the viewer's eyes. Influential critic David Sylvester (1924–2001) reviewed Riley's first solo exhibition at Gallery One, London in 1962, in which he described this sense of movement:

> Bridget Riley is a hard-edged abstractionist, painting in black and white, mostly using squares, circles and parallel lines as units in such a way that they seem to be jumping, flashing, bending. In one canvas, a sort of chessboard is, as it were, concertina'd to create a contrast, at once unnerving and reassuring, between all the frenetic activity that occurs where the squares are compressed and the serene stability of those which have retained their 'proper' proportions.[38]

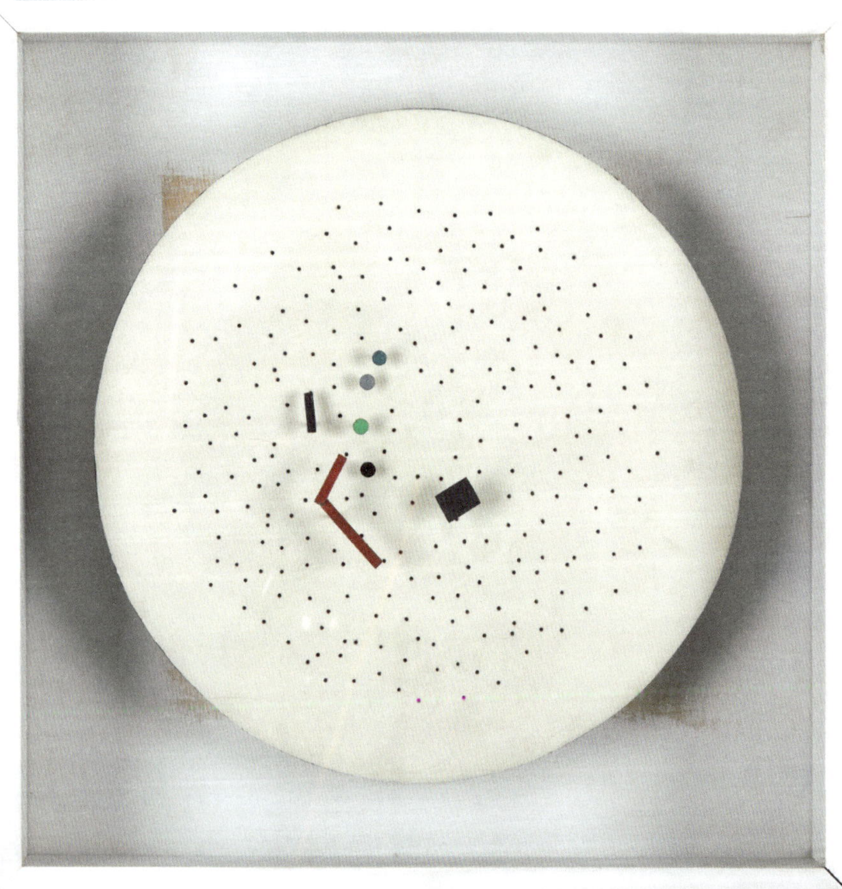

← Yaacov Agam
Movement on White
*c.*1955–66
Perspex, plastic and wood
Sainsbury Centre

→ Jesús Rafael Soto
Kinetic Construction
1965
Painted wood and nylon thread
Sainsbury Centre

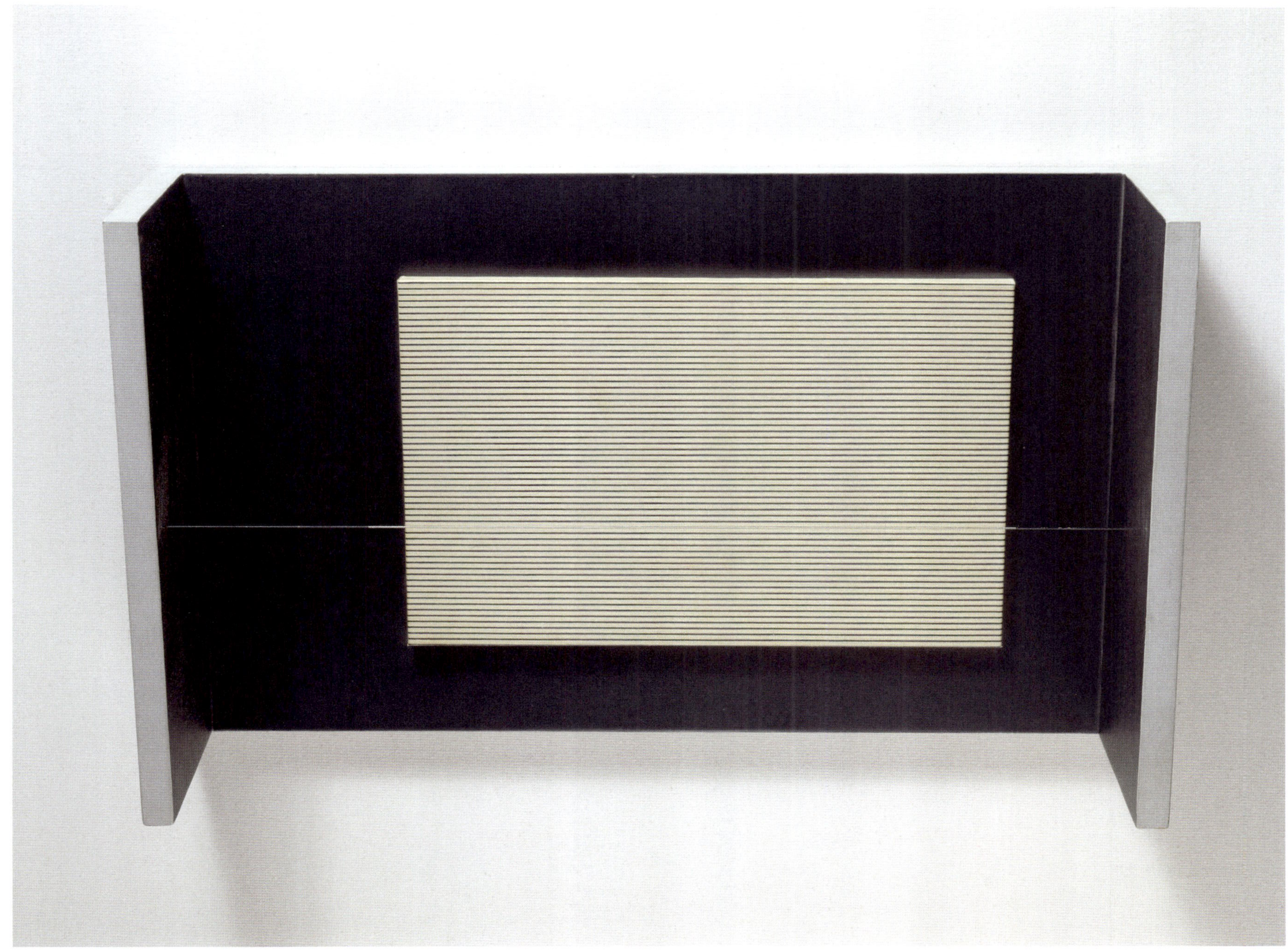

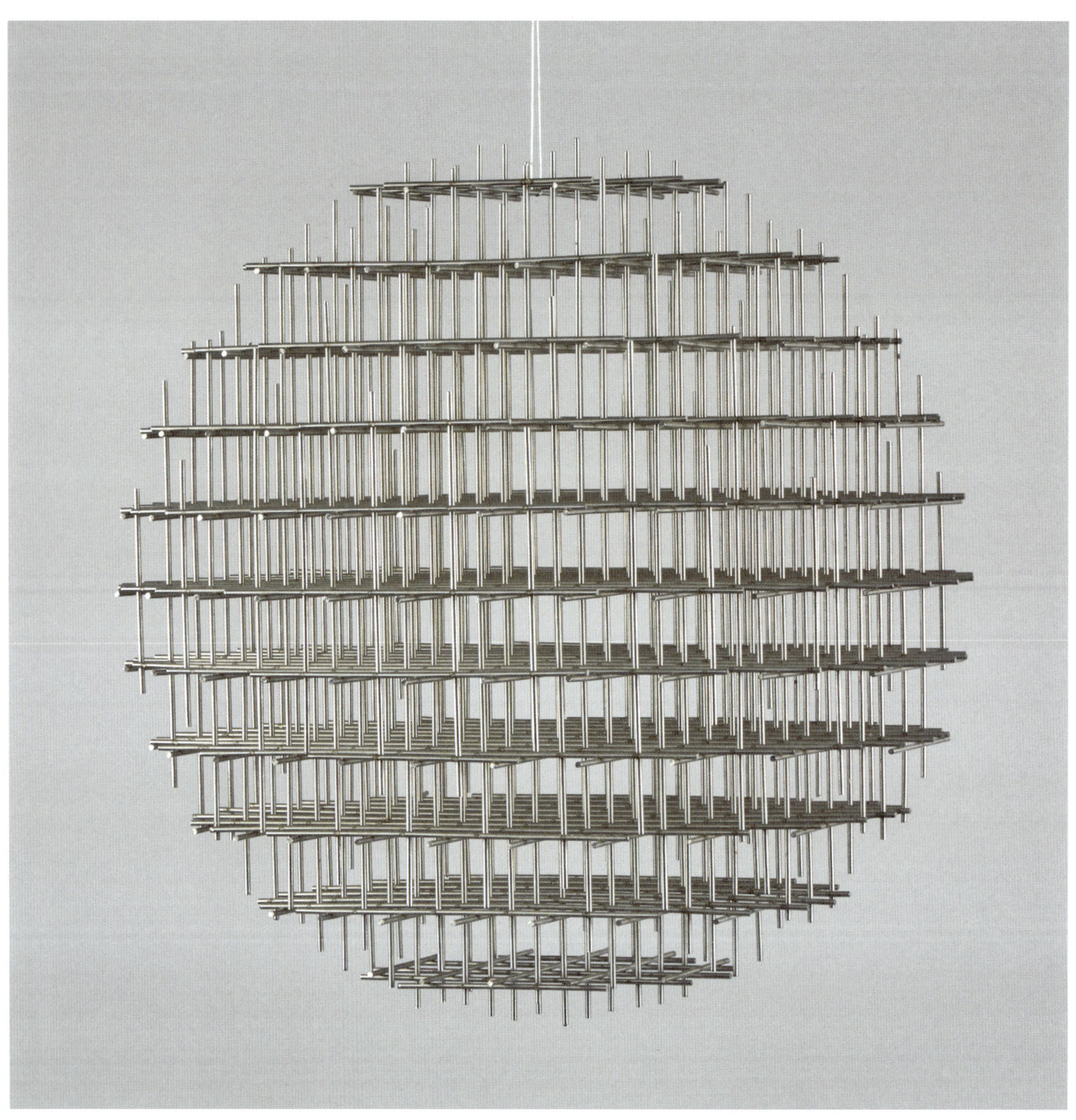

↑ François Morellet
Sphère-trame
1962
Stainless steel
Sainsbury Centre

→ Matthew Frère-Smith
Double Khombic
1965
Aluminium
Sainsbury Centre

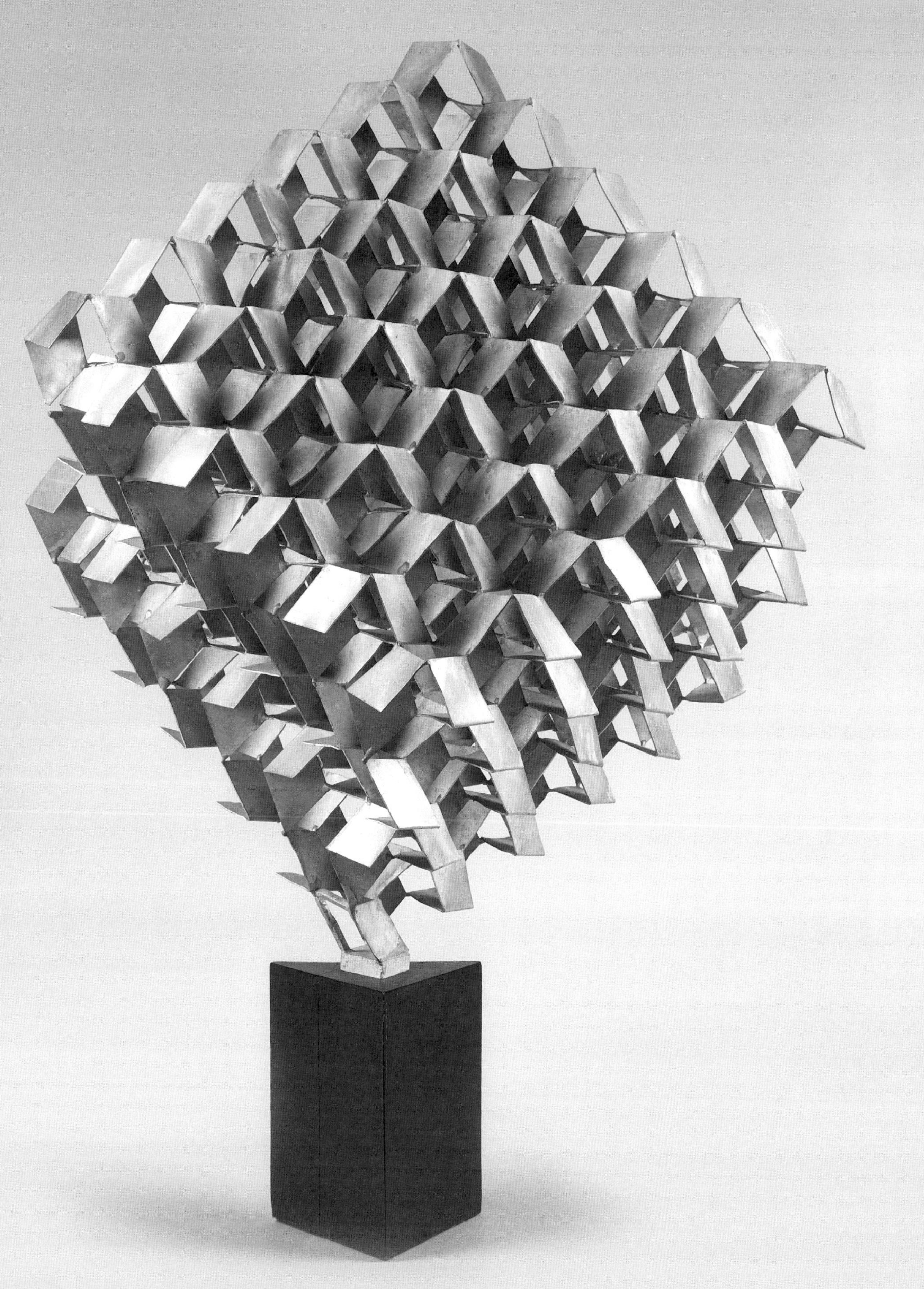

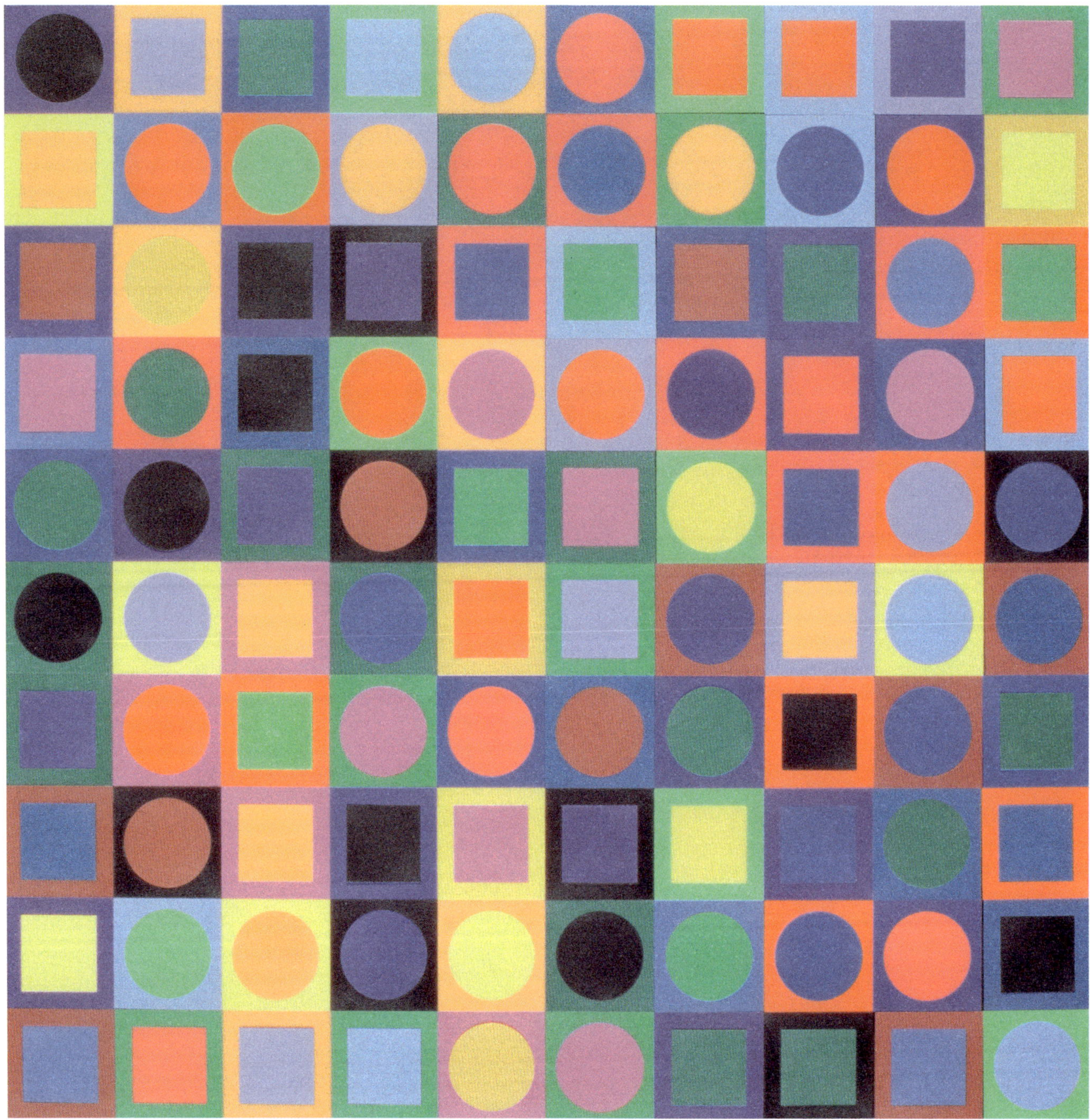

↑ **Victor Vasarely**
Planetary Folklore Participants No. 1
1969
Polystyrene, metal and magnets
Sainsbury Centre

→ **Li Yuan-Chia**
Cosmic Point Multiple
1968
Steel, styrofoam, cellulose paint
and barrium ferrite
Sainsbury Centre

Op Art was pioneered by Victor Vasarely and *The Responsive Eye* included his *Orion MC* (1963), composed of circles and ovals within squares. The proximity and repetition of the circles and ovals suggest a single form rotating, expanding and contracting. The repetition of circles within squares is also found in *Planetary Folklore Participants No.1* (1969). This is an interactive work in which each of the circles and squares could be interchanged to give different colour and form variations across the relief. Each piece is magnetic, so the internal shape and each square within which they sit could be changed. Therefore, not only do the colours change, but also where the circles and squares fall. This participatory work was made as a multiple, so there is endless variation amongst the reliefs themselves. The work came with an instruction manual and sheets encouraging the participant to try different variations and record them.

Li Yuan-Chia (1929–1994) also made a series of interactive reliefs in which the viewer would place metal shapes in a composition pleasing to them on a magnetic backboard. The title of *Cosmic Point Multiple* refers to Li's interest in the 'Cosmic Point', which he explored throughout his visual and participatory work. For him, the 'Point' was 'the origin and end of creation'.[39] It echoes Vasarely's interest in the cosmos as indicated by his own term, 'Planetary Folklore', which he used to define a world of colour, as was his aim for the built environment.[40] These reliefs by Li and Vasarely are both simple in their composition, with basic geometric shapes and a controlled number of colours. This allows the individual to produce aesthetically pleasing compositions within a predetermined layout. Both Li and Vasarely's works were made as multiples, which were gaining ground as a valid and creative art form in the 1960s. Gallerist Denise René produced multiples by artists such as Vasarely and François Morellet. They wanted to make art accessible to all, and demystify it as Morellet explained, when he aspired towards 'faith in progress, the demystification of art, systematic experimentation, a step towards a science of art, the ultimate hope'.[41]

In Switzerland, the company X Art Collections made multiples, such as Max Bill's *Three Equal Volumes* (1969) in an edition of 2,000. In Britain, the company Unlimited was set up by engineer and art collector Jeremy Fry (1924–2005) to produce multiples in collaboration with artists. Unlimited produced the relief *Rotation* (1968) by Mary Martin, and they worked with Brazilian artist Lygia Clark (1920–1988) to produce a series of her sculptures that she

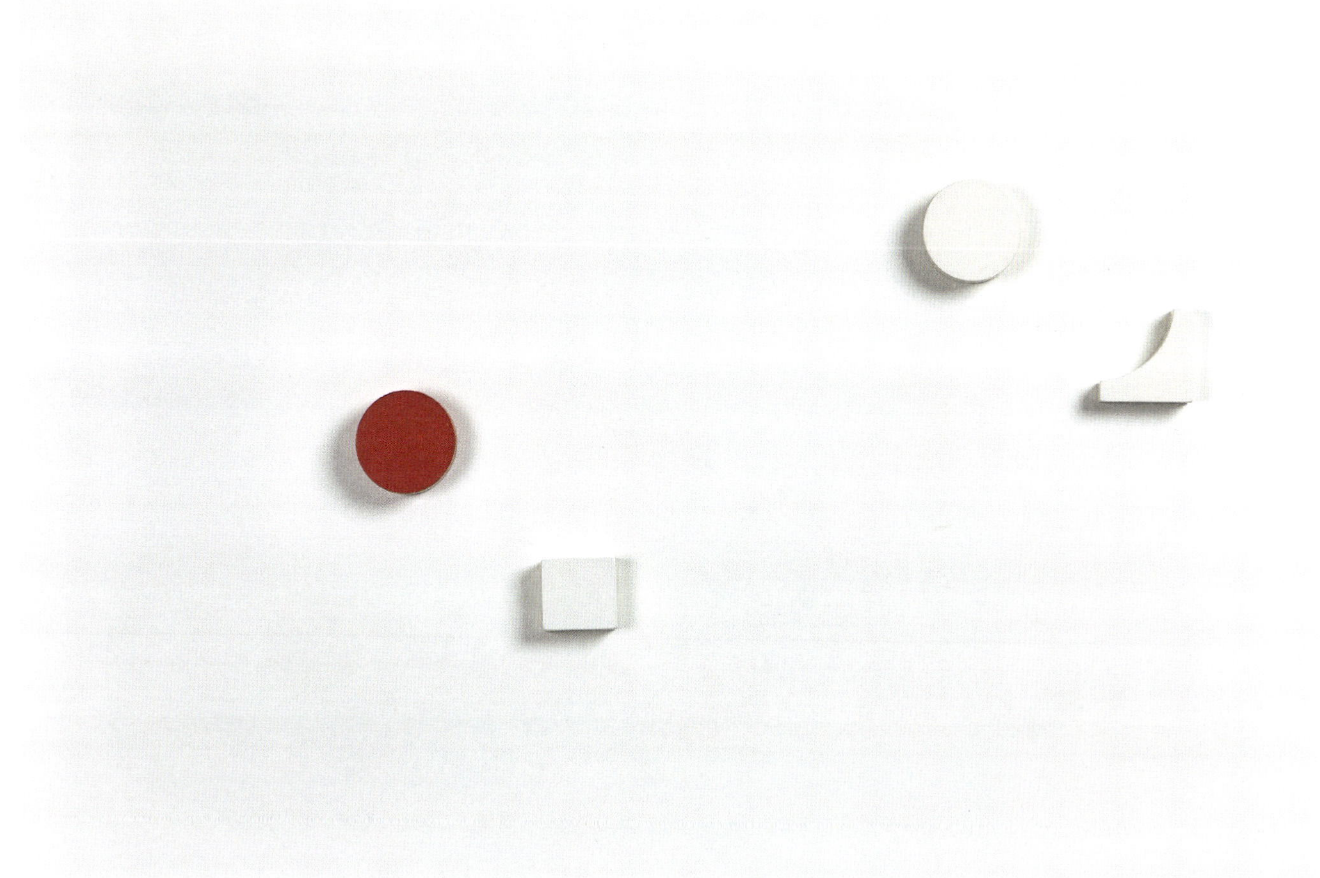

called *Bichos*, meaning 'little creatures', in an unlimited multiple in 1969. Like the works by Vasarely and Li, Clark's multiples were manipulated by a participant, this time to create various configurations of the aluminium planes on hinges. For Clark, it was this interaction from the viewer that brought about the creative expression. Via these works, those that had traditionally been the viewer became active participants. Furthermore, art now had an element of play. Due to the affordability of multiples, more people could live with works of art on a daily basis.

Unlimited also worked with Greek artist Takis (1925–2019) to create versions of his sculptural works collectively described as *Signals*. His *Signals* were slender poles topped with an object or light. With Unlimited, he created three versions with flashing lights in various colours on one or two poles. Earlier unique versions of the *Signals* had been topped with more complex swirls of metal, like calligraphy, or with a found industrial object. Takis and Fry simplified the *Signals* in order to develop them as a multiple for mass production. These examples illuminate why so many of the artists working in a Constructivist tradition may have translated their work into multiples: they were interested in the intersection between art and science; their work was composed of simple shapes, suitable for mass

↑ **Max Bill**
Three Equal Volumes
1969
Perspex
Sainsbury Centre

→ **Lygia Clark**
LC2
1969
Aluminium
Sainsbury Centre

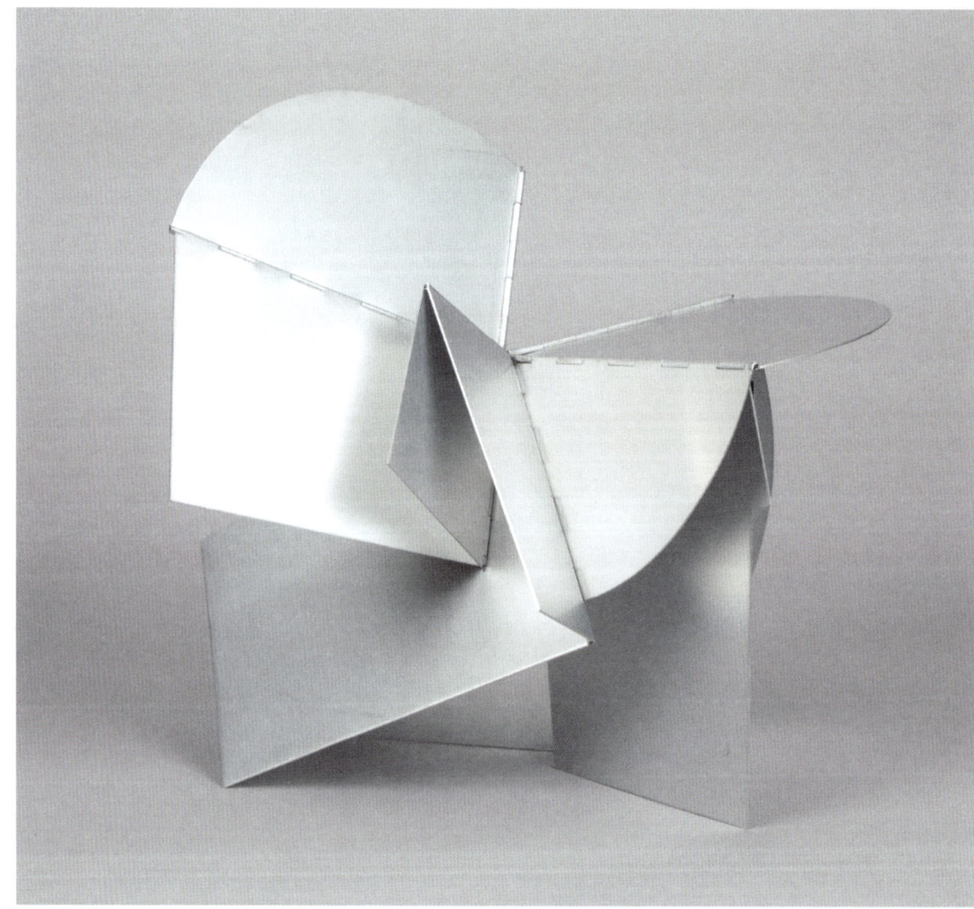

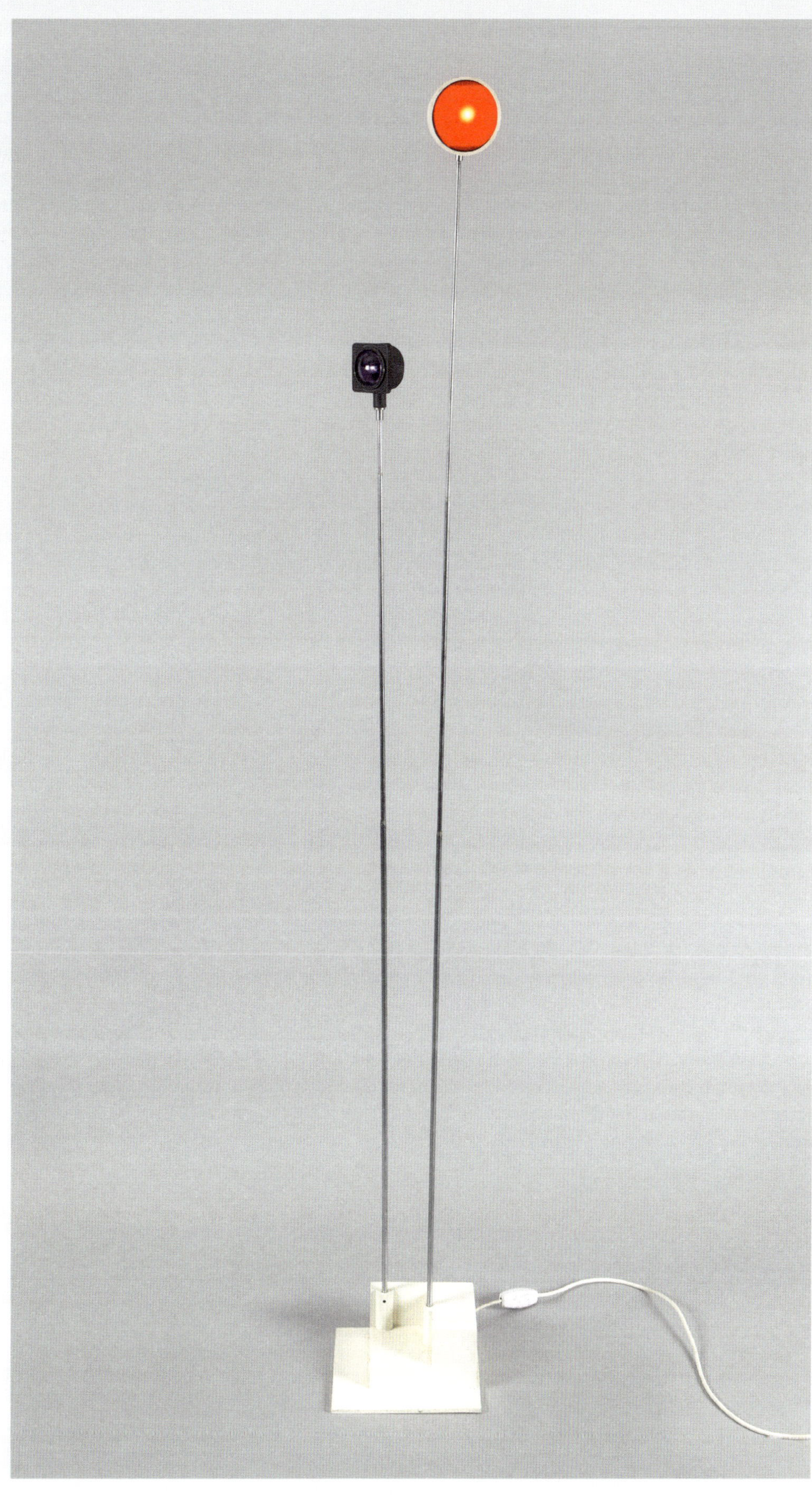

→ Takis
Signals Series II
1968
Steel, tubular chrome-plated steel,
acrylic, electrical components
and glass
Sainsbury Centre

production; but moreover, they had utopian views of art being integrated into the fabric of society, as set out by the foundations of Constructivism in Russia.

Takis' *Signals* were so fundamental to a group of artists, curators and critics in Britain that they named a gallery and publication after them. The Signals Gallery had its origins in the Newsbulletin founded by critic Guy Brett (1942–2021), curator Paul Keeler (b.1942), and artists Gustav Metzger (1926–2017), Marcello Salvadori (1928–2002) and David Medalla (1942–2020). Like many Constructivist artists, the group had ambitious aims to integrate art, technology, science and the environment, as set out in the first Newsbulletin.[42] First titled the Centre for Advanced Creative Study, the gallery was renamed Signals after the works by Takis. Other works by Takis incorporated magnets or sound; making invisible energies visible. The scientific yet enigmatic nature of Takis' work marks the aims of Signals' Newsbulletin and gallery. The gallery, which launched with an exhibition of Takis' work, ran from 1964 to 1966. Their activities remained experimental and groundbreaking, introducing artists such as Mira Schendel (1919–1988), Lygia Clark, Carlos Cruz-Diez (1923–2019) and Li Yuan-Chia to London.

It was his Signals exhibition that brought Li Yuan-Chia to London, after he had been living in Bologna. Li was Chinese and studied in Taiwan where he developed his abstract art before relocating to Italy. He has since been positioned by the Taipei Fine Arts Museum as 'one of Taiwan's earliest pioneers of abstract art and conceptual art'.[43] Following his invitation from the Signals Gallery, he lived in London between 1965 and 1968 before settling in Cumbria. There he established the LYC Museum and Art Gallery in the rural village of Banks, near Hadrian's Wall, as the neighbour of painter Winifred Nicholson (1893–1981). At his museum, he exhibited over 320 artists between 1972 and 1983. They included major names such as Barbara Hepworth and Paul Nash (1889–1946), as well as artists who were then little-known in Britain, such as Lygia Clark. The museum extended Li's interest in participatory practice to experimental exhibition-making.

COLOUR AND RHYTHM

Whereas artists such as Victor Pasmore, Kenneth Martin and Mary Martin had begun as painters, when they turned to abstraction they tended to adopt new sculptural materials for their reliefs, mobiles or constructions. From the 1960s, however, a generation of artists emerged that used painting or printmaking techniques in Constructivist styles using hard-edged abstraction. The term hard-edged abstraction was first used by Lawrence Alloway in reference to a group of Californian painters in 1960, but it was soon applied to painting in Britain, as in David Sylvester's quote regarding Bridget Riley above.[44] Whereas many of the constructions in plastics, metal and wood had maintained the original colours of the materials, and therefore often had muted palettes, by turning to paint, these later artists embraced colour for its emotive effects.

Much of this activity in painting emerged around the Systems Group, formed and named by artists Jeffrey Steele and Malcolm Hughes (1920–1997) after a 1969 exhibition *Systeemi • System: An exhibition of syntactic art from Britain* at the Amos Anderson Museum (Amos Rex) in Helsinki. Active members included Michael Kidner, Peter Lowe (b.1938) and Jean Spencer (1942–1998). John Ernest and Gillian Wise were also part of the group, breaking away from their connection with the Constructionists. Despite differences between the Constructionist and Systems artists, they followed in the Constructivist tradition in the logical geometry of their work.

The work of Jean Spencer marks a shift from working in parallel with Constructionism to an approach more in line with her Systems colleagues. From her time at Bath Academy of Art in 1960, where she was taught by Malcolm Hughes, until the mid-1970s she created shallow reliefs in a single shade of white. The forms stemmed from numerical systems as she searched for the number of possible variations that can come from overlapping identical squares. The system is not decipherable in the final works, but they are gentle studies in the variation of tone achieved from depth and form. The latter part of her career saw her embracing colour and tonal variations. She studied colour theory and the paintings of J. M. W. Turner (1775–1851), Kazimir Malevich

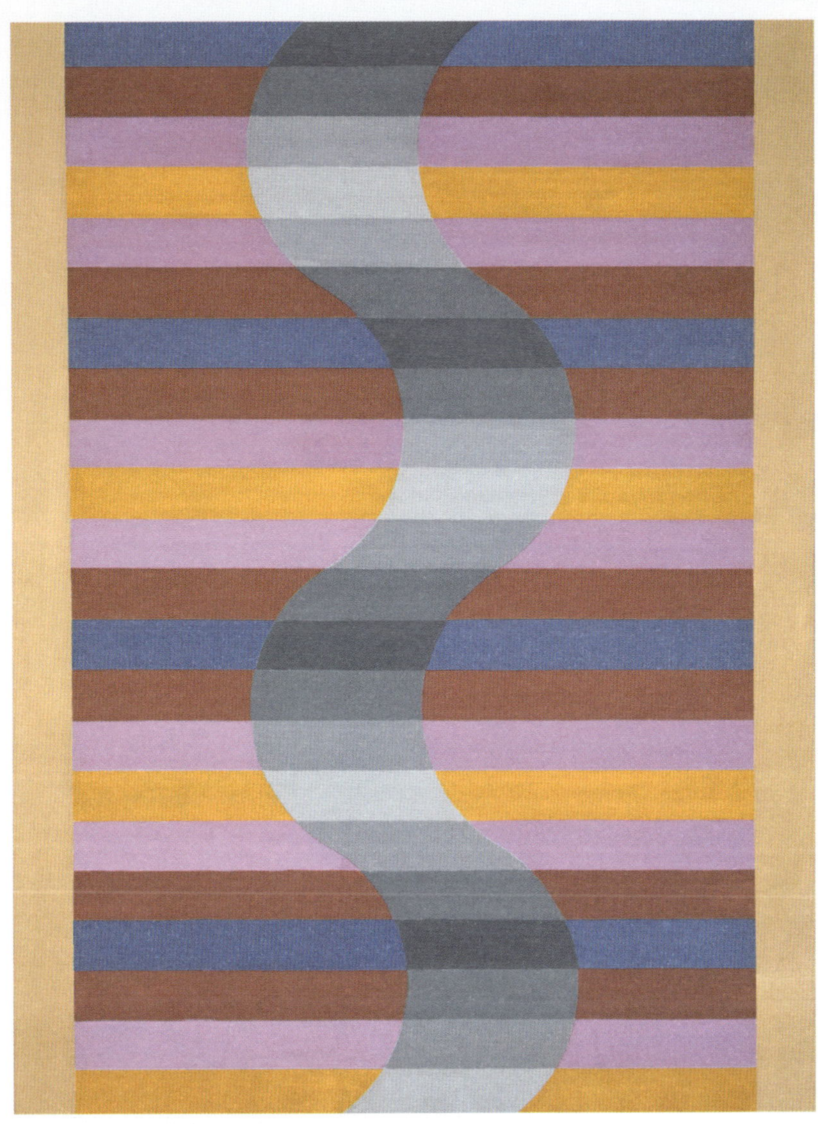

↑ **Michael Kidner**
Colour and Tone Wave
1967
Acrylic on canvas
Sainsbury Centre

→ **Richard Paul Lohse**
Six systematic colour movements
from yellow to yellow
1955–56
Oil on linen
Sainsbury Centre

(1879–1935), Piet Mondrian and Richard Paul Lohse. Swiss painter Lohse was a great influence on many Constructivist artists. He used modular forms, systematically varying the colours in standard-sized blocks. Lohse described the effect as 'Combined into free groups, the standardized elements mutually enter into opposition and become active carriers of energy. An objective rhythm on the basis of progressive and regressive movement develops'.[45]

The Systems artists disagreed in two key ways: firstly, in how much of the creation was intuitive or followed predetermined systems; and secondly, whether the viewer needs knowledge of the internal logic. One of the artists who faithfully followed her self-imposed mathematical processes was Natalie Dower (b.1931). Though her processes were mathematical, Dower admitted that her knowledge of maths was limited, but she used it to produce visually appealing effects. On the question of whether the viewer should understand the process, Dower believed either position was valuable:

> The methods are for myself and are often so intricate that without access to the preparatory working drawings they are difficult to deconstruct. If people do get pleasure from 'reading' the system that is a bonus, but my aim is to communicate and make a visual impact in visual terms.[46]

Dower differed from many of her Systems colleagues in that her work encompassed painting, reliefs and sculpture. Beginning as a painter (first training in the figurative tradition before turning to abstraction), she made her first relief in 1976 and her first sculpture in 1980. Her sculpture in fact stemmed from a preparatory drawing intended for a painting. In trying to solve a problem caused by one of her systems, she realised that it would have been resolved if it were for a three-dimensional work. In this, Dower followed the trajectory of the Constructionists, many of whom started as painters before beginning to create constructions. Dower's *Blue / Green Dudeney Relief* (1989) and sculpture *Dudeney Oyster no.2* (1985–2019) are

both based on the work of mathematician Henry Dudeney (1857–1930) and his best-known discovery that if you dissect an equilateral triangle into four, by rotating the shapes on their points, they form a square.[47]

In 1978 Rita Donagh (b.1939), Tess Jaray (b.1937), Liliane Lijne (b.1939), Kim Lim (1936–1997) and Gillian Wise selected the artists for the Hayward Annual. All these selectors, except Donagh, made purely abstract work. The all-woman panel was put together in response to criticism of a sculpture exhibition at the Hayward Gallery in 1975, which included thirty-six men and only four women. In the 1978 Hayward Annual exhibition, seventy percent of the artists were women, and the organisers aimed to showcase the 'undershown and underrated artists of all ages and stylistic persuasions'.[48] Wise curated a section of the exhibition devoted to Constructivist art, with work by Wise, Terry Pope (b.1941) and Susan Derges (b.1955). They created an octagonal framework, providing an installation reflective of the geometry of the artworks that was divorced from the brutalist architecture of the Hayward.

In 1986, sociologist Elizabeth Chaplin and Malcolm Hughes, co-founder of the Systems Group, organised the exhibition *Systematic Constructive Drawings* at the Wentworth Gallery, York. The Systems Group had already disbanded by the end of the 1970s, but this exhibition included work by some of the artists who had been part of the group, as well as related artists. The exhibition was part of Chaplin's research into the social, political and gender dynamics of artist groups, for which she had been interviewing British Constructivist artists. Two years later, Chaplin published 'Feminism and Systematic Constructive Art' in *Constructivist Forum*, the only journal dedicated to Constructivist art in the UK. In the article, Chaplin summarised the women artists' positions in relation to their work and feminism. Though the artists were listed, she did not attribute particular positions to specific artists. She describes one belief that, whilst an artist describes herself as a feminist, this does *not* apply to her work, which is objective and universal, therefore degendered. Chaplin herself discredits the claim of universality in the

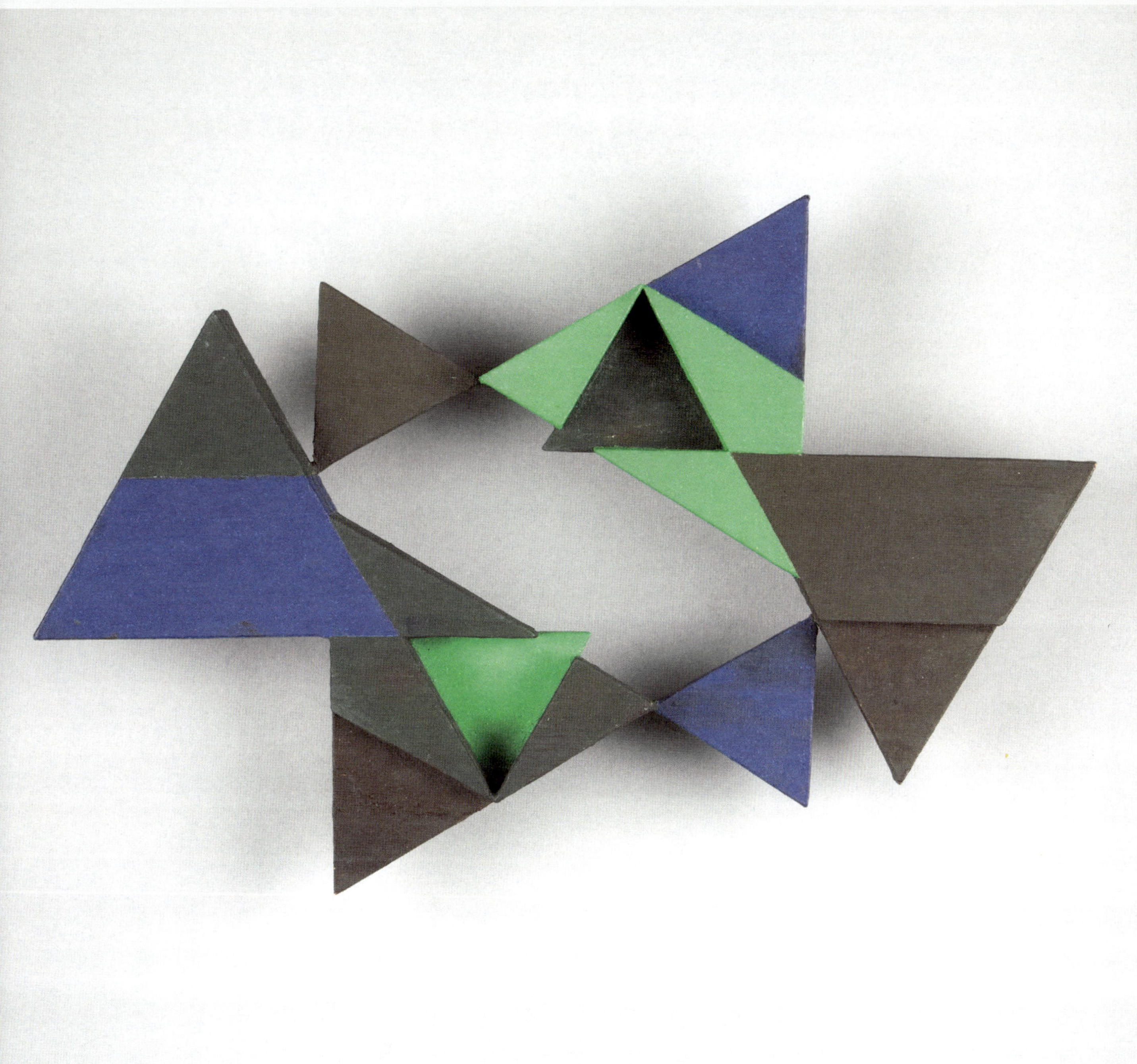

↑ Natalie Dower
Blue / Green Dudeney Relief
1989
Oil on wood
Sainsbury Centre

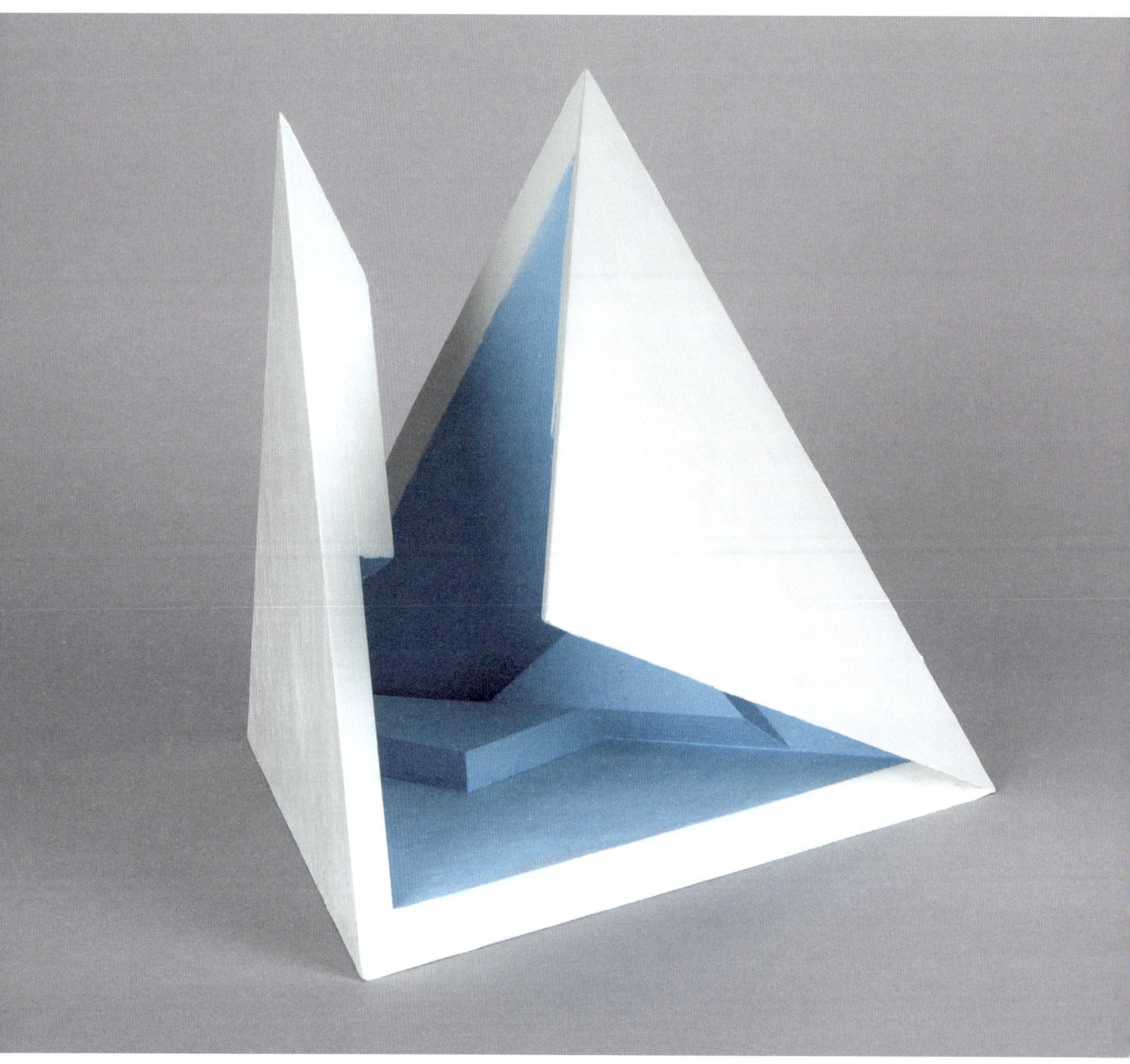

↑ Natalie Dower
Dudeney Oyster No. 2
1985–2019
Oil on wood
Sainsbury Centre

article, arguing that claims of universality and objectivity are rooted in patriarchal structures.[49] An opposing view offered is that their work *is* feminist, because it shows that the artist is embracing traits generally attributed to men: logic, rigour, rationality and abstraction.[50] Elsewhere in the article, Chaplin offers anecdotal evidence that the women artists have been told that their work 'looks male'.[51]

Three years later, Chaplin had two letters published in *Art Monthly* about her research. In one, she expressed concern that the feminist values of the artists are not expressed in their work:

> It almost seems as though they want feminism to come to them (in terms of a shift in socially connoted visual statements) rather than wanting to produce a shift in their own art so that it has a feminist element recognisable to other women/feminists.[52]

As a result of her work over a period of years, Chaplin founded the group Countervail with Jean Spencer. With the artists Nicole Charlett (b.1957), Judith Dean (b.1965), Natalie Dower and Susan Tebby (b.1944), the group aimed to disrupt the view that theirs was a masculine approach to art. Charlett described how this all-woman group offered a more open forum in which she could discuss the developments of her art as it shifted from a strictly Constructivist idiom.[53] In 1992 to 1993 they staged

an exhibition, *Countervail*, at the Mappin Art Gallery, Sheffield (now Weston Park Museum), then at the Mead Gallery, Coventry. Many of these artists considered how their works related to space, in making site-specific works, or showing works unframed as actual objects in space, so painting became installation. They collectively wrote in the exhibition catalogue, 'In all cases the environment is permitted (invited?) in some way to infiltrate the space of the object, to participate in its meanings'.[54]

Charlett invites the space of the gallery into her compositions through unframed groups of canvases comprising a single work. As she described:

> Painted panels of different widths are interspaced with measured intervals of wall space; the 'inter' or 'between' enabling some understanding of the position of separate panels in relation to others, and at the same time, being the result of their displacement. The separateness of panels highlights a notion that relations are not absolute or fixed to any one setting.[55]

(Dis)Placements: Corner Locus No.1 (1989) is a triptych of three canvases, each of different proportions and divided by different colour combinations. Together, the colours with the section of wall between them make a series of squares. Charlett made *(Dis)Placements: Corner Locus No.1*

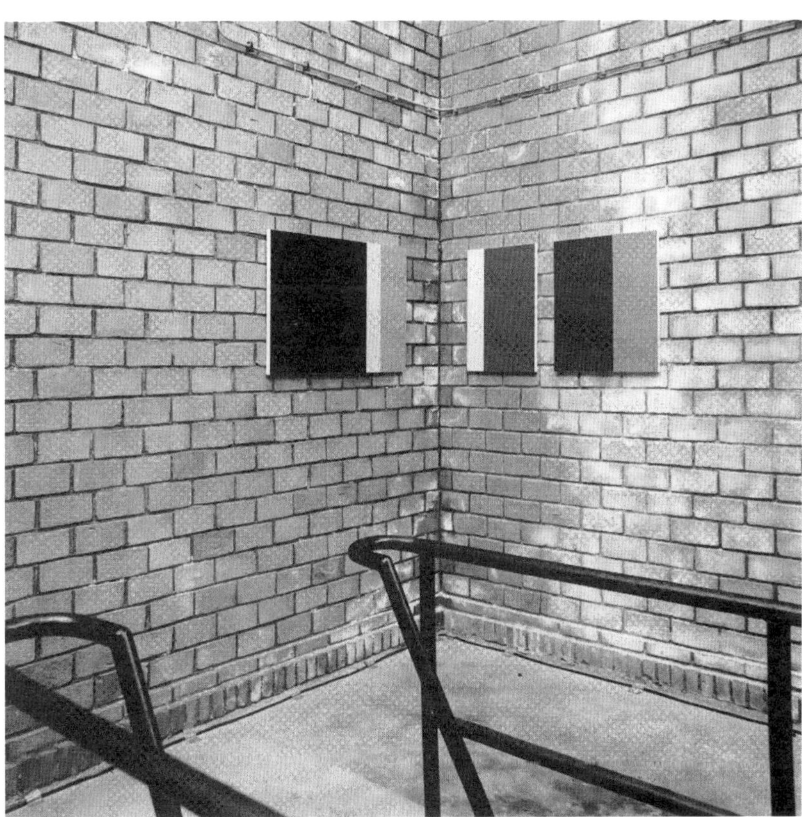

→ Nicole Charlett, *(Dis)Placements: Corner Locus No. 1*, 1989 in *Tape – Licht – Vert* at the Vlissingen Water tower, the Netherlands, 1989.

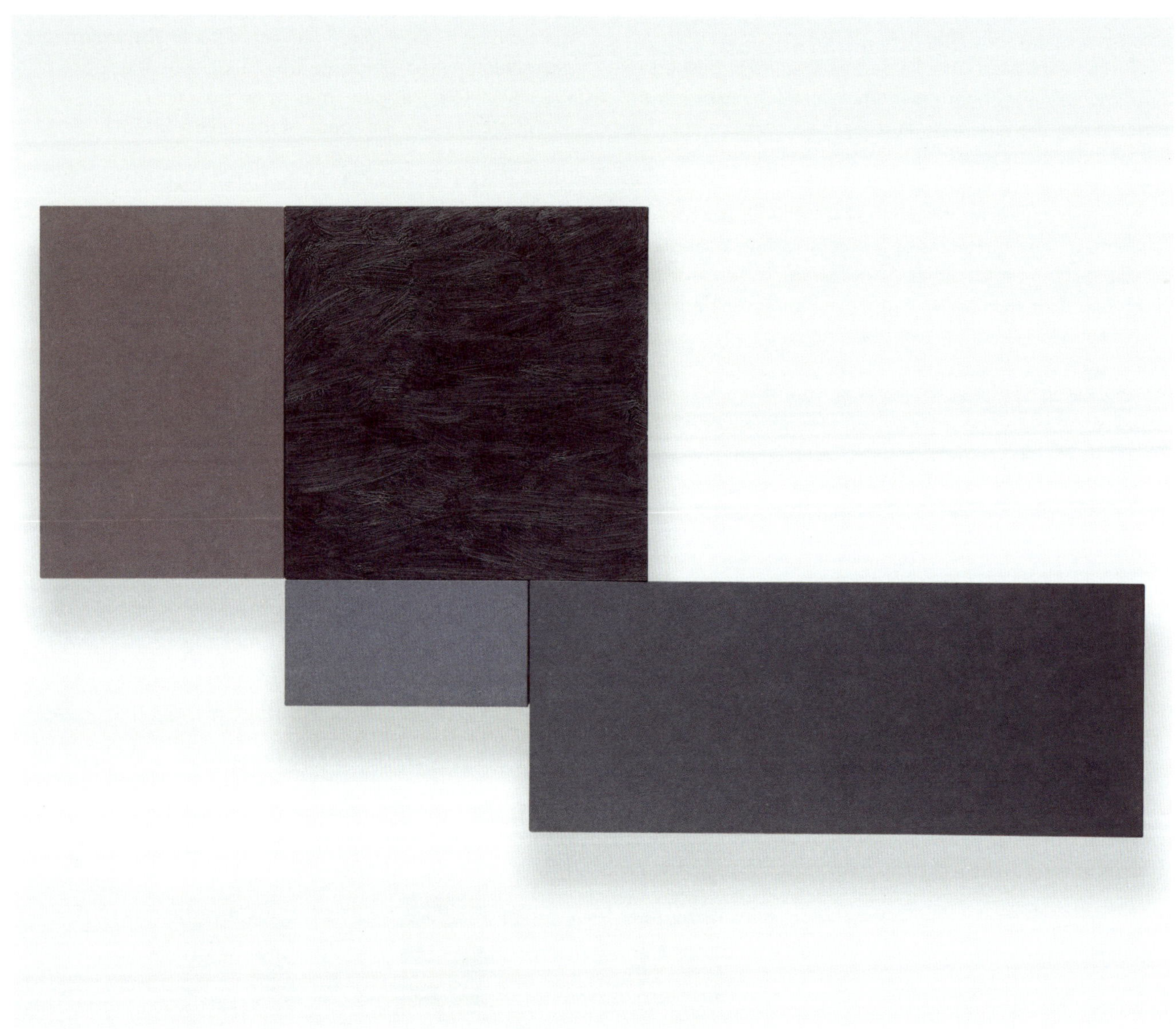

↑ Trevor Sutton
Painting A
1980
Oil and acrylic on canvas
Sainsbury Centre

for the exhibition *TAPE, LIGHT, VERF* in a disused water tower in the Netherlands. The footprint of the space was narrow so there were not long walls on which to show work, therefore Charlett created her only work for a corner. By incorporating space into the composition, the Countervail artists were developing the ideas previously described by Lohse. Lohse believed that by placing the pictorial elements in parallel to the edges of the canvas, the image and canvas became a structural whole: 'Thus the limits of the picture plane become an integral part of the formal picture'.[56] For the Countervail artists, not only do the edges of the picture plane become part of the picture, but so do the walls upon which they are placed.

Trevor Sutton (b.1948) also considered his painting in the context of space in piecing together different canvases to form an irregular shape, again transforming image into object. In his recent work Sutton has depicted architecture, but his earlier shaped abstract paintings demonstrate that architectural concerns have always been a fundamental part of his work. As he described, 'It's to do with constructing something... not just painting. It's actually bringing something into the world that has a structure, which seems to relate very powerfully to everything that's around us'.[57]

The use of colour and hard-edged abstraction was closely mirrored in sculptural developments at the time, particularly in the artists known as the New Generation. These young sculptors were taught by Anthony Caro (1924–2013) in the 1960s, and used industrial materials constructed, welded and painted in vibrant colours. In 2017, an Arts Council exhibition, *Kaleidoscope*, showcased art from the 1960s that employed 'sequence, repetition and symmetry'.[58] In the catalogue, exhibition co-curator Sam Cornish compares the New Generation to the earlier Constructionists, Mary Martin and Anthony Hill, in their use of repeated elements and industrial materials. Cornish argues that the sculptors of the 1960s used repetition more intuitively and flexibly than Martin and Hill, who had established predetermined rules. Moreover, Cornish argues that the Constructionists used industrial materials (aluminium, steel, Formica) for their precision, whereas the New Generation used plastics for their more whimsical qualities: 'plastic's irrationality, its ambiguous position between nature and artifice'.[59]

In an interview in 1966, Michael Tyzack (1933–2007) related the style of the New Generation to the movement in abstract painting with which he identified his work to be a part. He explained, 'I think in this country particularly that abstraction is moving towards a new baroque, if one is to judge by the work of people such as King and Tucker and possibly the more recent paintings of Denny and Kidner'.[60] His use of the term 'baroque' indicates an exuberance missing from the work of the Constructionist artists. The wavy patterns in such paintings as *Nickel Yard* (1967) demonstrate Tyzack experimenting with fluidity within a rigid structure. In other works, Tyzack's compositions broke out of the confines of the rectangle with shaped canvases echoing his wavy compositions.

Tyzack was a jazz musician as well as a visual artist, and is one of many abstract artists to find parallels between the two. Wassily Kandinsky (1866–1944), early pioneer in abstraction, is thought to have had synesthesia, where he associated particular musical sounds with colours.

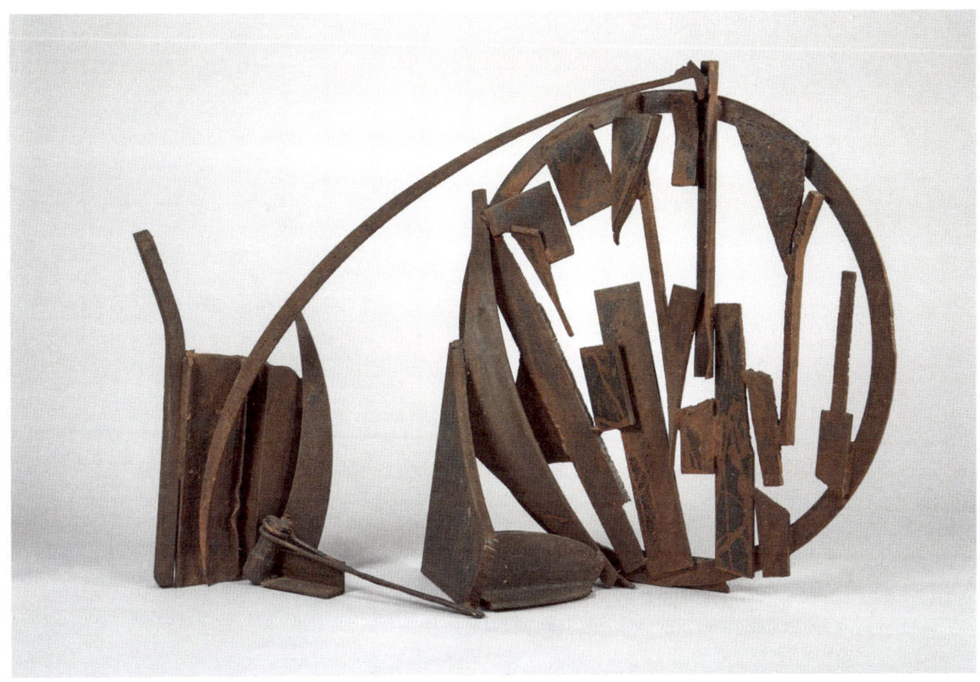

→ Anthony Caro
Table Sculpture CCCLXXI
1977
Steel, rusted and varnished
Sainsbury Centre

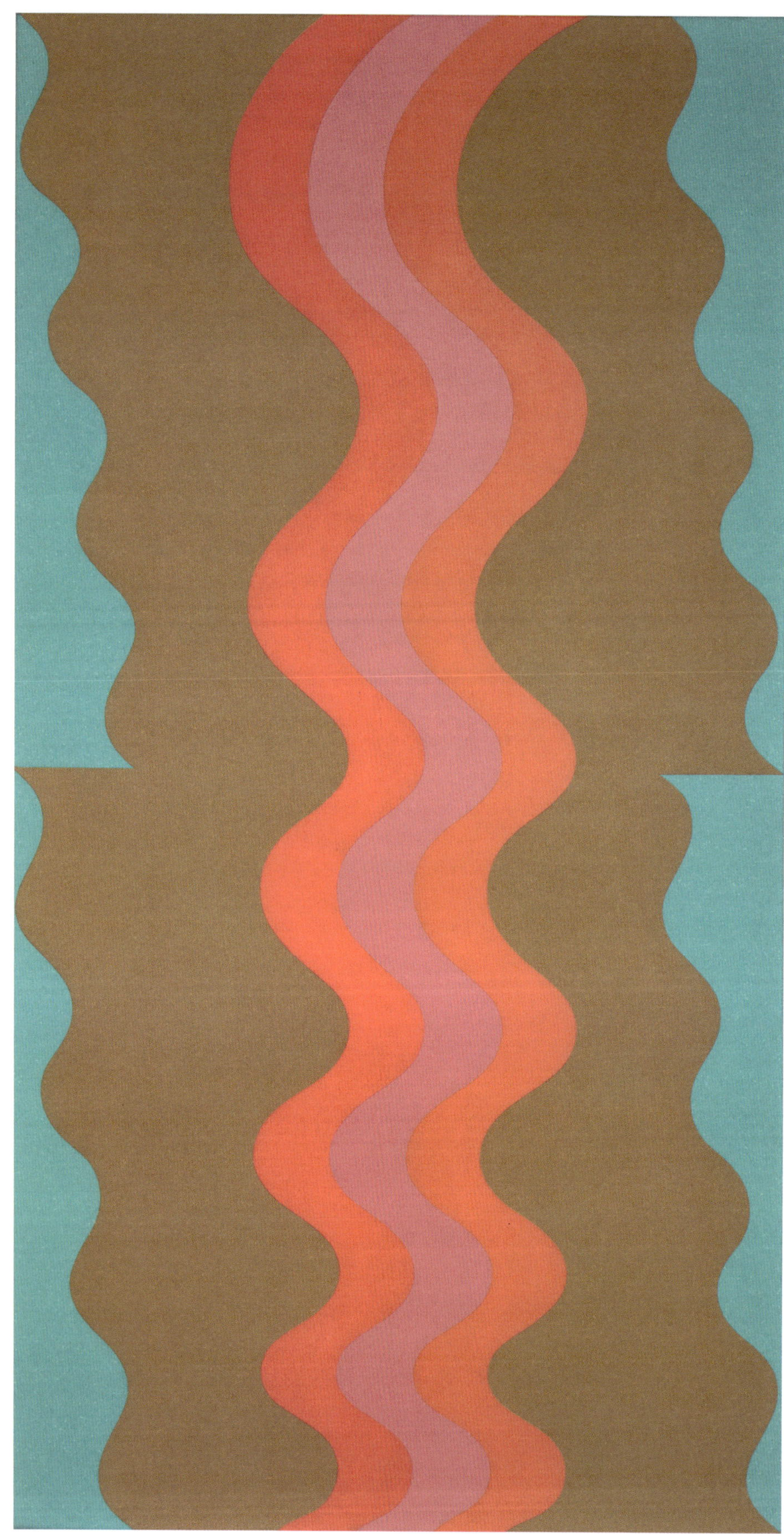

← Michael Tyzack
Nickel Yard
1967
Acrylic on canvas
Sainsbury Centre

↑ Mary Webb
Circle Line Series:
The Isle of Manhattan 2
1984
Screenprint on paper
Sainsbury Centre

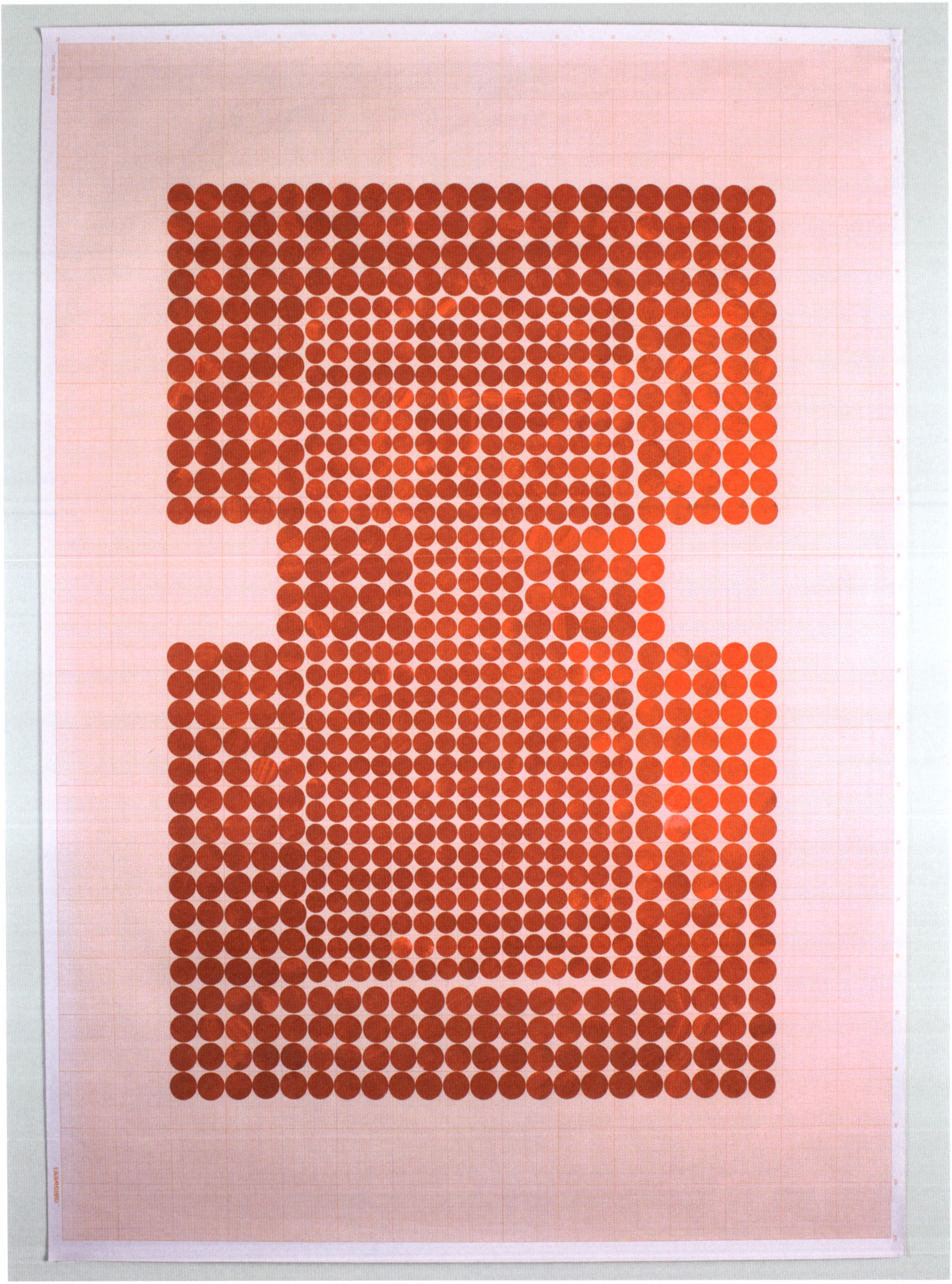

This is not a common phenomenon, but many artists identify parallels in the construction of music and visual art and their inherent rhythms. This is particularly true of abstract art, as Victor Pasmore wrote: 'Abstract painting emerges as a pictorial art closer to music than has hitherto been possible – an art essentially plastic in form but suggestive in effect'.[61] Richard Bell (b.1955) has described the parallels between making music and painting,[62] as has Mary Webb (b.1942), who found an equivalence in placing the intervals, pauses and emphasis in both.[63] Webb uses blocks of pure colour selected for their harmonious relationships. Her paintings and prints are always in the square format, so the movement comes from the colours and composition, without a rectangular form leading the eye from edge to edge. She was often inspired by her surroundings, whether the vibrant rocky geology of Utah or the austere skyscrapers of Manhattan: 'I like to call on the feelings I've had about a place over a period of time. Usually if I've been somewhere it's made a fairly big impression because it's very different from here'.[64] These artists demonstrate the emotiveness that can be achieved within the structures of Constructivist art.

Some artists now experiment with Constructivist art forms alongside very different styles. Lubna Chowdhary (b.1964), for example, in an exhibition at Jhaveri Contemporary in 2020, displayed a group of works on paper titled *Code*, which were ornamental and suggestive of Islamic art. A parallel series alongside them, *Switch*, was more austere and indicative of a Constructivist way of composing form. Together the titles delineate 'code switching', the act of shifting between languages in conversation. Both series are formed from patterns of red stickers on large sheets of graph paper. From afar they are painterly, with hand-painted stickers offering subtle variations in tone, but closer the graph paper demonstrates the underlying grid. Chowdhary usually works in ceramic, making installations of shaped and patterned tiles. Although not typically associated with the style, another artist whose ceramic work can be associated with Constructivism is Merete Rasmussen

(b.1974), whose distinctive sculptures twist and flow in a colourful Möbius strip. Early in her career, Rasmussen looked to mathematical models for inspiration; however, she no longer does and creates from intuition. Although she makes her ceramic works by hand, they have strikingly perfect finishes, often being mistaken as somehow machine-made.[65]

Rasmussen's work thus offers an interesting insight into the expectations of the hand-made and the machine-made that recur across Constructivist art. The linear and geometric style has often camouflaged irregularities in the hand-made works, making them seem closer to the machine. As critic John Berger (1926–2017) wrote of the first exhibition of Pasmore's reliefs in 1952:

> Their design is superb; their arrangement so right that one imagines them to be made with a precision which in fact they lack, their edges and joints often being blurred and clumsy. Yet for all this, they remain slightly funny – looking like bathroom fittings, and to all, except a few disciples, as inapplicable and irrelevant as the intimations of a hermit mystic.[66]

Constructivist art is no longer only comprehensible to a few disciples, as demonstrated by the works in this exhibition and book that span seventy years. Although at times this style may have seemed at the periphery of the prominent artistic trends – even by the artists themselves – there have always been artists who continue this tradition, and it evolves and re-emerges in ever surprising ways as demonstrated via the distinct headings within this chapter. The artists in *Rhythm and Geometry* demonstrate the variety in aesthetic, process and philosophy that can arise within the Constructivist tradition, even within the work of a single artist or series. What the artworks share is an internal rhythm within the geometry. □

← Lubna Chowdhary
'Switch' Series 2: Number 2
2020
Graph paper, adhesive paper
and acrylic
Sainsbury Centre

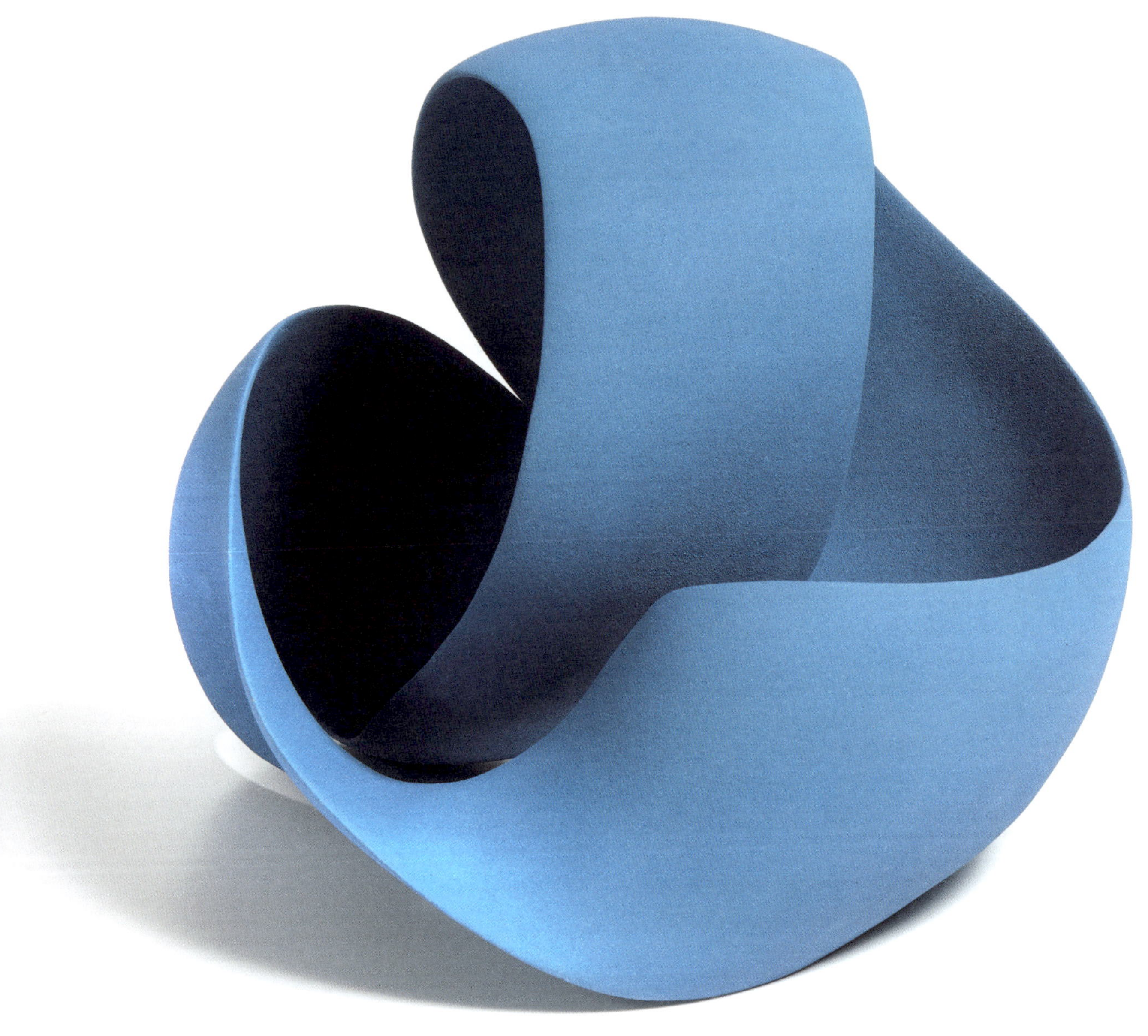

↑ Merete Rasmussen
Form
2011
Stoneware with blue slip
Sainsbury Centre

ENDNOTES

1   The debate was staged at the New Burlington Galleries before the ICA had a dedicated space.

2   'Notes of the discussion "The strange case of abstract art" held at 8pm on Tuesday 14th March 1950 at the New Burlington Galleries'. Tate archive TGA 955.1.7.

3   Namely in Alastair Grieve, *Constructed Abstract Art in England: A Neglected Avant-Garde* (New Haven and London: Yale University Press, 2005).

4   Sam Cornish, *Kaleidoscope: Colour and Sequence in 1960s British Art* (London: Hayward Publishing, 2017).

5   Lynda Nead, *The Tiger in the Smoke: Art and culture in post-war Britain* (New Haven: Yale University Press, 2017), p.133.

6   Lisa Tickner, *London's New Scene: Art and culture in the 1960s* (London: Paul Mellon Centre for Studies in British Art, 2020), p.107.

7   Charles Biederman, *Art as the Evolution of Visual Knowledge* (Minnesota: self-published, 1948).

8   Naum Gabo, Ben Nicholson and Leslie Martin (eds), *Circle: International Survey of Constructive Art* (London: Faber and Faber, 1937).

9   Naum Gabo and Antoine Pevsner, 'The Realistic Manifesto', in Charles Harrison and Paul Wood, *Art in Theory 1900–2000: An Anthology of Changing Ideas* (Oxford, Malden and Carlton: Blackwell Publishing, New Edition 8, 2007), p.299.

10 Martin Hammer and Cristina Lodder, 'The Abstract Utopia: The invention of abstract art', in Joanna Drew and Ann Jones, *The Non-Objective World* (London: South Bank Centre, 1992), p.31.

11 Heath's exhibitions are comprehensively described in Alastair Grieve, *Constructed Abstract Art in England: A Neglected Avant-Garde* (New Haven and London: Yale University Press, 2005), pp.17–27.

12 'Festival of Britain Sculpture', *The Times*, 16 January 1950, p.2.

13 *The Arts Council of Great Britain: Sixth Annual Report 1950–51*, p.7.

14 Victor Pasmore, 'A Jazz Mural', in Mary Banham and Bevis Hillier (eds), *A Tonic to the Nation: The Festival of Britain 1951* (London: Thames & Hudson, 1976), p.102.

15 Ibid.

16 Alastair Grieve, 'Pasmore's Constructed Abstract Art', in Neil Walker (ed.), *Victor Pasmore: Towards a New Reality* (London and Nottingham: Lund Humphries in association with Djanogly Gallery, Nottingham Lakeside Arts, 2016), p.59.

17 T. S. Eliot, 'The Hollow Men', 1925, was a response to the First World War.

18 Lawrence Alloway, *Nine Abstract Artists: Their Work and Theory* (London: Alec Tiranti, 1954), p.4.

19 D'Arcy Wentworth Thompson, *On Growth and Form*, Vol. II (Cambridge: Cambridge University Press, 1959 2nd edn).

20 Ellen K. Levy and Charrisa N. Terranova (eds), *D'Arcy Wentworth Thompson's Generative Influences in Art, Design and Architecture: From Forces to Forms* (London: Bloomsbury, 2021).

21 Charles Biederman, 1948, quoted in *The Structurist*, no. 5, 1965, p.11.

22 Biederman, 1948, p.388.

23 Jasia Reichardt, 'Computer art', in *Cybernetic Serendipity: the computer and the arts* (London: Studio International, 1968), p.71.

24 Interview with Vera Molnár, *Studio International*, 6 June 2018, https://www.studiointernational.com/index.php/vera-molnar-interview-computer-art-paris-mayor-gallery accessed 4 April 2021.

25 Each machine produced around twelve drawings each hour, which could be purchased by the exhibition's visitors.

26 Between 1979 and 1983, Dominic Boreham edited the Computer Arts Society's *PAGE* bulletin.

27 Stephen Willats in conversation with the author, 16 October 2020.

28 See George Rickey, *Constructivism: Origins and Evolution* (London: Studio Vista, 1968), p.193.

29 Gabo and Pevsner in Harrison and Wood, 2007, p.300.

30 Kenneth Martin, 'On Architecture and Mobile', *Architectural Design*, vol. 26: 1 (July 1956), p.234.

31 Mary Martin, 'Reflections', in *Mary Martin Kenneth Martin* (London: Arts Council of Great Britain, 1970), republished in Gerhard von Graevenitz, *Pier + Ocean: Construction in the art of the Seventies* (London: Arts Council of Great Britain, 1980), p.23.

32 Alastair Grieve, *The Sculpture of Robert Adams* (London: Lund Humphries, 1992), p.76.

33 Alastair Grieve, *Robert Adams 1917–1984: A Sculptor's Record* (London: Tate Publishing, 1992), p.16.

34 Denise René, *Denise René à Londres* (London: Redfern Gallery, 1968), p.4.

35 Mathew Frère-Smith, 'Focus in Space', March 1969, statement in the Sainsbury Centre Archive.

36 Margit Rosen, 'The Art of Programming: The New Tendencies and the Arrival of the Computer as a Means of Artistic Research', in Margit Rosen (ed.), *A Little-Known Story about a Movement, a Magazine, and the Computer's Arrival in Art. New Tendencies and Bit International, 1961–1973* (Karlsruhe: ZKM/Center for Art and Media, 2011), p.27.

37 William Seitz, *The Responsive Eye* (New York: MoMA, 1965), p.41.

38 David Sylvester, 'Bridget Riley', *New Statesman*, 25 May 1962, reprinted in Bridget Riley (Edinburgh: National Galleries of Scotland, 2019), p.29.

39 Biography, Li Yuan-Chia Foundation, http://lycfoundation.org.uk/li-yuan-chia/biography/ accessed 9 August 2021.

40 Victor Vasarely, *Planetary Folklore* (Greenwich: New York Graphic Society, 1973), unpag.

41 François Morellet, quoted in Rosen, 2011, p.123.

42 Julian Zinovieff, David Medalla and Paul Keeler (eds), *Signals: newsbulletin of Signals* (London: Centre for Advanced Creative Study, 1964).

43 'View-Point: A Retrospective Exhibition of Li Yuan-chia', Taipei Fine Arts Museum, https://www.tfam.museum/Exhibition/Exhibition_page.aspx?id=498&ddlLang=en-us accessed 9 August 2021.

44 Thomas Crow, *The Hidden Mod in Modern Art: London 1957–1969* (New Haven and London: Paul Mellon Centre for Studies in British Art, 2020), p.105.

45 Richard Paul Lohse, 'Elementarism. Series. Modulus', 1966, in Anthony Hill (ed.), *Directions in Art, Theory and Aesthetics: An anthology* (London: Faber and Faber, 1968), p.61.

46 Natalie Dower, note 2010, published in *Natalie Dower: Line of Enquiry* (London: EMH Arts, 2012), p.11.

47 Dower came across Dudeney in Martin Gardner, *More Mathematical Puzzles and Diversions* (London: G. Bell and Sons, 1963), p.16.

48 Lucy R. Lippard, 'The Anatomy of an Annual', in *The Hayward Annual* (London: Hayward, 1978), p.1.

49 Ibid., p.7.

50 Elizabeth Chaplin, 'Feminism and Systematic Constructive Art', *Constructivist Forum*, issue 8, 1988, p.9.

51 Ibid., p.7.

52 Elizabeth Chaplin, 'Constructivism and Feminism', *Art Monthly*, no. 125, April 1989, p.22. The second letter is Elizabeth Chaplin, 'Towards Constructive Androgyny', *Art Monthly*, no. 129, September 1989, p.30.

53 Nicole Charlett in conversation with the author, 5 August 2021.

54 'Introduction', in Tam Giles et al., *Countervail* (Sheffield: Mappin Art Gallery, 1992), p.9.

55 Nicole Charlett in Giles, 1992, p.18.

56 Lohse in Hill, 1968, p.58.

57 Trevor Sutton in conversation with the author, 30 June 2021.

58 Jill Constantine, 'Foreword', in Cornish, 2017, p.6.

59 Sam Cornish, 'One, Two, Three, Four: Sequence, Symmetry and Sculpture', in Cornish, 2017, p.50.

60 Barrie Sturt-Penrose, 'Michael Tyzack: Profile', *The Arts Review*, date unknown, p.102, cutting in the Sainsbury Centre Archive.

61 Victor Pasmore, 'Abstract Painting', in *Abstract and other paintings* (London: Redfern, 1948), quoted in Grieve, 2005, p.61.

62 Richard Bell in conversation with the author, 20 July 2021.

63 Mary Webb in Sarah Bartholomew, 'A Conversation with Mary Webb', in Mel Clark and Alastair Grieve, *Mary Webb: Journeys in Colour* (Norwich: Sainsbury Centre, 2011), p.61.

64 Webb in Bartholomew, 2011, p.58.

65 The author in discussion with clients and visitors when previously working with Rasmussen's work.

66 John Berger, 'Victor Pasmore, at the Redfern', *New Statesman and Nation*, 17 May 1952, p.586, quoted in Alastair Grieve (ed.), *Victor Pasmore: Writings and Interviews* (London: Tate Publishing, 2010), p.59.

construction & collaboration

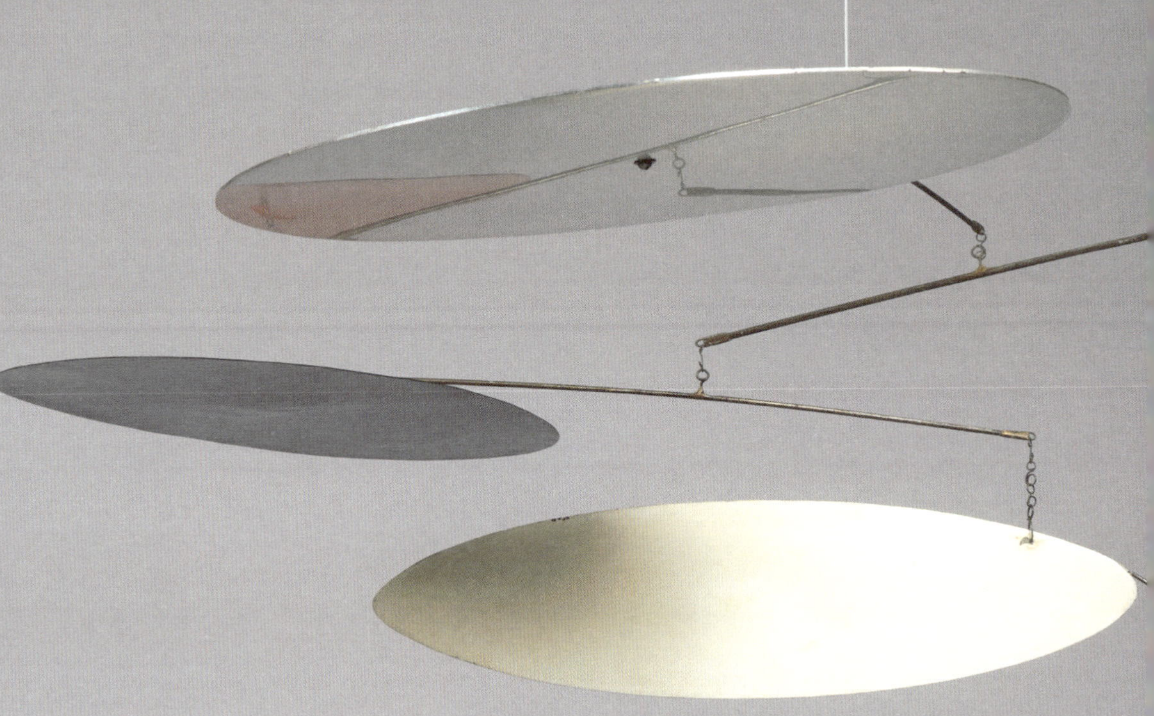

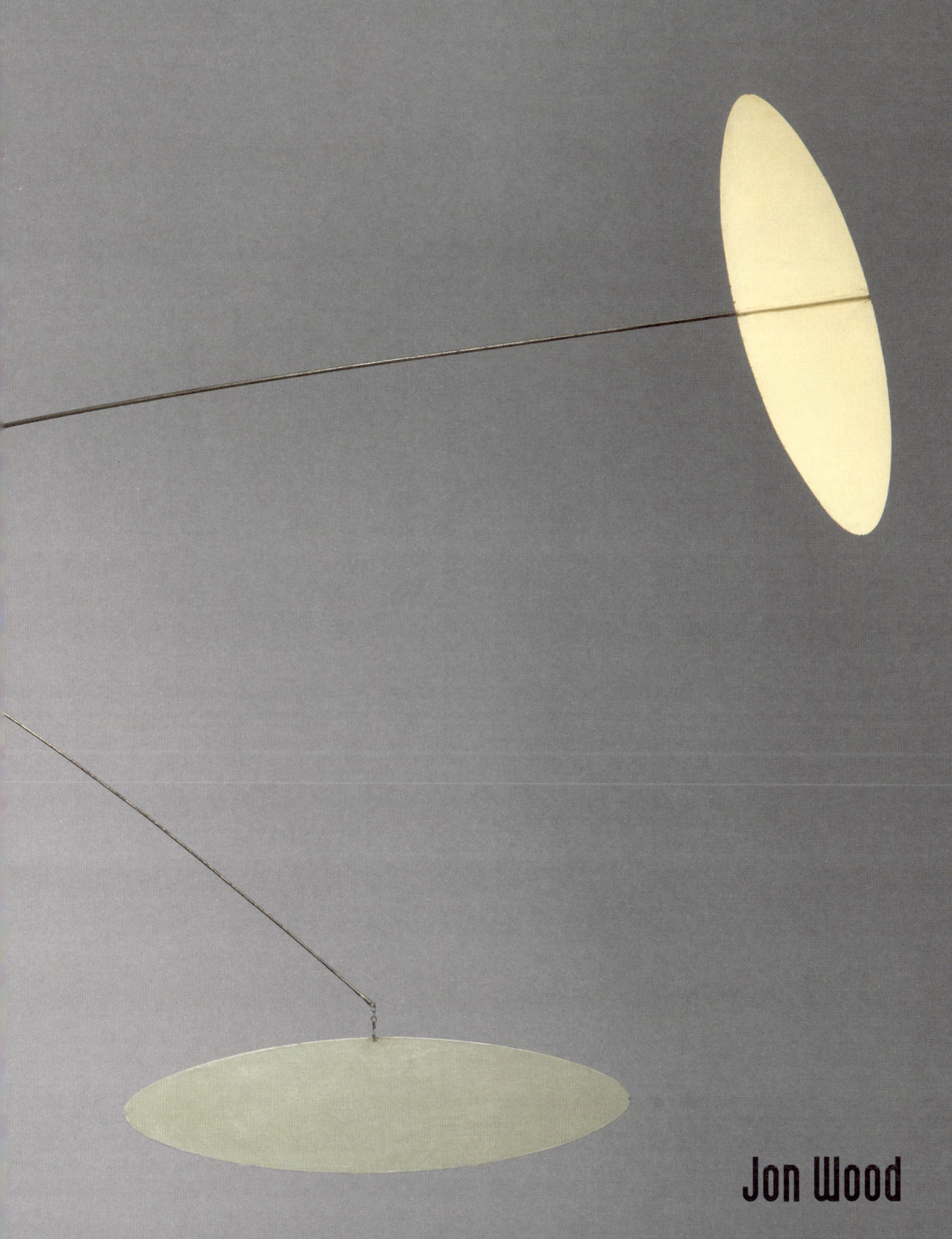

Jon Wood

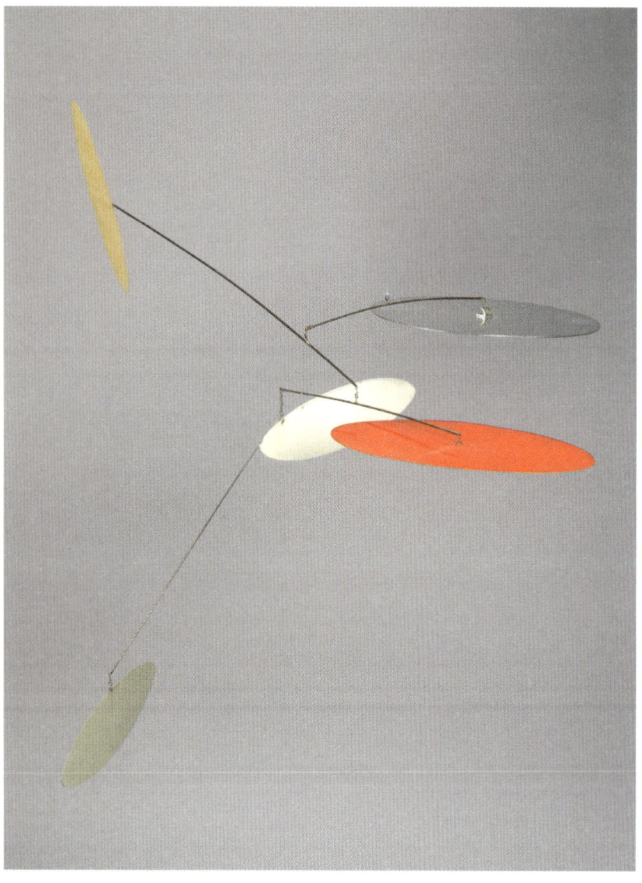

'Individual freedom must not
be allowed to destroy itself
through isolation'.[1] Victor Pasmore

FROM THE 1930S into the post-war decades and beyond, the story of Constructed abstract art in England is, on one level, a story of individual talents. All of the artists associated with this kind of art in the early post-war years – Robert Adams (1917–1984), John Ernest (1922–1994), Stephen Gilbert (1910–2007), Adrian Heath (1920–1992), Anthony Hill (1930–2020), Kenneth Martin (1905–1984), Mary Martin (1907–1969), Victor Pasmore (1908–1998) and Gillian Wise (1936–2020) – are represented in the collection of the Sainsbury Centre and their works are shown in *Rhythm and Geometry: Constructivist Art in Britain since 1951*.

In this new exhibition and publication, we are given a unique opportunity to consider the individual achievements of these artists, but most strikingly – and of relevance to this present essay – to look also at them comparatively and in dialogue. We can, for example, focus on the architectonic approach to construction and colour pursued by Stephen Gilbert in his free-standing *Construction* (1954) in painted aluminium, while comparing it to the kinetic treatment of metal, light and space found in Kenneth Martin's *Screw Mobile* (1953) and *Mobile Reflector* (1955), each made one year either side of it. We can encounter the very different approaches to relief explored in Victor Pasmore's *Transparent Relief Construction in Black, White and Ochre* (1956–57), Mary Martin's *White-Faced Relief* (1959), Anthony Hill's *Five Regions Relief* (1960–62), Gillian Wise's *Black and White Relief with Prisms* (1961) and Robert Adams' *Emperor Relief* (1964). Each work displays different treatments of colour, surface, plane construction and compositional orientation and logic. Each offers up different kinds of rational and intuitive thought, and different rhythms, geometries, directional energies and dynamic procedures. All are also powerfully connected (through both visible and less visible threads) via a shared belief in art as a common visual language: one that could be extended into the world beyond the immediate physical limits of the material objects themselves. *Rhythm and Geometry* gives glimpses into such shared concerns, pointing to some of the group and collaborative dynamics at work.

Mobile Reflector, Elliptic Motif
1955
Steel, duralumin and aluminium
Sainsbury Centre

Construction
1954
Painted aluminium
Sainsbury Centre

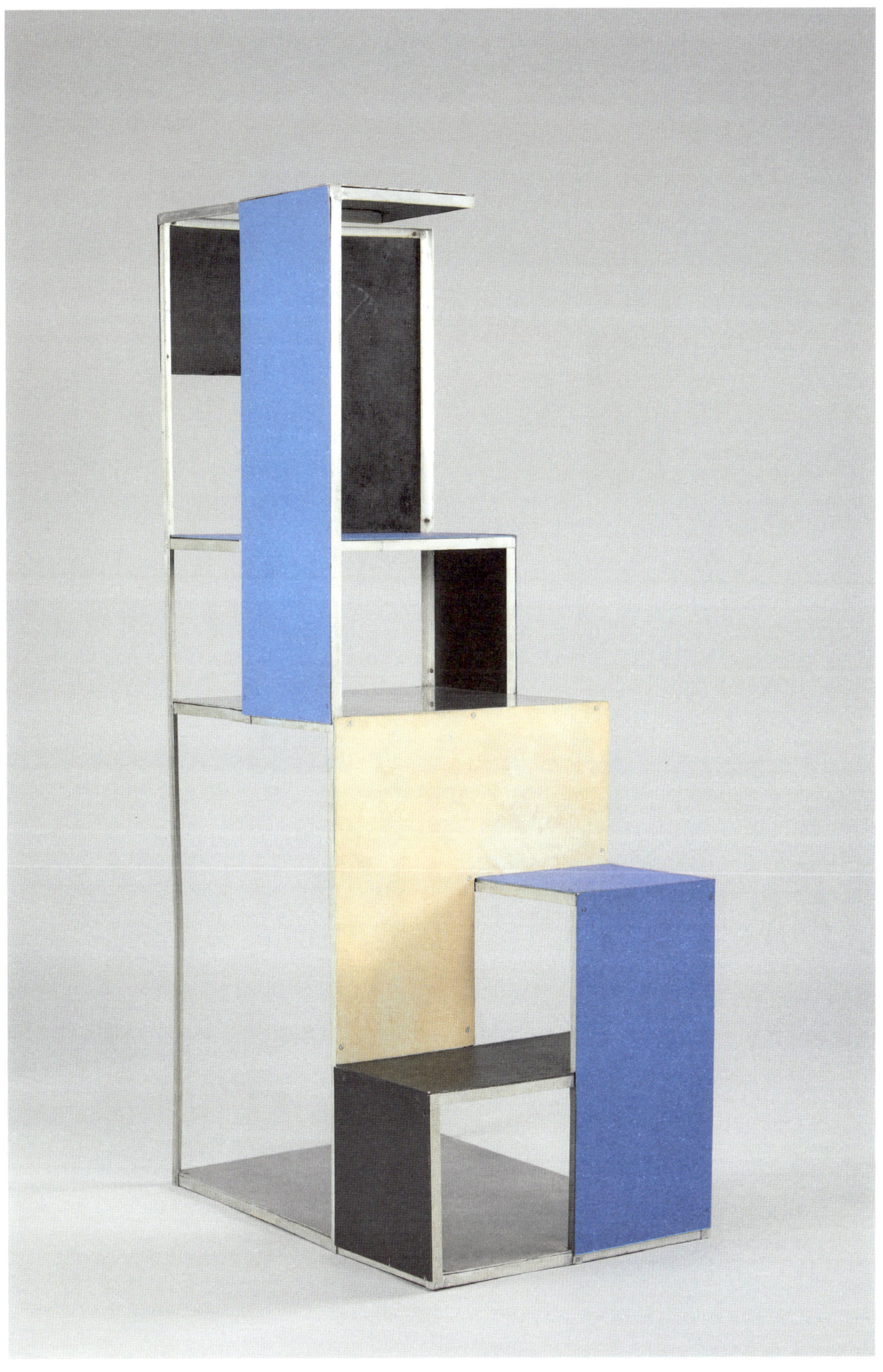

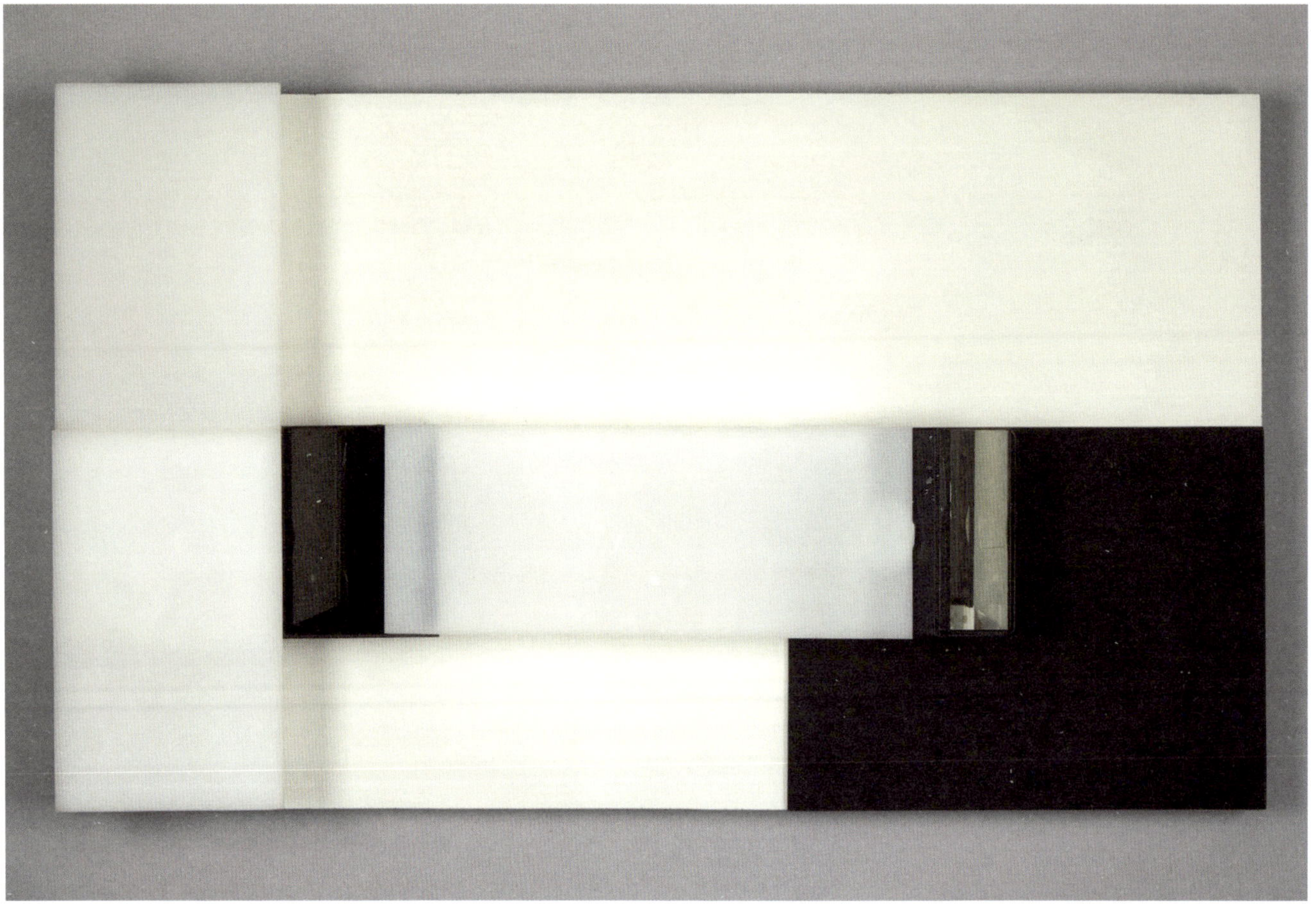

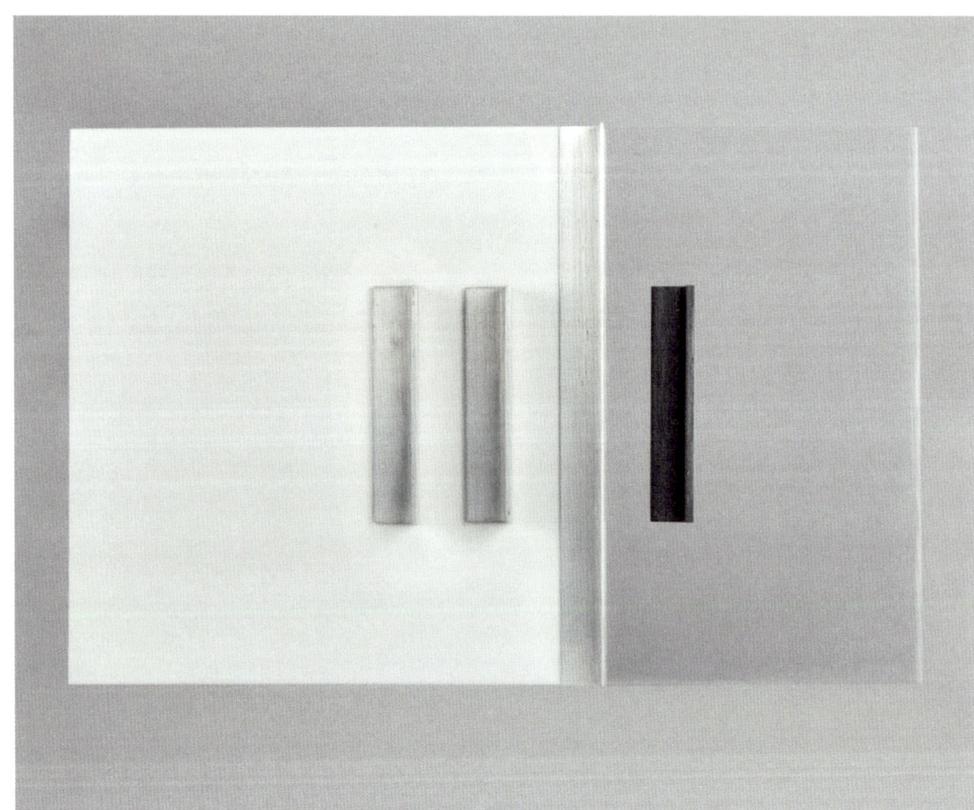

↑ **Gillian Wise**
Black and White Relief with Prisms
1961
Perspex, glass and Formica
Sainsbury Centre

→ **Anthony Hill**
Relief Construction
1956–60
Perspex, aluminium and plywood
Sainsbury Centre

Alastair Grieve's important book on this subject, *Constructed Abstract Art in England: A Neglected Avant-Garde* (2005) gives valuable insight into this subject. It was also based on years of research that have had a close and synergetic relationship to the collection formed at UEA. He approaches each of these post-war artists as individual subjects with various artistic orientations and trajectories, whilst introducing them all through a consideration of an emerging group dynamic. Across the chapters, he points to a history of friendships, of social networks, as well as affiliations through statements, publications and exhibitions. As he states in his Introduction, it was 'necessary to form a group in 1951, as the opposition to abstract art, especially to constructed abstract art, was strong'.[2] There was strength in numbers, as debates over the competing merits of figurative and abstract increasingly charged contemporary artistic thinking. At a time when the post-war spirit of reconstruction and rebuilding was ascendant, Constructed art itself, with its additive, combinatory and multipartite elements, was highly amenable not only to this progressive mentality, but also to a cooperative way of thinking and making: collective endeavour standing as a robust alternative to the single-handed, self-expressive heroics of romantic models for art making.

As the artist Peter Lowe (b.1938) has reflected recently: 'British Art schools discouraged abstract art. It was not tolerated as part of the curriculum until the 1960s. This situation shaped a defensive attitude conducive to the formation of artistic groups. Systems artists had no manifesto, but a unifying tenet was that visual information should be recoverable via the artifact'.[3] The early 1960s and the new Diplomas in Art and Design brought educational change that enhanced the discursive life of Constructivist art across the country. Constructed art (and then Systems art) could be used and applied, read, researched and discussed, and their shared languages generated considerable interaction and exchange – from the art school and out into the world, within Britain and beyond.

The collaborative impulse animated much Constructed art, and many of its artists – and the exchanges and

cooperations fostered – led to some of its most interesting post-war achievements, as well as generating a number of its disagreements. These often focused on questions of synthesis and integration, and how best to secure a role for dynamic visual art at the centre of society. There were both inclusions and exclusions, fallings-in and fallings-out. In a sense, this was all part of the political life of the collaborative experience: its potentiality and creative energy. Membership – and protocols of belonging – played an important role, perhaps more so, as time went by. This had positive and negative ramifications for artists. As George Meyrick (b.1953) has reflected recently:

> I think the difficulty for me is that in Britain there was a strong desire for purity and a wish to connect to the past and it adds to that feeling that working in this way put you into a distinct, circumscribed grouping, which of course was backed up by the creation of these tightly knit groups that attempted to define who or what was to be included.[4]

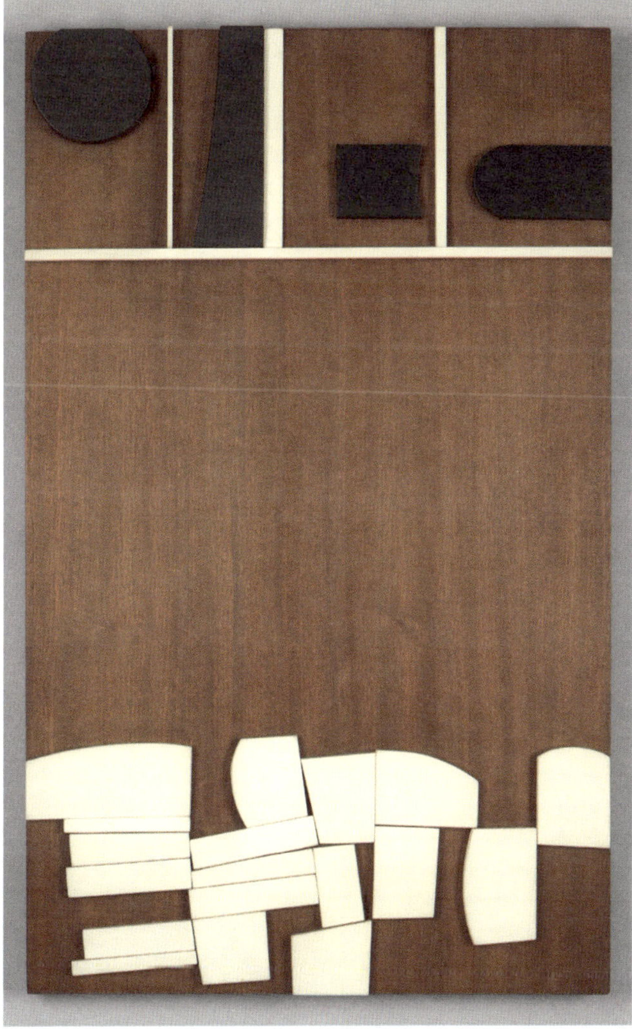

This short essay looks briefly at some of the collaborative strands of Constructivism in Britain and its associated tendencies, looking at how collaboration was not only explored by this first generation in the 1950s and 1960s, but also by younger artists making Constructed art in the 1970s, 1980s and beyond. As this exhibition also reminds us, Constructed art very much has an ongoing life today with new voices being heard and new directions explored. In the post-war period as in the 2020s, the degrees to which connections to earlier art works are directly and indirectly cited is a fascinating subject in its own right. The cross-generational life of Constructed art in Britain is sometimes fraught with complications, as different generations of artists see different qualities in earlier works and place different emphases on their various aesthetic and political concerns.[5]

In focussing here on collaboration and construction in the second half of the twentieth century, this essay touches upon the publications, exhibitions, architecture and public art projects with which they were all engaged. Artistic testimony gives voice to some of the intricacies of these projects and issues. Some accounts are by some of its older figures, others by a handful of later generation artists, such as Norman Dilworth (b.1931), Peter Lowe, Susan Tebby (b.1944) and Richard Bell (b.1955).[6] What emerges are not only different types of artistic collaboration – artists working with architects, curators, writers and fellow artists (often of different generations) in and between the studio, the gallery and the seminar room – but also very different conditions and contexts for it.

Such issues have an interesting contemporary resonance. 'Collaboration' has increasingly acquired new and positive values in recent years: it has come to signal co-authorship, cross-disciplinarity, relationality, reciprocity and dialogical exchange between people and organisations.[7] The idea of cross-generational artistic exchange has caught the eyes and minds of many artists, as well as curators and art historians. Collaborative endeavours are seen as fair, helpful, shared, mutual and collective. At the same time, the exact meanings and values of collaboration have become further nuanced, as the complicated overlaps and differences between various contributing activities have been better understood. Collaboration, then as now, is a complicated matter, and the acts of contribution and commonality are sometimes tricky to discern, full of intangibilities.

Constructivist artists in the 1950s in Britain were working, as was understood early on, with an awareness of models of avant-garde activity from the 1920s and 1930s: from Russian Constructivism and De Stijl, to Abstraction-Création in Paris. Through their reading of publications such as *Unit One*, *Circle* and *Axis*, they saw the value of magazines, books and exhibition catalogues. *Nine Abstract Artists* published in 1954 by Tiranti Ltd on Charlotte Street was instigated by the nine artists themselves: Robert Adams, Terry Frost (1915–2005), Adrian Heath, Anthony Hill, Roger Hilton (1911–1975), Kenneth Martin, Mary Martin, Victor Pasmore and William Scott (1913–1989). As Lawrence Alloway (1926–1990) states at the end of his introductory essay: 'It was not my idea to collect these reproductions and statements together – the first move was made by the artists concerned. They do not constitute a movement, though six of the nine do belong to a single, loosely-knit group'.[8] These artists, in part, were taking their avant-garde bearings from the pre-war ethos of Hampstead's 'nest of gentle artists' and cultures of support that sustained Gabo (1890–1977), Moholy-Nagy (1895–1946), Mondrian (1872–1944) and others living there as refugees in the 1930s. Many of these younger post-war artists also socialised together around Fitzroy Street and Charlotte Street in central London, neighbours sharing the same postcode, often working in each other's studios and frequenting the same cafés and bookshops, such as Alex Tiranti's art bookshop, which offered access to contemporary publications from Paris and elsewhere. As well as continental, there was a powerful metropolitan image at work in this new art too which placed Constructivist artists apart from St Ives and West Country artists.[9]

This convivial dynamic was important, and many of the artists shared more personal relationships too.

→ Adrian Heath
Composition: Red and Black
1954–55
Oil on canvas
Sainsbury Centre

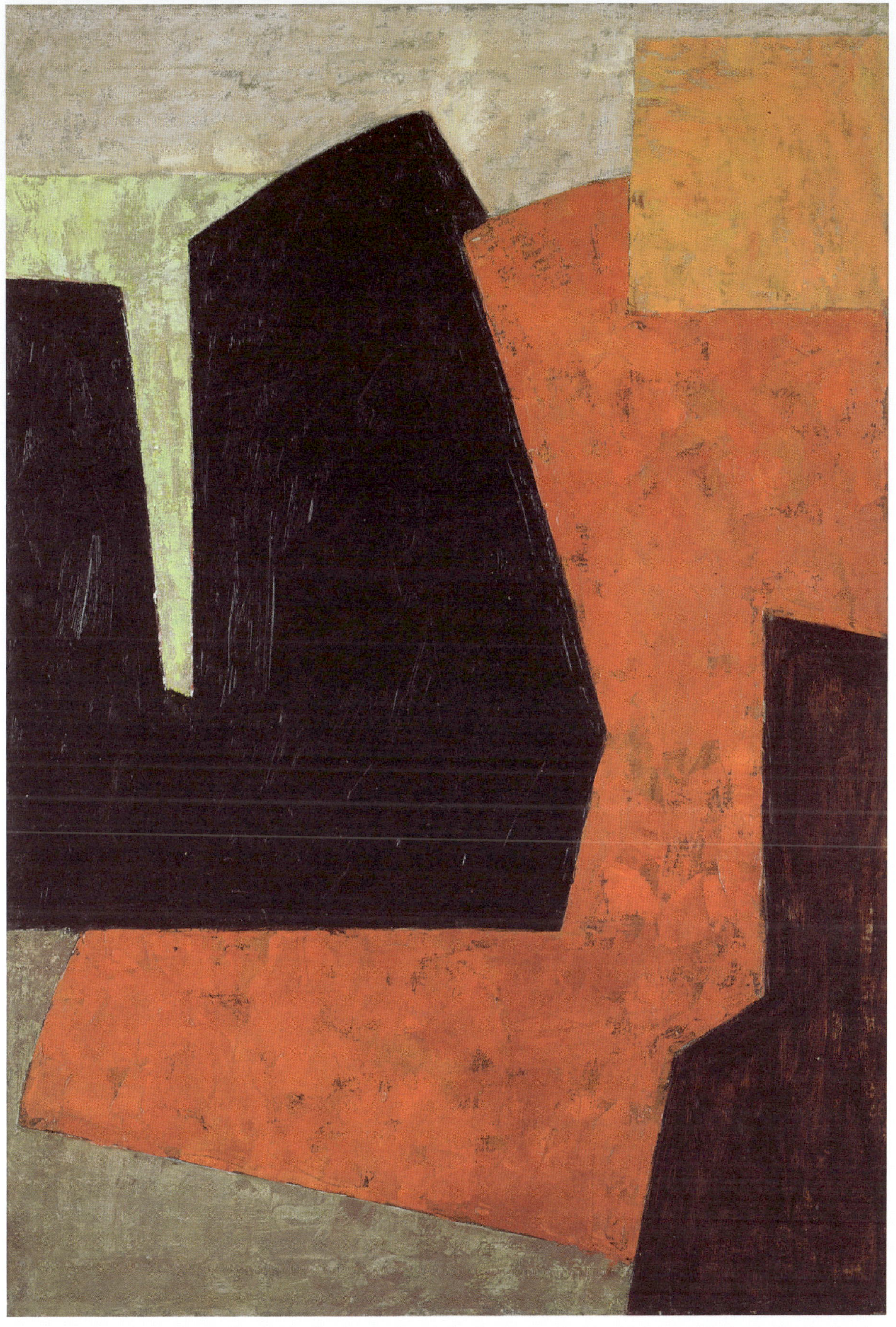

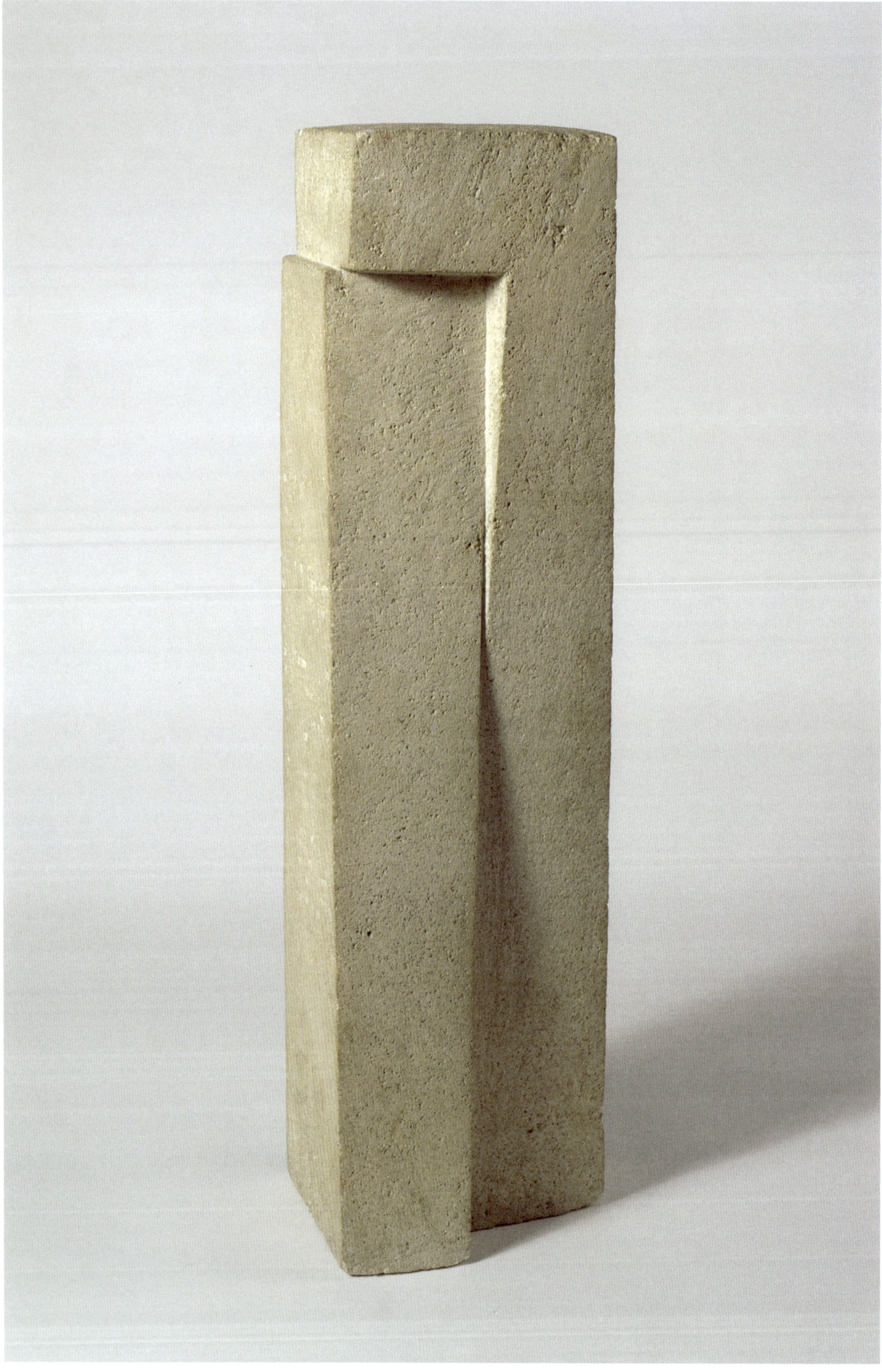

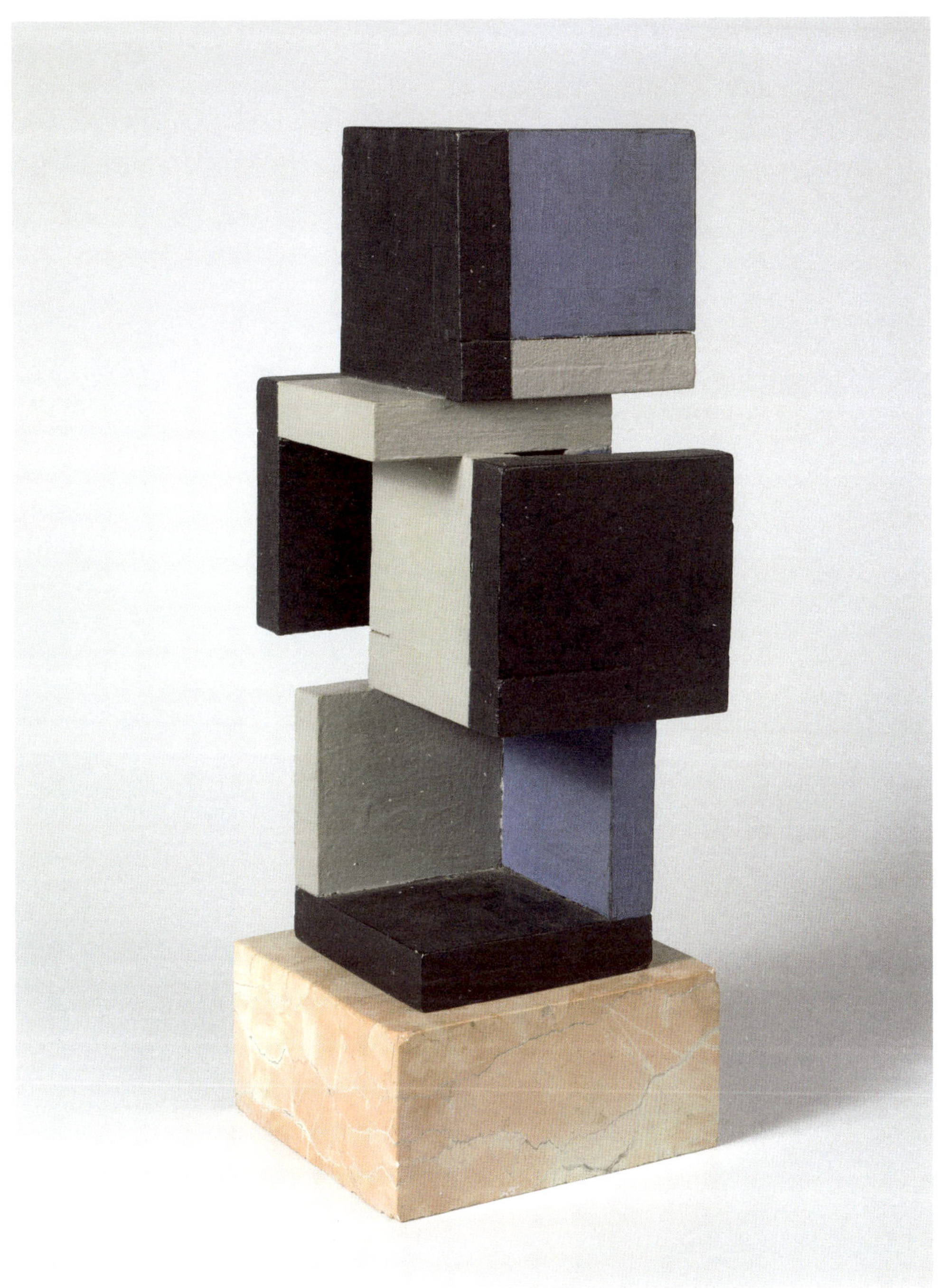

← Jocelyn Chewett
Untitled
1950
Limestone
Sainsbury Centre

↑ Jocelyn Chewett
Construction
1965
Painted wood
Sainsbury Centre

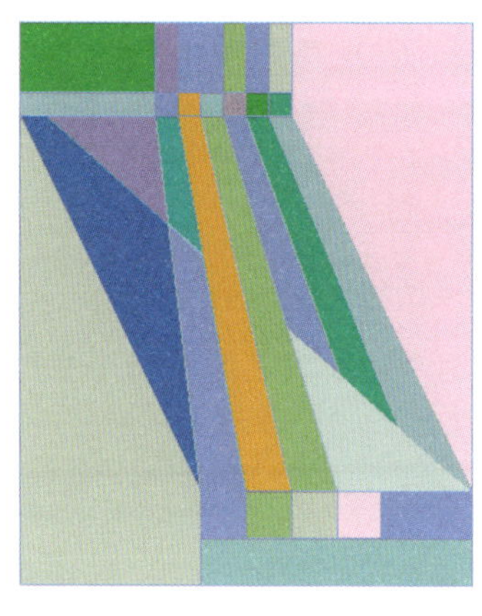

STARATS 1

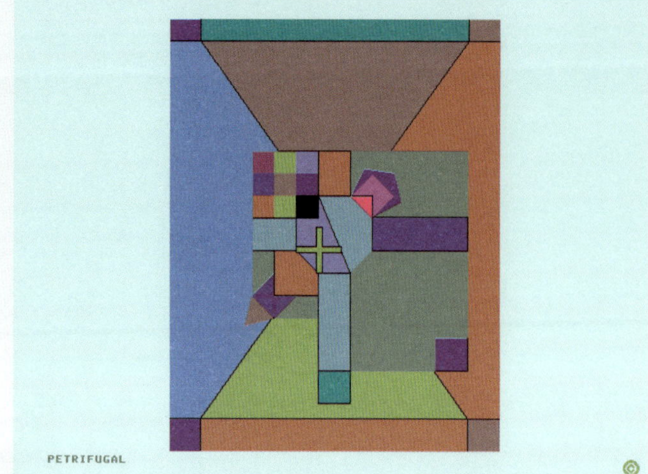

PETRIFUGAL

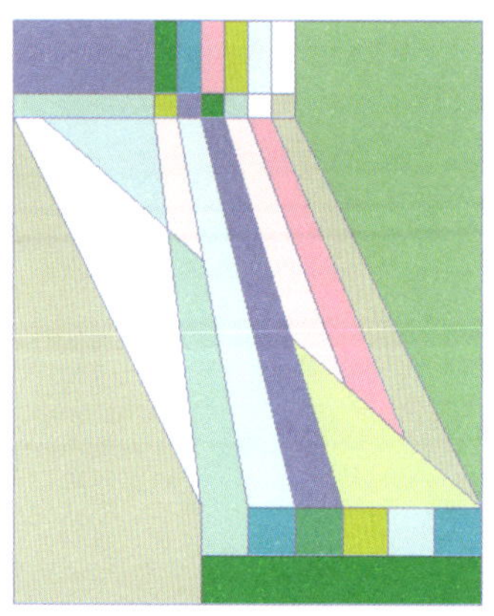

STARATS 3

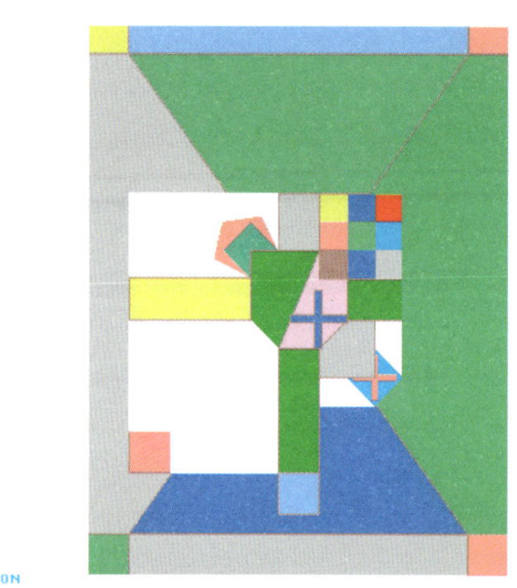

PULSATION

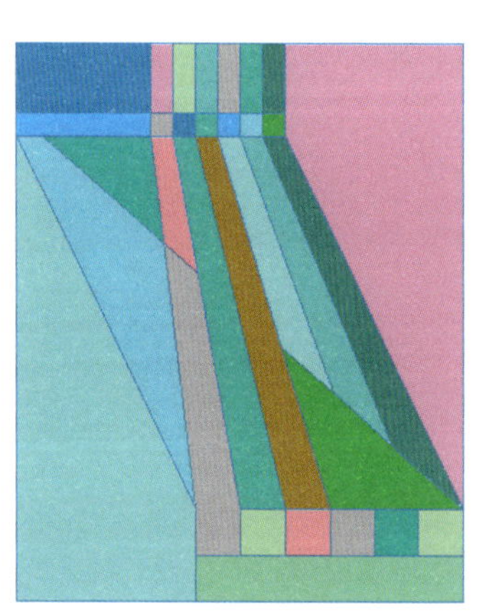

STARATS 2

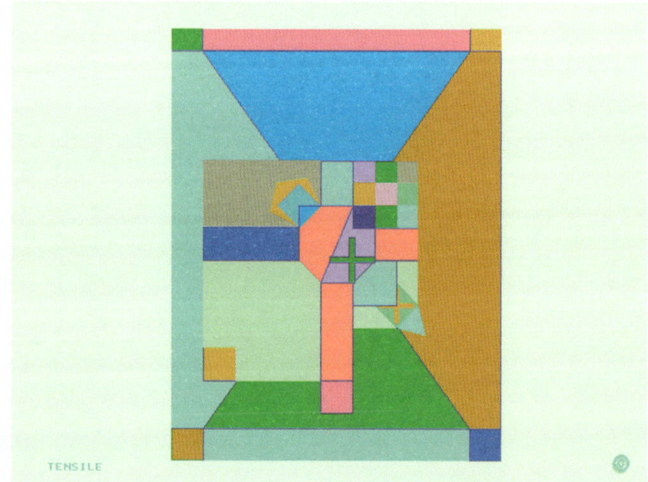

TENSILE

↑ **Gillian Wise**
Textum Ars
1991
Digital drawings
Sainsbury Centre

Looking back, this is a striking characteristic of this moment and milieu. Partnerships between men and women – sometimes married, sometimes not – were often at the heart of artistic endeavours. Mary Martin and Kenneth Martin, Gillian Wise and Anthony Hill, Stephen Gilbert and Jocelyn Chewett (1906–1979) all made work separately, whilst enjoying personal exchange. Such art could be made jointly by men and women and through different contributions. These artists worked together and showed together too, and collaborations were developed for publications, exhibitions, architectural and public art projects and commissions.

Wise worked closely with Hill on various projects, including the publication for the International Union of Architects Sixth Congress at the South Bank in London in 1961 – a project to which she also contributed an ambitious glass relief measuring 24 feet. On occasion they also made a jointly authored work – a rare instance of direct collaboration on shared art work. A few years later they also worked together on *DATA: Directions in Art, Theory and Aesthetics*, published in 1968, with Wise contributing a text on 'the art work as an object' to this anthology, a compilation that brought together essays and statements by twenty-five artists and texts by other specialists.[10] It was (and still is) an extraordinary book, beautifully designed by their mutual friend Richard Hollis (b.1934), and a bold act of transdisciplinary field-creation, placing contemporary Constructed and Concrete art at the centre of debates. As well as working with Wise, Hill also created an artistic pseudonym called 'Achill Redo', as an outlet for the Duchampian side of his interests and his sense of humour. Redo can be read, in a way, as a kind of internal collaboration with dimensions of Hill's creativity that couldn't be easily placed within the more official and public-facing side of his work.

Later Wise married the architect, Adrian Ciobotaru, adding his name to hers and becoming known as Gillian Wise Ciobotaru for many years. She travelled extensively, working in the United States, including spells at the University of Illinois (in 1970–71) and at the Center for

Advanced Visual Studies at MIT (in 1983), before settling in Paris. Wise was deeply interested in what she called 'the original avant-garde aims of creating "circles" in which architects, artists, scientists, writers and musicians discuss ideas without benefit from minders'.[11] In 1970 she joined the Systems group set up by Jeffrey Steele (1931–2021) (whose work is considered elsewhere in this publication in Andrew Bick's essay) and in the mid-1970s she founded the short-lived ARS (Arts Research Syndicate) with Hill. Her interest in the longer histories of Constructivism and the cultural politics of the Modern movement more generally took her on a UNESCO fellowship to Prague in 1968 and on a British Council scholarship to research the Soviet Modern movement in Leningrad in 1969 and 1970.

Stephen Gilbert and Jocelyn Chewett, British and Canadian by birth respectively, married in 1935 and moved to Paris soon after, settling there permanently in 1946. Their work was complementary: Constructed and carved respectively (although Chewett did make the occasional wooden construction as can be seen in her small painted wooden *Construction* (1965). Gilbert commented in 2005,

It was never a case of being a team or an artistic partnership…I've owed a lot to her. She was always a less physical explorer of the plastic arts than me. The best thing I could do was very organic; the best she could do was very formal. My best formal works were very 'one off'.[12]

In the 1950s, though, both oeuvres coincided and both artists were briefly united in making not only 'formal work', but also geometric, abstract sculpture. Gilbert's work then involved the construction of colourful metal sculptures and 'space frames'. These metal constructions articulated elaborate and subtle spatial compositions that hovered between sculpture and architecture – a combination that was deeply in tune with his architectonic sculptural imagination and that Gilbert went on to explore further in the mid-1950s with a number of proposals for houses and apartment blocks, collaborating with an

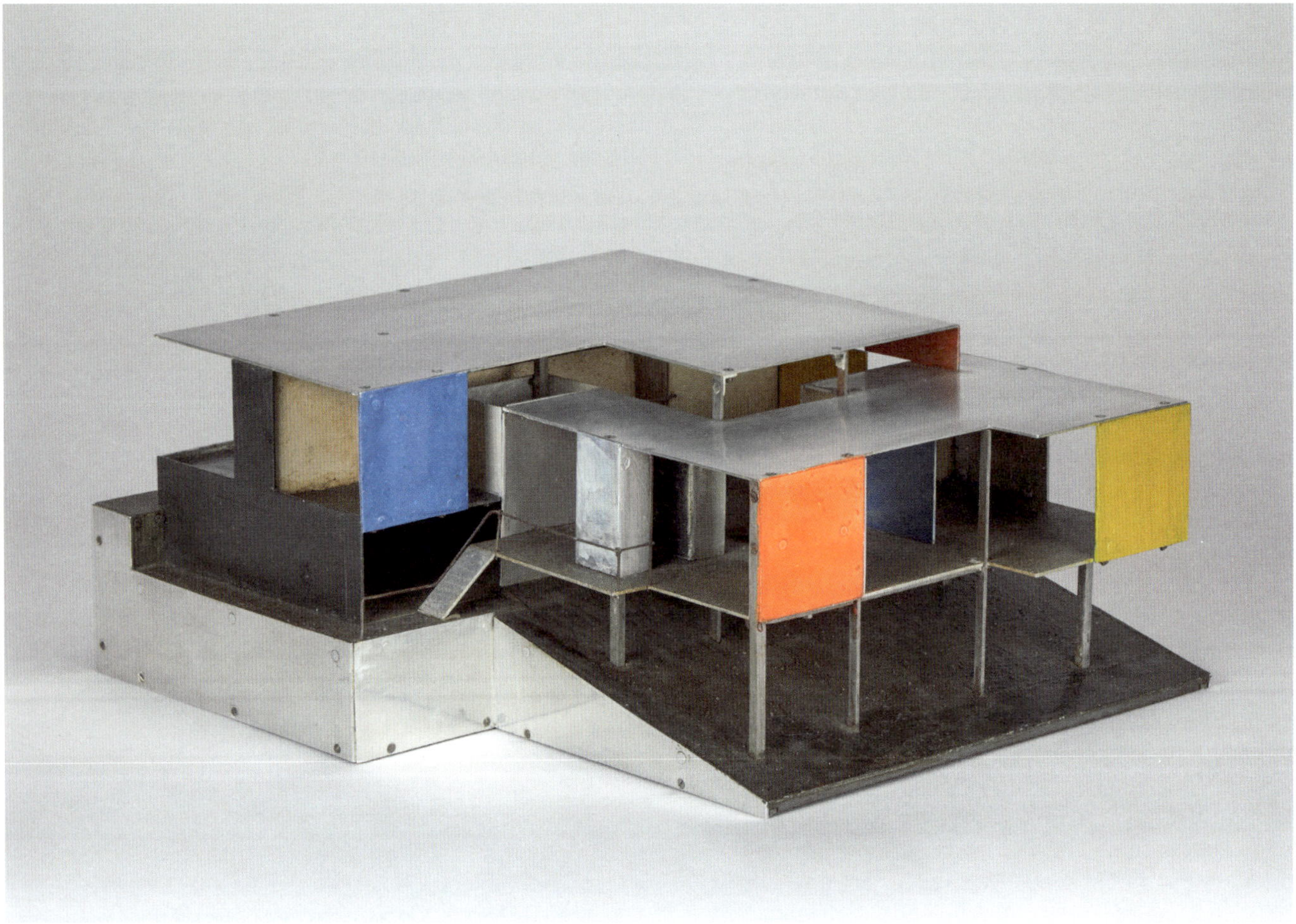

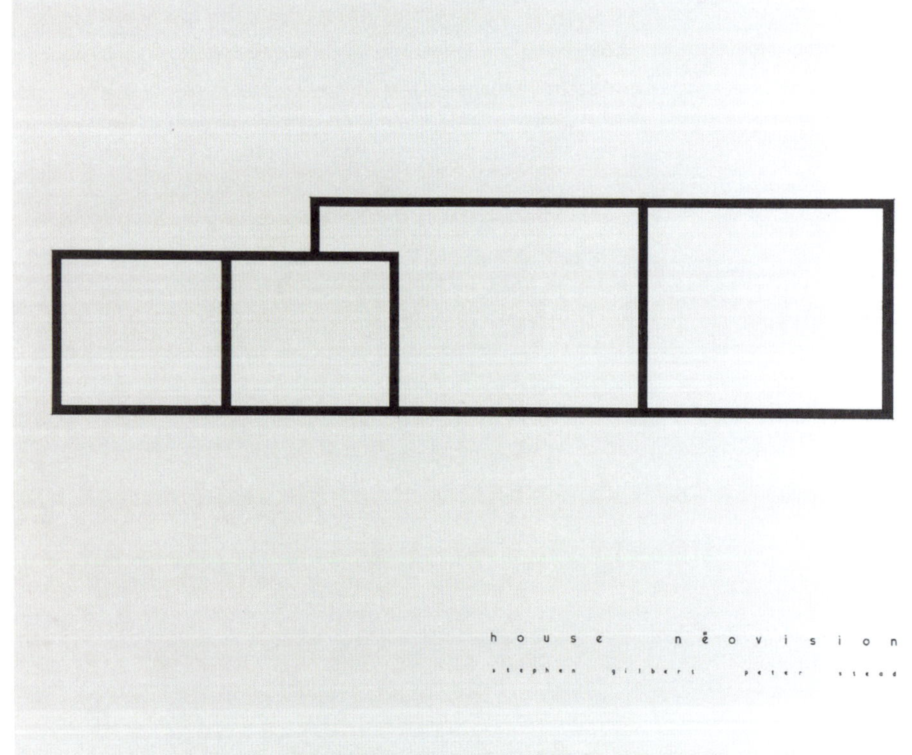

↑ **Stephen Gilbert**
House model 'Néovision'
1955
Aluminium, steel and paint
Sainsbury Centre

← **Stephen Gilbert** and
Peter Stead
House Néovision
c.1955
Ink on paper
Sainsbury Centre

→ **Mary Martin**
White-Faced Relief
1959
Wood, plywood, paint, plastic and
white PMMA
Sainsbury Centre

architect. Chewett carved subtle, small-scale sculptures which, though multipartite at first glance, were often highly crafted and deceptively 'all of a piece'.

The model for Gilbert's *House Néovision* (1955) is part of the Sainsbury Centre collection. It is a compelling object that gives a vivid account of the artist's interest in 'putting colour into space'.[13] The thinking behind this project occurred in Paris amongst his Néovision colleagues, Constant (1920–2005), Schöffer (1912–1992) and Parent (1923–2016) around 1954 and 1955. They took him to Huddersfield in 1955–56, where he spent time on a number of extraordinary, but sadly unrealised projects for the architect Peter Stead (1922–1999). *Rhythm and Geometry* includes a fascinating line drawing that Gilbert and Stead made jointly for the project. For Gilbert, this was a chance to try out some of his architectural proposals on new terrain. Although he saw his projects as continuing the pre-war work of Le Corbusier (1887–1965), van Doesburg (1883–1931) and Rietveld (1888–1964), he had not however foreseen the difficulties involved in building Modernist architecture in Yorkshire in the mid-1950s. As he stated in 2005:

There is very fine modern architecture in the former colonies that would be rejected in England. When I went to Huddersfield it was forbidden to have a flat roof, but in Nigeria they built exemplary architecture that would have looked splendid in Huddersfield, or anywhere else in England.[14]

Gilbert's collaborative work with Peter Stead was one of many such artist-architect collaborations explored by these artists. Each has different stories and outcomes, and each carries varying experiences of synthesis and integration. Many of them cast longer, more influential shadows that continue into the present. Amongst them, we find Victor Pasmore's Apollo Pavilion at Peterlee, and later Gillian Wise's *Alice Walls* at the Barbican Arts Centre in London, a mural on two walls and across three storeys within the cinema staircase. Both works have since been the subject of restoration campaigns and championed by supporters.

Kenneth Martin and Mary Martin – or 'Kenneth and Mary', as they were often affectionately called – also worked on several larger, outdoor projects, some in the public domain. Interestingly, both made fountains, working with water as an active part of the work. Kenneth Martin made works for colleges and university contexts, including *Fountain* (1960) at Brixton College, *Construction in Aluminium* (1967) at the Engineering Laboratory of Cambridge University, and a large column in Sheffield for his contribution to the

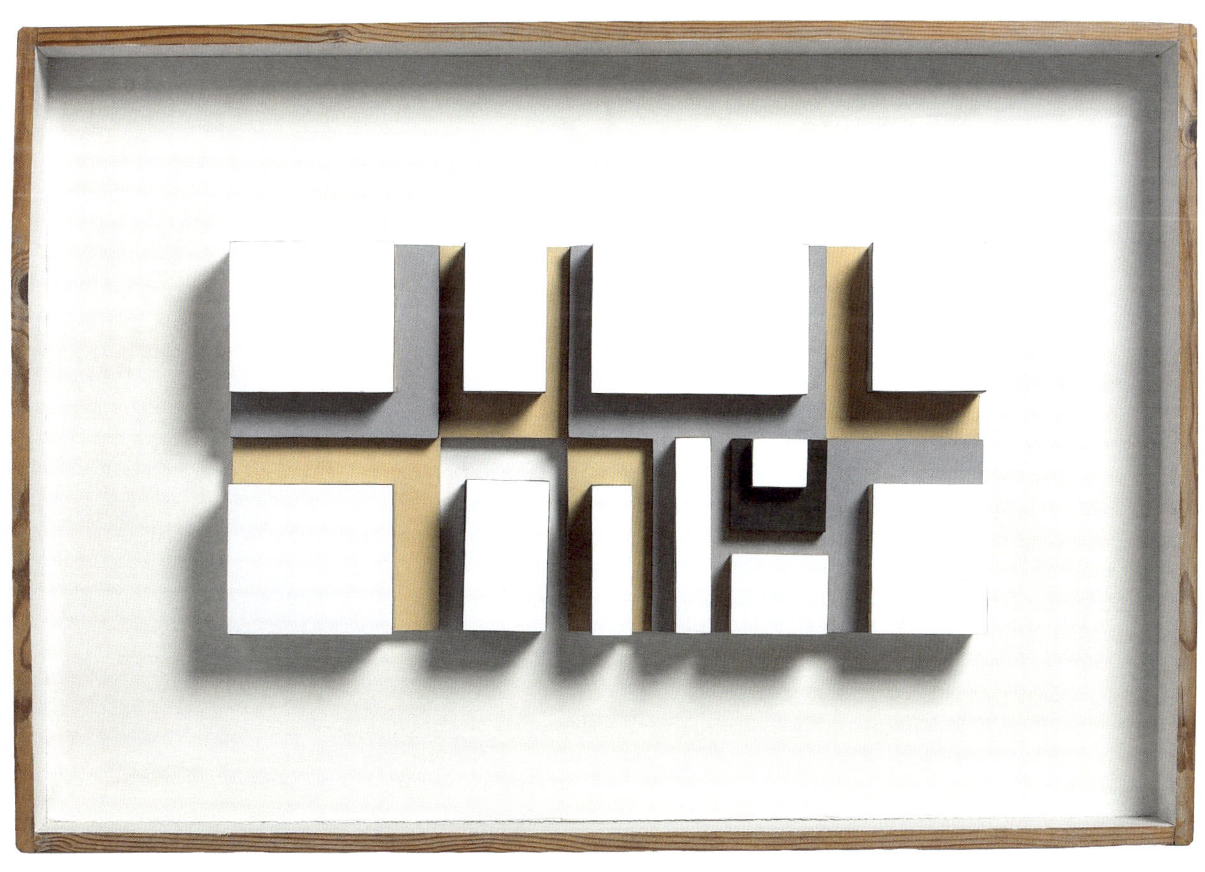

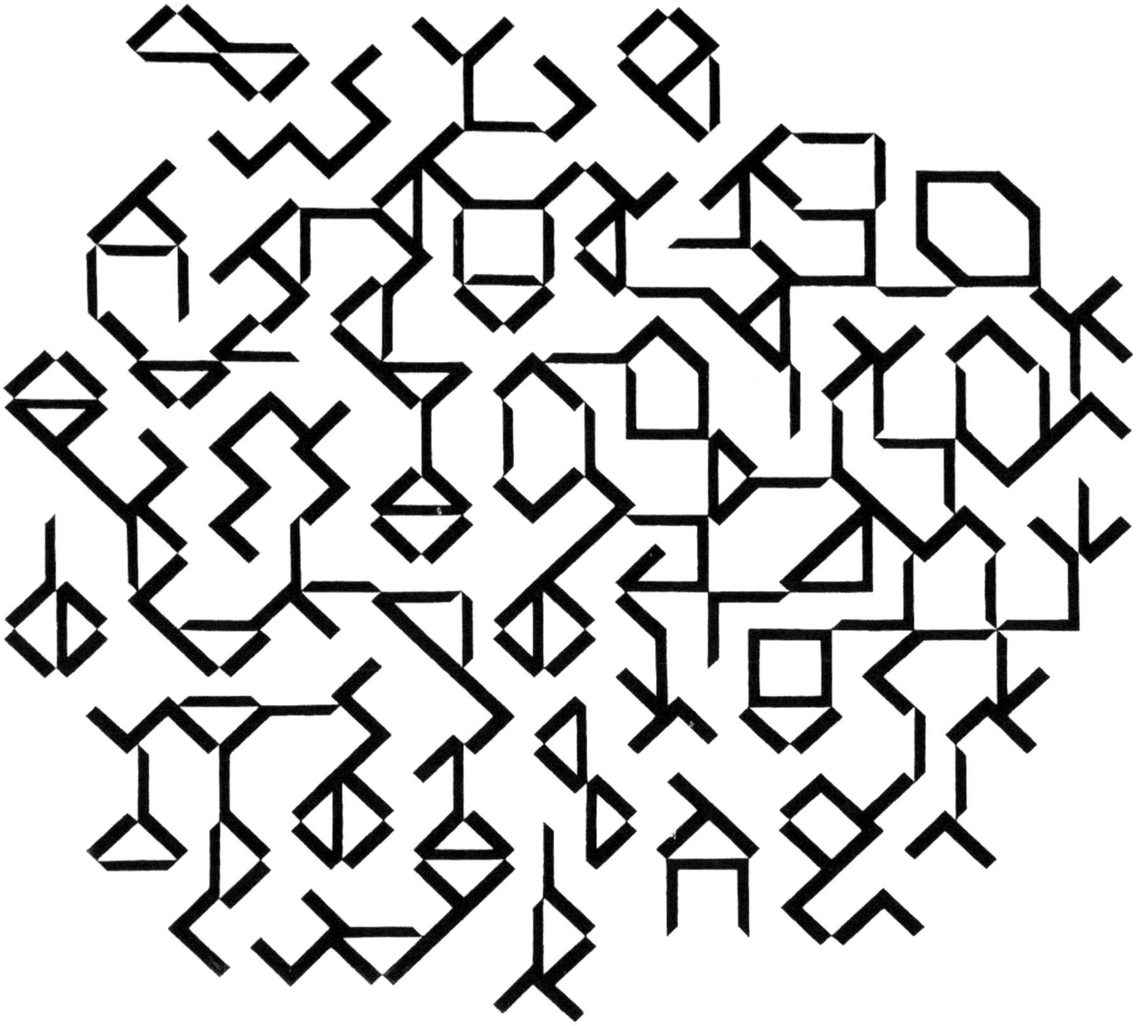

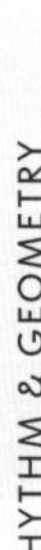

↑ **Kenneth Martin**
Black Sixes
1967–68
Oil on canvas
Sainsbury Centre

City Sculpture Project in 1972.[15] Mary Martin's more public works included a relief for Musgrave Park Hospital in Belfast (1957), and also a series of six reliefs based on tidal movements for the staircase of the *S.S. Oriana*, part of the P&O Navigation Company, in 1960. In addition, she worked on a maquette for a fountain for the BP headquarters in 1965, that was eventually unrealised.

Back in the studio, both artists worked apart, while at the same time sharing ideas together. The art critic and curator Guy Brett gave a useful reading of this kind of artistic togetherness in his review in *The Times* of the Arts Council touring exhibition of their work in 1970, a year after Mary Martin's death, writing:

> This exhibition is more than a convenient opportunity of grouping together two artists who happen to have been married. It makes one simultaneously aware of two things: close sympathy, or equality, between two artists and great differences in temperament. The work shares the same measure, the same unforced feeling, and often, as a basis, the same ideas, while taking final forms of quite different character.[16]

It was a striking comment. A further fascinating insight into their studio practices is offered by Susan Tebby, who worked as an assistant to both artists. She started first with Kenneth Martin, recalling his use of her sculptural skills:

> I was fortunate to become assistant to Kenneth in summer 1966 until his death in 1984. He had been my tutor at Goldsmiths, when we met in 1962, and seen my development first-hand: welding, use of a lathe, and other machinery and hand tools, materials, and perhaps most of all, recognised that my interests were firmly located within his own abstract constructive milieu. The first task he gave me in his studio was to file off excess brazed silver from a brass construction for the Arts Council in 1966: neat, technical and

to his exacting standards. This progressed to my proposing solutions to practical problems and to drawing illustrations for his *Leonardo* article.[17]

Tebby's passion for their work and her collaborative disposition stood her in good stead with these two artists. She still helps today in restoring the work of both artists for exhibitions. This is something she has been doing for many years, having restored works for their retrospectives at the Tate Gallery in 1975 (Kenneth Martin) and 1984 (Mary Martin) (as well as working on the latter's catalogue design), and for more recent exhibitions in the 2000s. Looking back and reflecting upon what 'collaboration' meant in this earlier studio context, she highlights both manual skills and verbal exchange. She reflects:

> There was always a difference between simply contributing to something, and *collaborating* with Kenneth. Coming from a different background with other experiences meant that Kenneth could combine things that I brought to studio discussion and work that he would not otherwise have considered or even known about, that changed some things radically, generated new situations and solutions. "Working with": the true meaning of collaboration.[18]

Both artists had come from backgrounds in two-dimensional art making, whereas Tebby had recent training in three dimensions (as well as being brought up with a background in engineering through her father). Working with Mary Martin was different to working with her husband. She states:

> Mary had also been one of my tutors at Goldsmiths. I came to work for her in a different capacity from Kenneth. This was far more to do with finishing work that she had begun as I was able to spend more time on producing elements and surfaces than she could allow time for.[19]

constructive context

An exhibition selected by Stephen Bann
from the Arts Council Collection

Warehouse Gallery
52 Earlham Street, London W.C.2.

29 March—19 April. Tuesdays—Saturdays 10am—6pm
Closed Sundays and Mondays
Admission free

Arts Council
OF GREAT BRITAIN

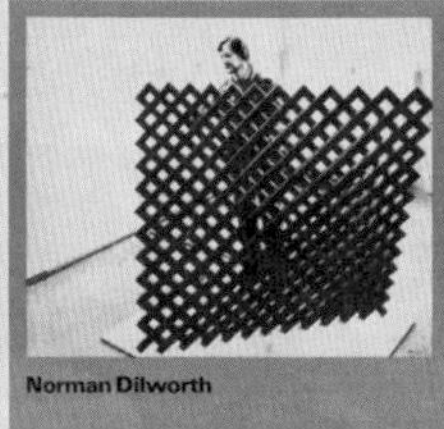

Norman Dilworth

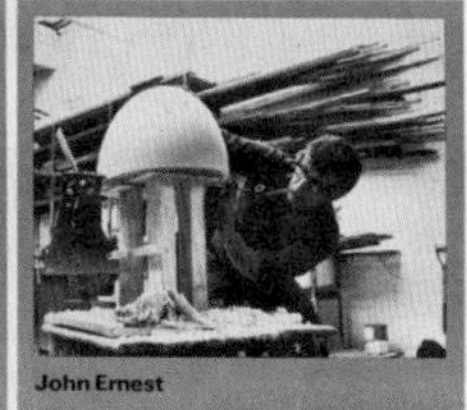

John Ernest

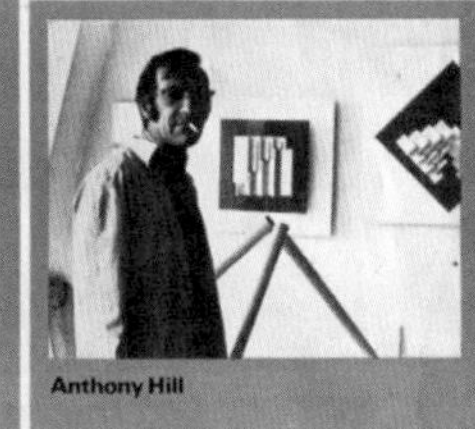

Anthony Hill

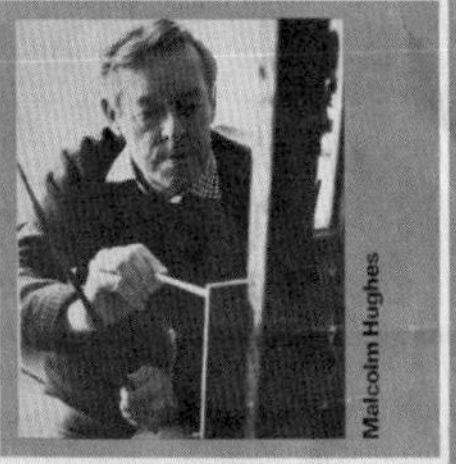

Malcolm Hughes

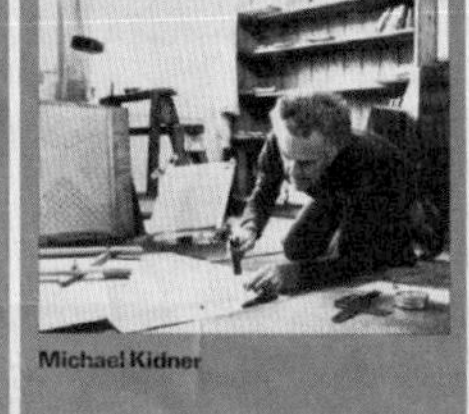

Michael Kidner

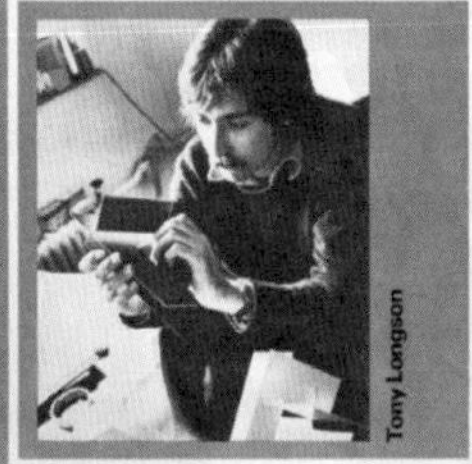

Tony Longson

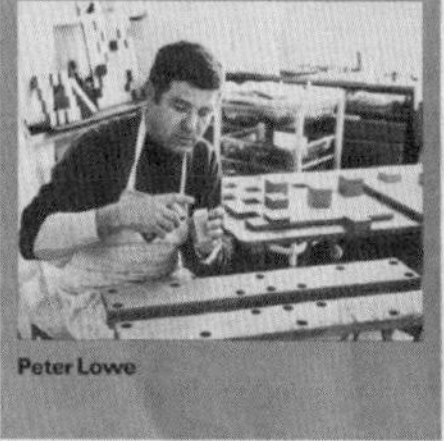

Peter Lowe

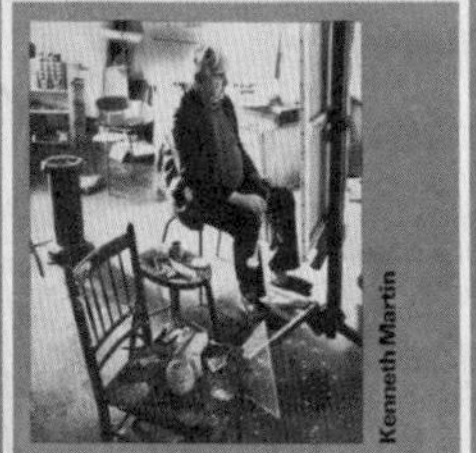

Kenneth Martin

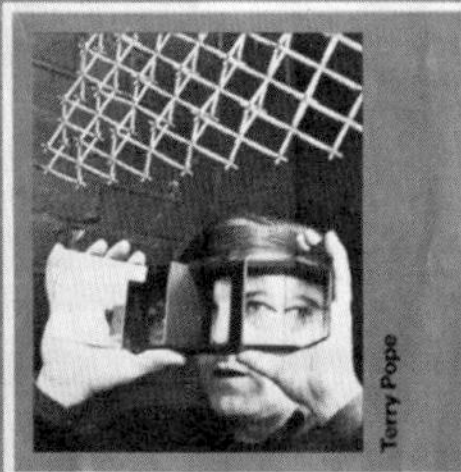

Terry Pope

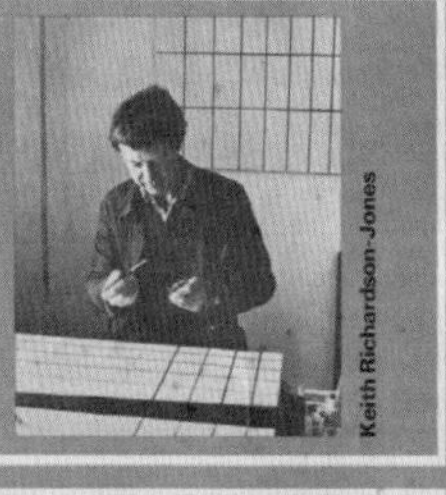

Keith Richardson-Jones

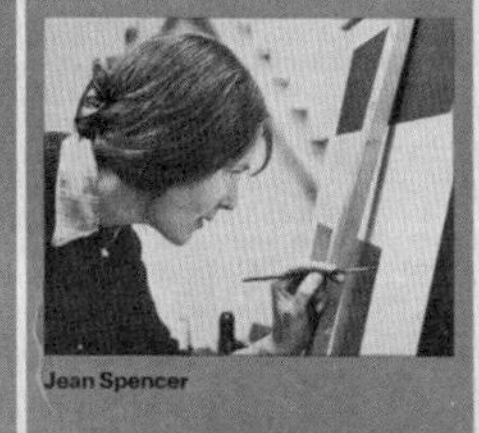

Jean Spencer

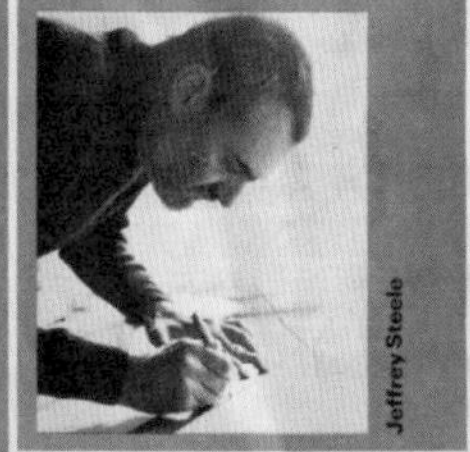

Jeffrey Steele

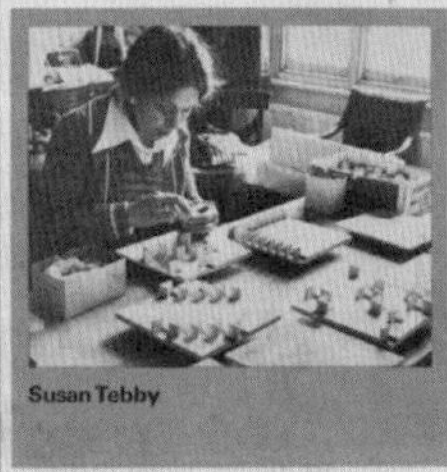

Susan Tebby

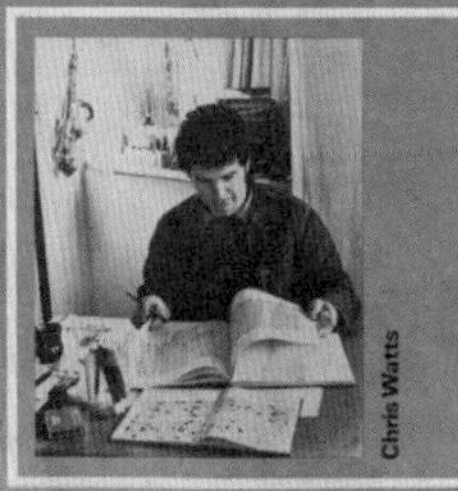

Chris Watts

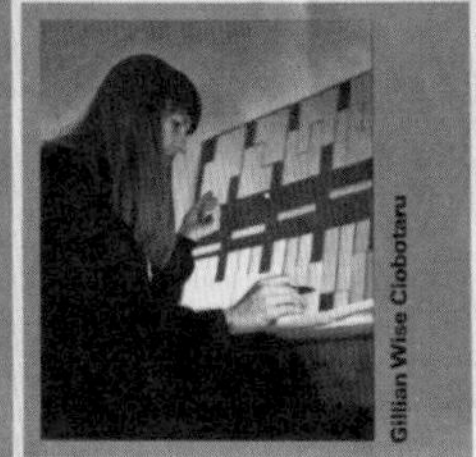

Gillian Wise Ciobotaru

Tebby has also recalled helping Mary prepare her work for exhibition and sometimes offering possibilities for hanging work in the gallery.[20] Working with 'Kenneth and Mary' gave Tebby herself very useful training for her own career as an artist. It is interesting to see just how strongly collaboration has charged her work over the years. Working on public sculpture projects and collaborating with architects and urban planners has been her main field of activity over the last forty years. She has written about it many times, perhaps nowhere more strikingly than in a text called 'The Collaborative Process', written in 1994 in the context of an exhibition at King's Manor Gallery at the University of York, which deals with her water projects for Chatham High Street and Quarry House, Leeds. She concludes her essay:

> In spite of the fact that the work here has my name on it, it is appropriate to acknowledge that the final commissioned work is a summation of many contributions, and is therefore a truly collective work: collaboration, interaction, experimentation, negotiation, implementation, each stage involving degrees of the others and each stage necessarily involving other people.[21]

Exhibition design had a special place in the thinking of the Martins early on. They had worked with the architect John Weeks (1921–2005) on part of the display for *This is Tomorrow* (1956), and his transportable systems of free-standing walls were used by them after this in the 1970–1 touring show of their work.

Questions of collaboration and affiliation played crucial and fascinating roles within group exhibitions of Constructed art, helping shape circles of involvement and recognition, sometimes consolidating national contexts and at other times rightly stressing European and international connections and inter-artistic exchanges. Exhibitions such as *Construction: England 1950–1960* at the Drian Galleries in 1961 showed a decade of endeavours. Something of a generational turning point was made by *unit series progession: an exhibition of constructions* in 1967.[22] This Arts Council exhibition combined younger and senior artists, men and women, showing works by Malcolm Carder (b.1936), John Ernest, Anthony Hill, Colin Jones (b.1934), John Law (b.1941), Peter Lowe, Kenneth Martin, Mary Martin, Waldemar d'Orey (b.1940), Terence Pope (b.1941), Jean Spencer (1942–1997), Susan Tebby and Gillian Wise. This exhibition, which was shown in Cambridge and Nottingham that year, placed an emphasis on the mathematical and three-dimensional qualities of these artists' works, as well as pointing to the interaction of the rational and intuitive sides of their endeavours.

Later group exhibitions such as *Rational Practice* (1978), curated by Norbert Lynton at the Gardner Centre Gallery in Falmer, Brighton, and *Constructive Context* (1978), another ambitious Arts Council touring exhibition, curated by the art historian Stephen Bann (b.1942), who was an influential spokesperson for Constructivist work in Britain, offered other ways of considering the dynamic life of this approach to art. *The Tradition of Constructivism*, an anthology of texts he edited, came out in 1974 and he'd also curated the *Systems* show in 1972–73. *The Tradition of Constructivism*, an anthology of texts Bann edited (the final chapter of which included writings by Anthony Hill and Kenneth Martin), came out in 1974 and he also curated the *Systems* show in 1972–3.[23] The early 1970s witnessed a generational shift, but also a shift in orientation for many to systems based work, away from earlier post-war, Constructivist concerns.

Constructive Context toured throughout 1978 and 1979 (including at UEA early that year), showcasing recent and contemporary work, including the work of Norman Dilworth, John Ernest, Anthony Hill, Malcolm Hughes, Michael Kidner, Terry Longson, Peter Lowe, Kenneth Martin, Terry Pope, Keith Richardson-Jones, Jean Spencer, Jeffrey Steele, Susan Tebby, Chris Watts and Gillian Wise Ciobotaru. Bann's catalogue text highlighted earlier inheritances, from early experiments in Russia and the De Stijl movement through to the work of the American artist Charles Biederman (1906–2004), whose *Art as the Evolution of Visual Knowledge* (1948) had a powerful

← Poster for the Arts Council exhibition *Constructive Context*, Warehouse Gallery, London, 1978.

impact on several artists involved. *Constructive Context* included works by different generations of artists, which enabled continuities and affiliations to be considered, but also pointed to the lively present and future life of this approach to art. Although Bann saw the present context of Constructivist art in Britain as active within a 'system of oppositions and affiliations', what he saw as shared concerns were interests in displaying 'the fabrication of the work as a procedure', attention to 'the course of an investigation' and an affiliation with scientific processes of 'hypothesis and experiment'.[24]

The 1970s and 1980s also witnessed much activity among Constructivist and Systems art groups. 'Exhibiting Space' in London represented a serious and lively forum for meetings and debate, as well as display and response. Active between 1983 and 1989, it was hosted by artists Ray (G. R.) Thomson and Martine Lignon in their place on Gower's Walk in Whitechapel, participants also included Trevor Clarke (b.1949), Catherine Pearson, Nicole Charlett (b.1957) and Richard Bell and Susan Tebby. Guest visitors were also invited to take part in discussions, which addressed art, philosophy and politics. A publication of their activities called *CONSPECTUS* was produced in 1986.

Subsequent groups, Countervail and 'Postal Academy', were formed by some of the female members of this group. The later 1980s also witnessed many publications and symposia, including the *Constructivist Forum* publication, produced by Nathan Cohen (b.1962) and Tim Johnson. Text and documentation played a crucial part in the discursive life of Constructivism and sat in active relation to the material objects these artists made and displayed.

Richard Bell, who took part in 'Exhibiting Space', has recently reflected on what collaboration meant to him, commenting on the importance of dialogue. He learned about the British Systems group and the collaborative thinking of this period from discussions with Jeffrey Steele, and Bell was particularly drawn to collaborative developments in Constructive and abstract art.[25] He states:

> For me, a 'collaborative practice' was not to aspire to a single unity of purpose or style. Contradiction and change are often at the heart of the collaborative dialectic. Differences in approach and aesthetic decision-making are vital to the process. I was increasingly aligning my approach with the abstraction and thinking of such artists as Ad Reinhardt, Agnes Martin, and Peter Joseph. I thought there was potential for a hybrid method within a collaborative and constructive model.

Concluding:

> On reflection, collaboration was largely confined to dialogue, sharing texts and organising/curating exhibitions. I believe its benefits are to be found as a formative process. It enables collective thinking and discrete group dialogue and events to come about, and it gives rise to significant moments of individual transformation.[26]

Collaborations with artists abroad were becoming increasingly interesting to British artists, offering opportunities to show their work and share ideas.

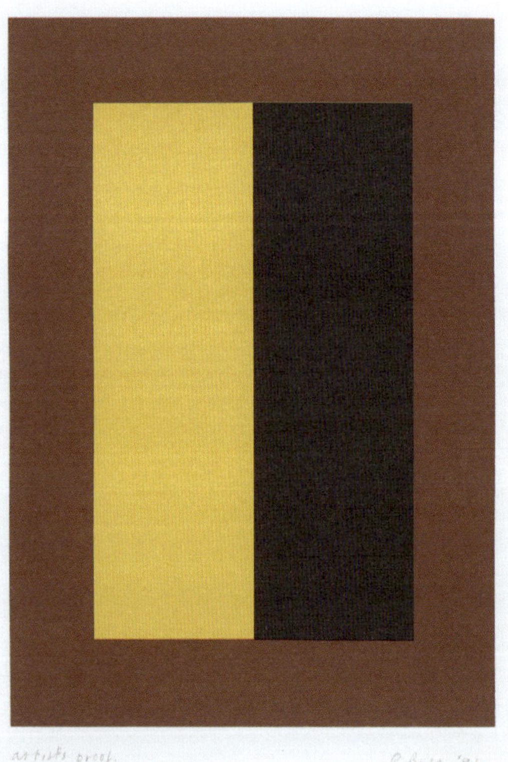

artist's proof   R.Bell '91

← Richard Bell
Untitled
1991
Screenprint on paper
Sainsbury Centre

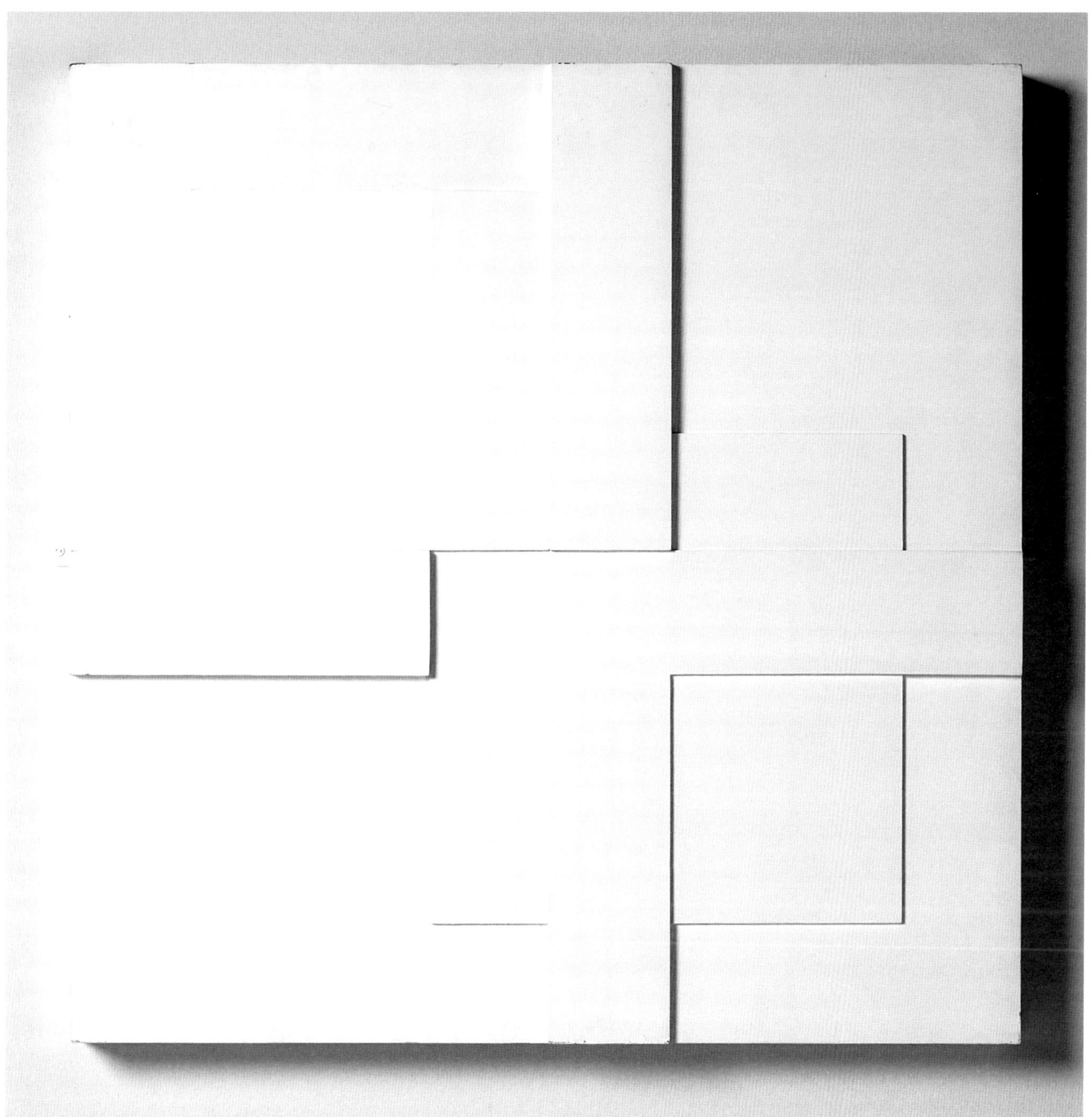

↑ Jean Spencer
Square Relief 4
1968
Wood with PVA
Sainsbury Centre

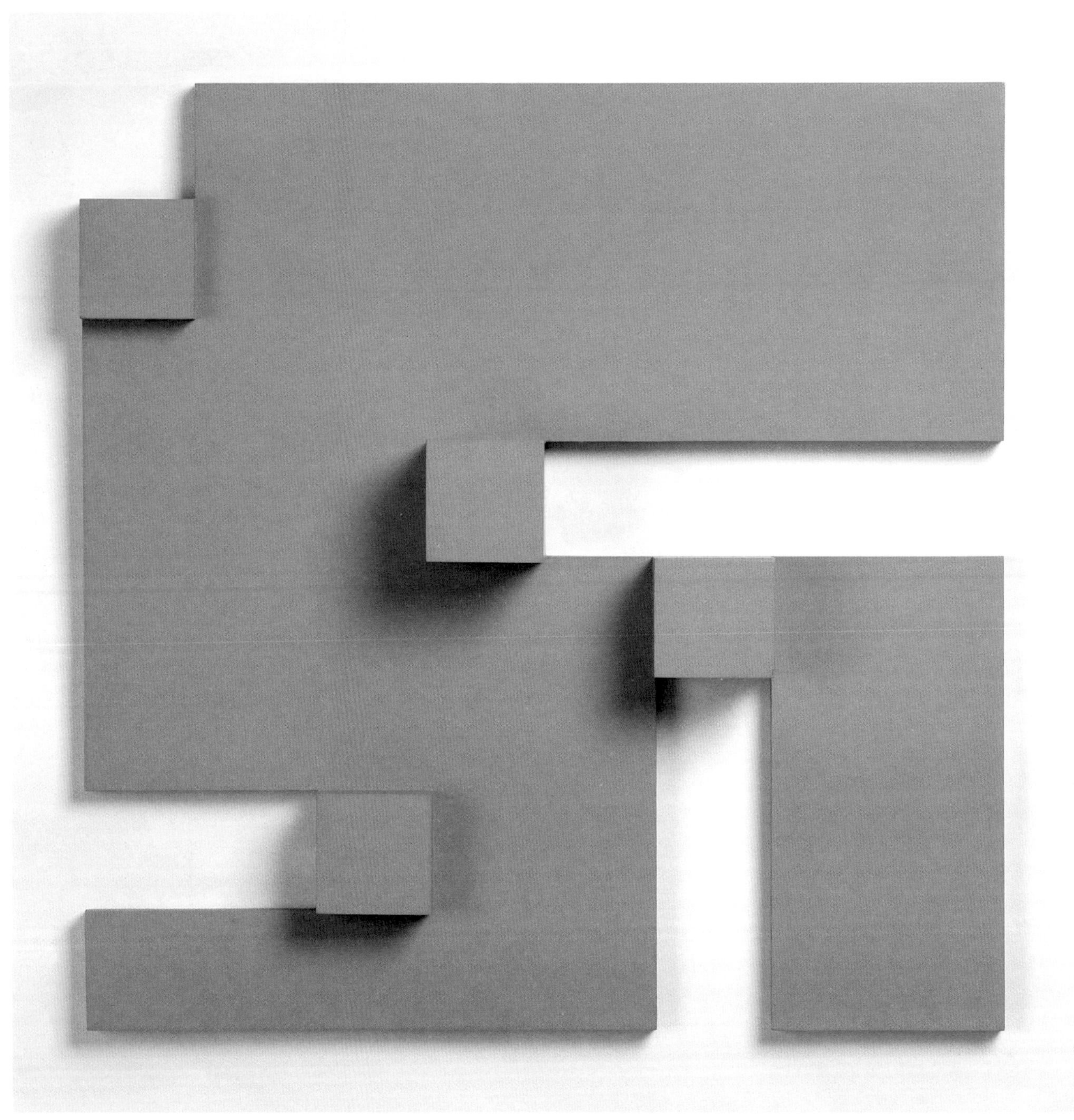

↑ **Peter Lowe**
Relief, Series A, No. 10
1974
MDF, paint and melamine
Sainsbury Centre

Many artists, including Norman Dilworth, Peter Lowe, John Carter (b.1942), Jeffrey Steele and Gary Woodley, were particularly engaged with exchanges and collaborations with non-British counterparts. John Carter enjoyed regular contact and liaison with European concrete and Constructivist art and artists from the mid-1980s, taking part in conferences and symposia as well as exhibitions.[27] These included PRO conferences in the 1980s and many other pan-European collegiate endeavours. During the 1980s and 1990s such interests also connected exhibition projects, both in Britain and in Europe; they helped develop different understandings of the scale, scope and reach of Constructed art and its developing intellectual and artistic ambitions. They also gave a much-valued extension of exhibition opportunities to artists working in Britain.

One of the most fascinating was the ambitious and international *Pier + Ocean* exhibition at the Hayward Gallery in 1980, which travelled to the Rijksmuseum Kröller-Müller in Otterlo.[28] The exhibition was selected by artists Norman Dilworth and Gerhard von Graevenitz (1934–1983). Through three main concerns – 'Concepts of Space', 'Chance System Endlessness' and 'Gravity' – it brought together a wide range of artists from around the world, placing Constructivist and Systems tendencies in the company of other sculptural, conceptual and environmental ones. Dilworth recalls:

> I chose *Pier + Ocean* as the title because it encapsulated the concept of a construction in relation to its environment, and also enabled us to include works that previously had appeared to have nothing in common. To arrive at a work of art through construction (a construct of elements), this we inherited from the constructivists and with this in mind we could look at what construction meant to a contemporary generation.[29]

Such internationalist and contemporary considerations were also reflected in one of the most striking groupings of this period, namely the 'International Workgroup for Constructive Art' (*internationaler Arbeitskreis für konstruktive Gestaltung* or Arbeitskreis for short).[30] This was established in Antwerp in 1972 by artists Pierre de Poortere, H. D. Schrader and Guy Vandenbranden, and its Constructivist-related activities ran for just over a decade. Arbeitskreis travelled annually to different cities with themed concerns. It involved a number of artists from Britain, notably Jean Spencer and Peter Lowe, whose *Square Relief 4* (1968) and *Relief, Series A, No. 10* (1974) are included in *Rhythm and Geometry*.

Lowe was a student of Kenneth Martin (who was also an honorary member of Arbeitskreis) and interested in collaboration from early on. He recalls: 'In 1962 Colin Jones and I showed reliefs at the Artists' International Association in London. We worked on a mutually agreed theme of positive and negative for one year with "Plus Minus" as the exhibition title'.[31] Following this, Jones took things a step further, beyond London, contacting Joost Baljeu (1925–1991), the editor of *Structure*, who invited them to submit an article describing the results of their dual approach.

Lowe's reflections on the openness and opportunities which Arbeitskreis offered a decade later make compelling reading today. He writes: 'One of many positive things about Arbeitskreis was Internationalism and respect that united several nationalities. In order to facilitate collaborative projects, including themed exhibitions and symposia, Arbeitskreis adopted a policy of inviting local non-members to participate on a temporary basis'.[32] Lowe's recollections of the realities of such collaborations also serve to remind us today how difficult were the conditions for collaborations. He writes:

> The internet had yet to be invented when the group was forming and we depended on postal services. The UK was not a member of the European Community at the time. Customs posts at border crossings were an impediment when transporting works to and from the UK. Days before our exhibition was due to open in Amersfoort, the works were impounded by customs

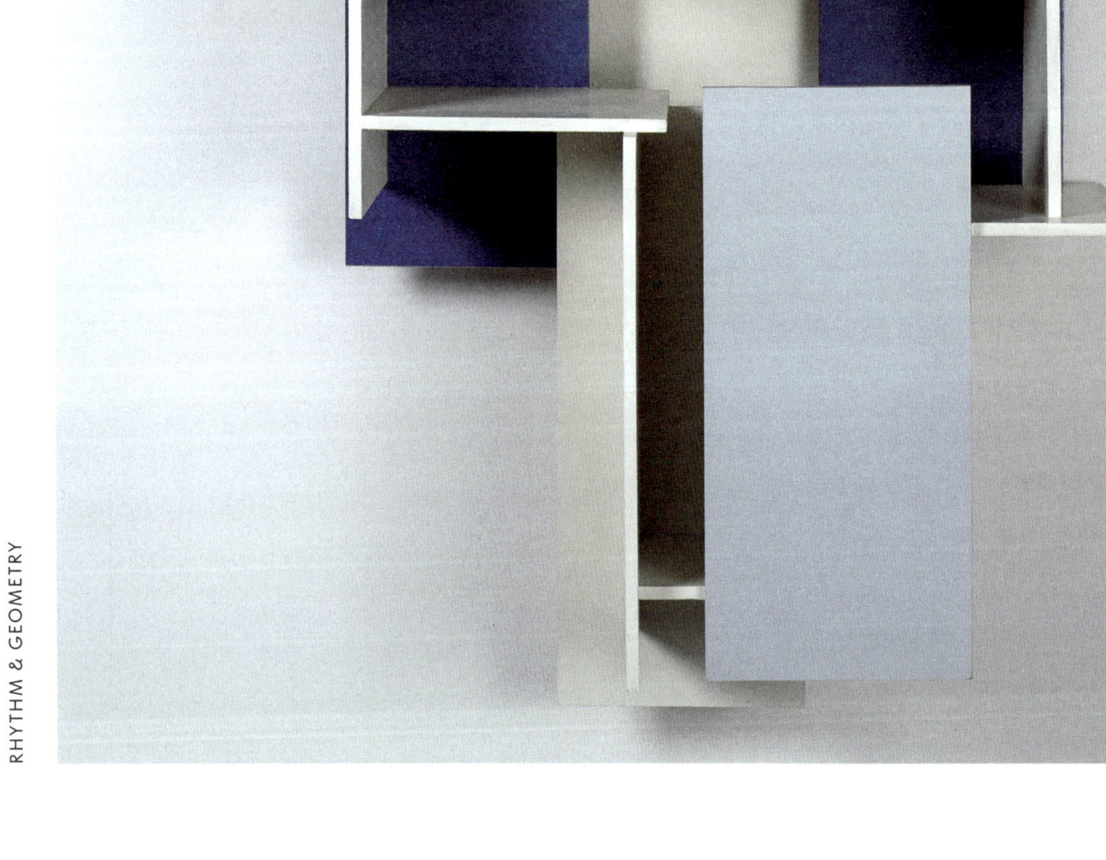

and locked in a bonded warehouse. The Cold War made it difficult or near impossible to cross certain borders with work. These obstacles were challenges to be overcome and we became adept at getting our work through. This was possible because constructed art doesn't usually resemble conventional art. Otherwise, the bureaucracy involved was a disincentive to exhibiting abroad.[33]

Such statements help shine a light on the works shown in this exhibition and the collaborative spirit shared by so many of the artists who made them. From the early achievements of an older generation in the 1950s through to the endeavours of later generations, Construction and its various branches and associated approaches embraced collaboration in a variety of different ways. Part of the job – and interesting challenges – of being an artist was to be open-minded and amenable to such ways of thinking. Many reached out, often against all odds, animated by a deep-seated belief in the power of exchange and what it could do to build bridges not just between artists and different sensibilities, but between different communities and countries. Looking back over the last seventy years of work, this internationalist dimension, which has, across generations, been such a powerful component in these artists' outlooks and shared endeavours, has very much continued into recent decades. Constructivism has always been a movement of continuity, of different stages and different groups, of commonalities and differences, with one element leading to another. Sometimes painting takes centre stage, at other times the more sculptural questions of three-dimensional work lead the way, depending on who the primary organisers were. However, it has also always been a movement of international exchange and dialogue: artists and the art works they make participating in a broader artistic community beyond national boundaries. □

← Joost Baljeu
Synthetic Wall Construction
1964
Wood and paint
Sainsbury Centre

ENDNOTES

1. Quoted in Jasia Reichardt, *Victor Pasmore*, Art in Progress series (London: Methuen, 1962) unpag.
2. Alastair Grieve, *Constructed Abstract Art in England: A Neglected Avant-Garde* (London and New Haven: Yale University Press, 2005), p.9.
3. Peter Lowe, letter to author, 28 July 2021.
4. George Meyrick, letter to author, 4 July 2021.
5. The art historian Steven Gartside has written on this subject in interesting ways. See, notably, his exhibition and its catalogue: *Model Forms: Sculpture/Architecture in 50s and 60s Britain* (Leeds: Henry Moore Institute, 2003).
6. The publication for *Nine Abstract Artists* was republished in facsimile form in 2005, to accompany the *Nine Abstract Artists Revisited* exhibition staged at Osborne Samuel Gallery, which ran from 11 March to 9 April 2005.
7. See, for example, Charles Green, *The Third Hand: Collaboration in Art from Conceptualism to Postmodernism* (University of Minnesota Press: Minneapolis, 2001) and Ellen Mara De Wachter, *Co-Art: Artists on Creative Collaboration* (London and New York: Phaidon, 2017).
8. Lawrence Alloway, *Nine Abstract Artists: their work and theory* (London: Alec Tiranti Ltd, 1954), p.16.
9. This is also discussed by Alan Fowler and Brandon Taylor in *Elements of Abstraction: Space, Line & Interval in Modern British Art* (Southamton: Southampton Art Gallery, 2005).
10. Anthony Hill (ed.), *DATA: Directions in Art, Theory and Aesthetics* (Greenwich, Connecticut: New York Graphic Society Ltd), 1968.
11. Gillian Wise, 'Gillian Wise', in *Low Frequency* (Textum Set 1, Paris, 2003), p.72.
12. Stephen Gilbert, letter to author, 11–12 November 2005.
13. Stephen Gilbert to Constant, 4 December 1983, reprinted in *Stephen Gilbert*, exhibition catalogue (Den Haag: Galerie Nova Spectra, 25 February–18 March 1984). See also *Shaping Modern Sculpture: Stephen Gilbert and Jocelyn Chewett in Post-War Paris* (Leeds: Henry Moore Institute, 2006).
14. Stephen Gilbert, letter to author, 11–12 November 2005. Alastair Grieve's 2005 book provides an excellent account of Gilbert's work in Huddersfield and of his involvement with Stead and the Symon Quinn Gallery. For a fascinating collection of writings on Stead's work, see: Lynne Green and Robert Hall (eds.) *Peter Stead: A Life in Equilibrium* (Huddersfield: Huddersfield Art Gallery, 2006). This publication also contains Sam Gathercole's essay 'Space / Time + Colour = 2 Houses', pp. 84–94.
15. For a recent publication on this project, see *City Sculpture Projects 1972, Henry Moore Institute Essays on Sculpture*, issue 76 (Henry Moore Foundation, 2016).
16. Guy Brett, 'Two who rose to the occasion', *The Times*, 20 August 1970.
17. Susan Tebby, 'The Studio Context for Artist and Assistant Collaboration' (2021), unpublished, correspondence with the author, summer 2021. See 'Construction and Change on a group of works made between 1965 and 1967', *Leonardo*, vol. 1, 1968 (drawings 1–2, 4–6, Susan Tebby, 1967).
18. Tebby, 2021.
19. Ibid.
20. For example, Mary Martin's solo exhibition at the Axiom Gallery in 1968.
21. Susan Tebby, 'The Collaborative Process', King's Manor Gallery, University of York, 1994, p.4.
22. *unit series progression: an exhibition of constructions*, Arts Council, 1967. 'Introduction' by Hugh Evans.
23. Stephen Bann (ed.), *The Tradition of Constructivism, The Documents of 20th-Century Art* (London: Thames and Hudson, 1974).
24. Stephen Bann, 'Introduction', in *Constructive Context* (London: Arts Council, 1978), p. 5.
25. For instance, the Russian Constructivist avant garde had redefined the role of the artist in the revolutionary period; the De Stijl movement's impact on architectural modernity; and how the Art Konkrete movement, CoBrA and Supports/Surfaces groups had been driven by interests in critical theory, social-political and aesthetic change.
26. Richard Bell, statement/letter to author, 21 August 2021.
27. For a useful book on John Carter's work, see Chris Yetton, *John Carter* (London: Royal Academy of Arts, 2010), with contributions by Mel Gooding, Britta E. Buhlmann and Klaus Staudt.
28. For a recent text on this exhibition, see 'New Beginnings: Groups and Exhibitions in the 1960s and 1970s: Norman Dilworth in conversation with Jon Wood', in *Concrete Parallels/Concretos Paralelos: British Constructivism and Brazilain Concrete and Neo-Concrete Art* (São Paulo: Cultura Inglese, 2012), pp.321–27.
29. Ibid., p. 325.
30. See: http://iafkg.com/ accessed 21 August 2021.
31. Peter Lowe, letter to author, 28 July 2021.
32. Ibid.
33. Ibid.

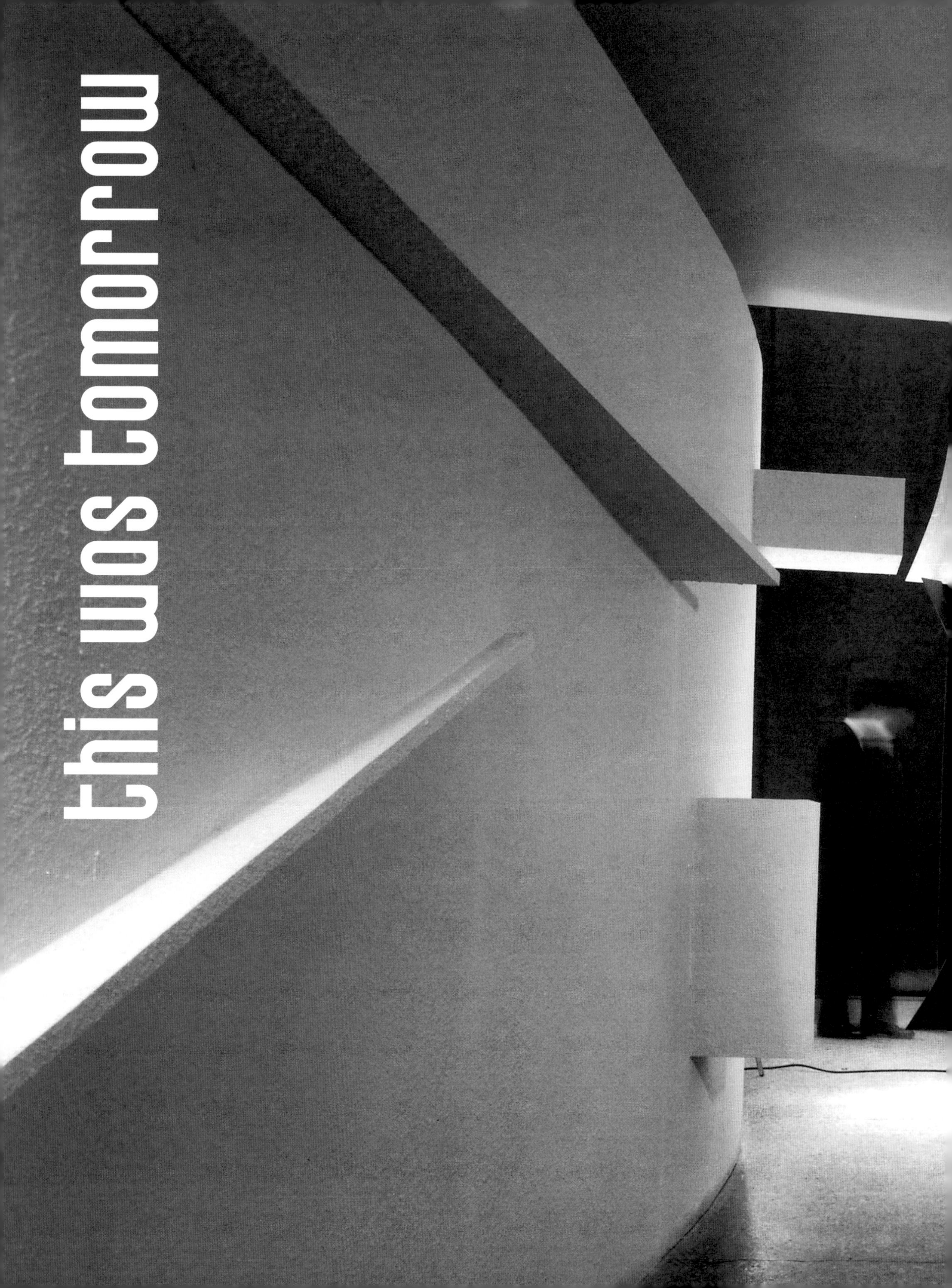

this was tomorrow

adventures in a brave new world
Calvin Winner

THIS IS TOMORROW, the iconic 1956 exhibition, has been much mythologised but more typically with reference to the emergence of Pop Art. However, *This is Tomorrow* in fact included a significant number of artists working in variant forms of abstraction and constructed art, many of whom are represented in the collection at the Sainsbury Centre. This essay re-examines the exhibition and presents an alternative perspective on its content and the aims and objectives of the contributing artists. By constructing a narrative based on those artists making abstract and constructed art, this essay presents a new understanding of the iconic exhibition. It will explore its impact and legacy in the trajectory of constructed art practice over the subsequent years. The protagonists saw this as a progressive tendency in British art and no doubt believed theirs was the art of the future that the provocatively titled exhibition promised.

The pioneers of the interwar years explored the possibilities of abstraction in a radical series of innovations that formed a synthesis between painting and sculpture. They attempted alignment between fine art, decorative art, architecture and design practice. In the main, they were utopian, often politically motivated and believed in the agency of art to change society for the better. After the Second World War, a dominant theme was the application of geometry and mathematics. There was a call to reconnect art to science and integrate technology. This was highlighted by C. P. Snow (1905–1980) in his famous thesis from 1959, the *Two Cultures*, where he argued against the detrimental effect of a separation between science and the humanities.[1] Advances in technology led many artists to experiment with new materials such as lightweight metals and plastics. Artists strived to produce art that both reflected and was part of industrialised society.

This is Tomorrow was held at the Whitechapel Art Gallery between 9 August and 9 September 1956. The premise was to explore the ways that artists and architects could work more closely together; for practitioners to explore shared concerns as well as probing the boundaries between art and architecture; and to see how they could better collaborate in a time of post-war reconstruction. This was fertile ground as disparate individuals and groups debated, argued and sometimes disagreed over the degree of synthesis that best suited the moment. A collaborative spirit had been inspired by the artist Theo van Doesburg (1883–1931) and De Stijl, the movement he founded in the Netherlands. He had preached for the amalgamation of painting, sculpture and architecture into a universal language. This was a language of non-objective art consisting of the straight line, the square and the rectangle (and later the diagonal).[2] The individual personality of the artist would be limited in the serving of these general principles.

For *This is Tomorrow*, the thirty-eight participants were divided into twelve groups consisting of artists, architects and designers. Each were allocated space in the gallery and worked independently of each other. The groups were identified numerically and ordered in the exhibition according to the intended visitor route through the gallery. Eight groups (1,2,5,6,7,9,10 and 11) included artists working in abstract and constructed art and are examined in detail here, whilst the remaining four groups (3, 4, 8 and 12) exist outside the realms of this study. In this essay, the relevant artists and groups are discussed to support the narrative rather than numerically or in the order they appeared in the exhibition. The exhibition was hugely popular, attracting almost 1,000 visitors per day.[3] Its popularity may have had something to do with its provocative title which gained the attention of mainstream news broadcasts.[4] The exhibition is commonly discussed as the inaugural moment in the emergence of a proto British Pop Art. Reyner Banham (1922–1988) described it as the 'first Pop Art manifestation to be seen in any art gallery'.[5] It was also the first visualisation of Banham's 'New Brutalist' agenda as proposed by him in the *Architectural Review* in 1955.[6] Both these elements had grown out of the Institute of Contemporary Arts (ICA) in London. The participants of *This is Tomorrow* are often assumed to occupy two distinct tendencies: firstly, the Constructivist artists, or 'Constructionists' as they preferred to be called, who

← Group 10 (Robert Adams, Peter Carter, Frank Newby and Sir Colin St John) installation at *This is Tomorrow*, Whitechapel Gallery, 1956.

→ Group 7 installation at *This is Tomorrow*, Whitechapel Gallery, 1956 with reliefs by Victor Pasmore.

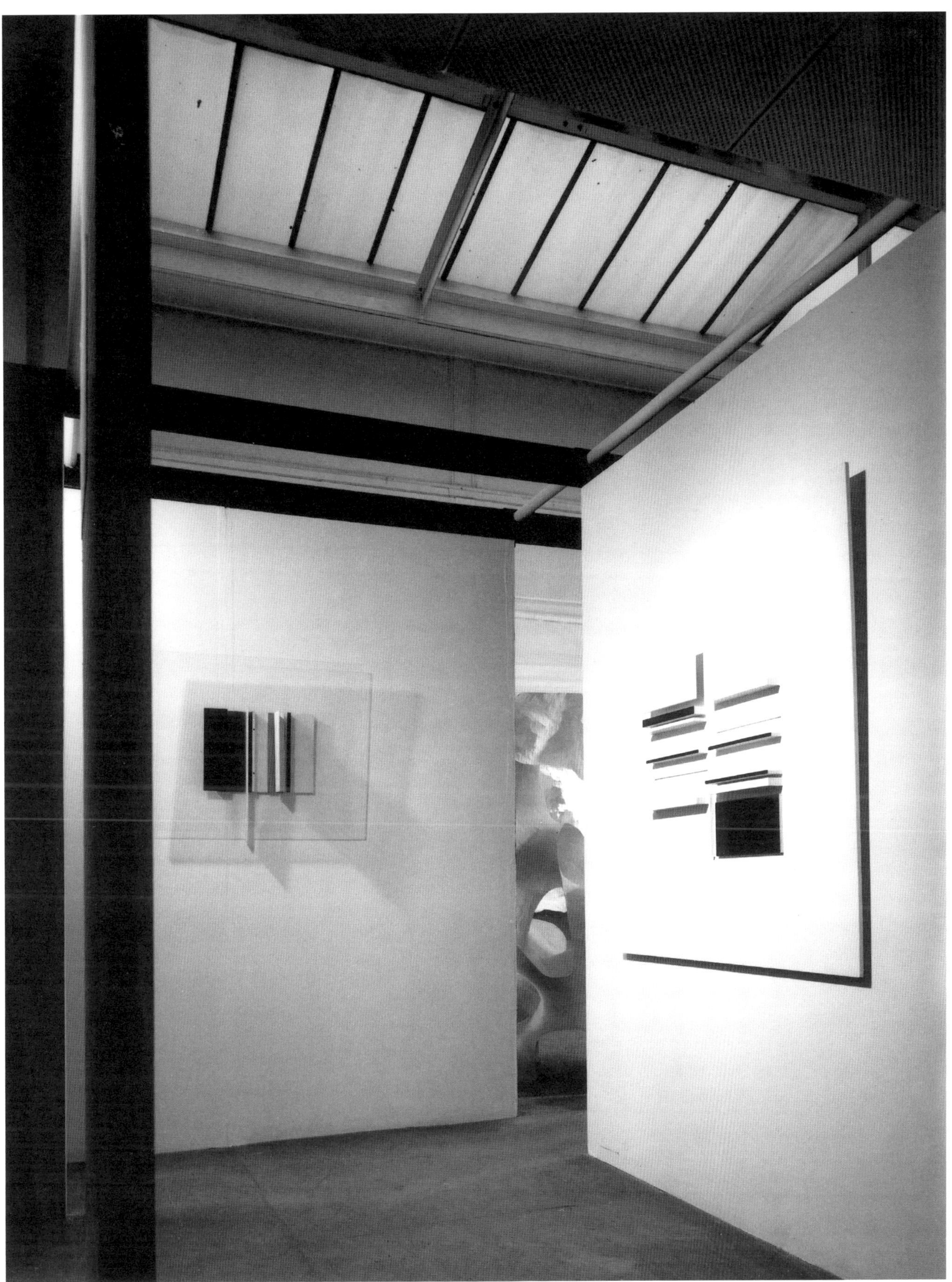

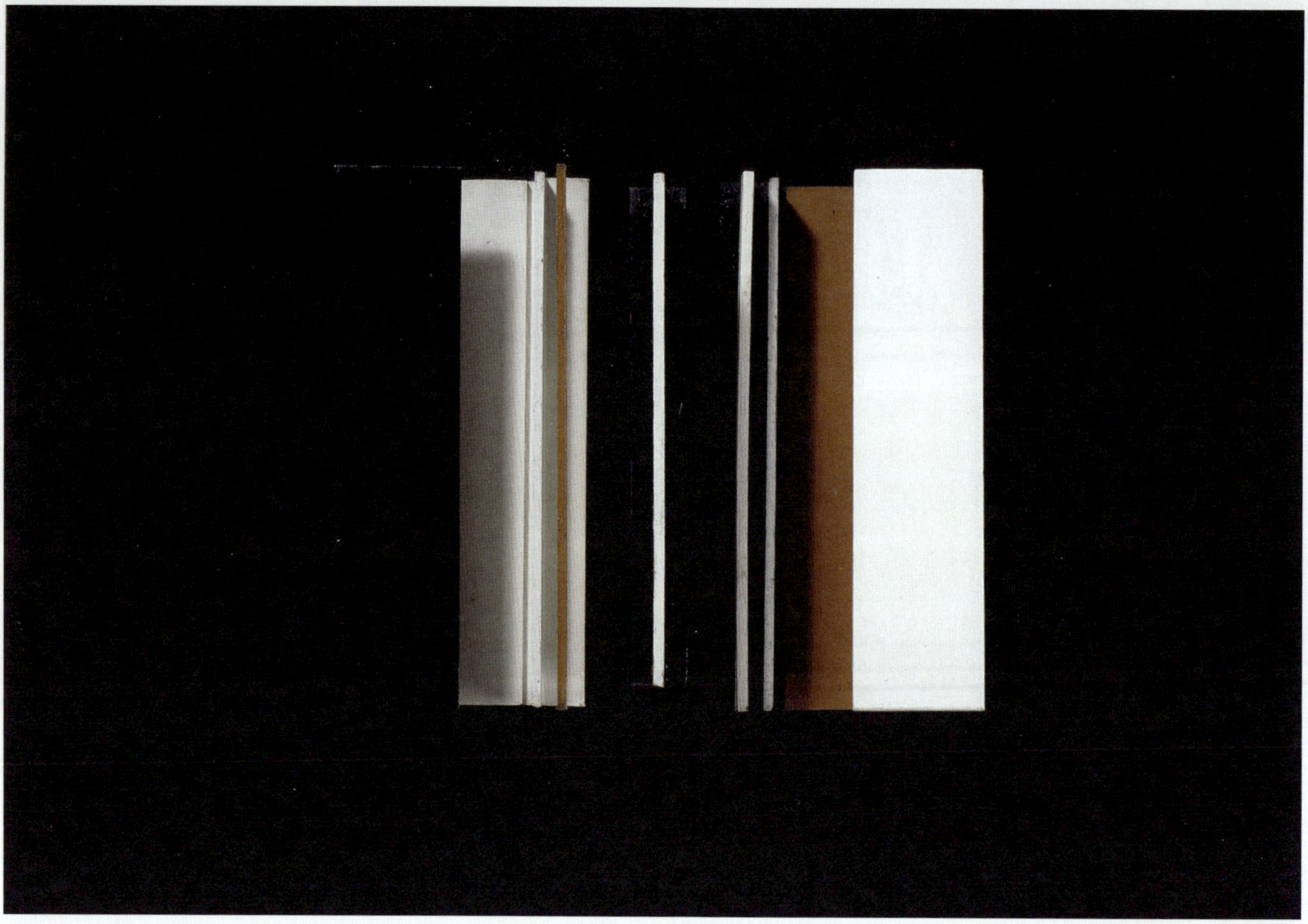

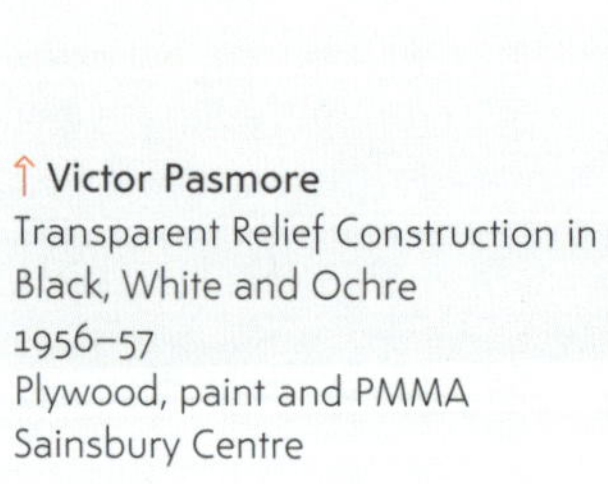

↑ **Victor Pasmore**
Transparent Relief Construction in
Black, White and Ochre
1956–57
Plywood, paint and PMMA
Sainsbury Centre

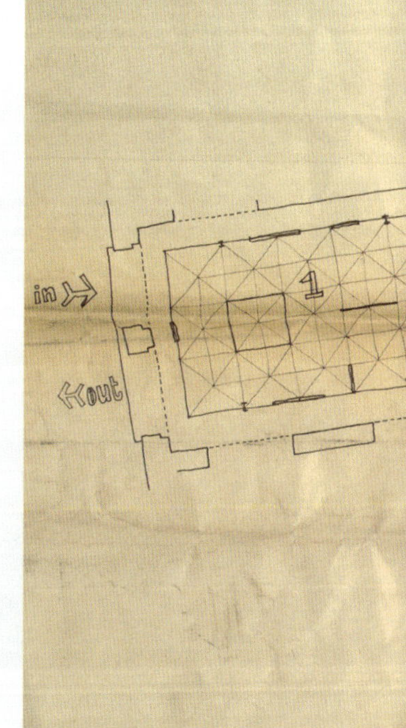

→ Colin St John's drawing of the
layout for *This is Tomorrow*.

engaged in abstract and constructed art;[7] secondly, the artists and architects associated with the ICA, who identified as the Independent Group, and had a fascination with technology and popular (American) culture.[8] But some artists defied this two-camp categorisation, such as Richard Hamilton (1922–2011), Eduardo Paolozzi (1924–2005), William Turnbull (1922–2012), John McHale (1922–1978) and Denis Williams (1923–1998). There had already been considerable cross-fertilisation of ideas in various exhibitions and in the London art schools, notably Central School of Art and Camberwell College of Arts, where artists from both tendencies were either teaching or students.[9]

The artist Adrian Heath (1920–1992) played an important role in the birth of *This is Tomorrow*. In 1951, Heath had organised the seminal exhibition, *Abstract Paintings, Sculptures and Mobiles* at the gallery of the Artists' International Association (AIA). Alongside Heath, contributing artists included Victor Pasmore (1908–1998), Robert Adams, Kenneth Martin (1905–1984), Mary Martin (1907–1969), Anthony Hill (1930–2020), William Turnbull and Eduardo Paolozzi.[10] The exhibition was accompanied by the publication *Broadsheet No. 1*, where Kenneth Martin contributed an important statement on abstract art.[11] This publication also included texts by Anthony Hill discussing Alexander Calder's (1898–1976) mobiles; Misha Black (1910–1977) and Alexander Gibson (1906–1977) wrote 'New Architecture and Abstract Art'; and the architect John Weeks (1921–2005) wrote about Piet Mondrian (1872–1944)

and Ludwig Mies Van der Rohe (1886–1969). Heath went on to host three weekend-long exhibitions at his London studio at 22 Fitzroy Street in March and July of 1952 and May 1953.[12] The artists who appeared in the AIA exhibition were present and architect Trevor Dannatt (1920–2021) created the design. The third exhibition arranged by John Weeks included Nigel Henderson (1917–1985) and Denis Williams who would all appear in *This is Tomorrow*. In January 1955, the exhibition *Nine Abstract Artists* was held the Redfern Gallery in London. Curated by Lawrence Alloway (1926–1990), it included work by Heath, Adams, Hill, Mary and Kenneth Martin and Pasmore. Alloway wrote a text in the exhibition catalogue and each artist made a statement about their work.[13] Alloway attempted to establish the sense of a new generation of British abstract artists. He presented this as a development distinct from the pre-war publications such as *Unit One* (1933), *Axis* (1935) and *Circle: International Survey of Constructive Art* (1937), which attempted to end Britain's isolation from trends in international art.[14]

At a meeting in Heath's studio early in 1955, the seed was sown that would eventually result in *This is Tomorrow*.[15] This occurred out of the ashes of previous discussions for an exhibition organised by artist Paule Vézelay (1892–1984) in an attempt to link British artists with Le Groupe Espace in Paris. This association of geometric abstract artists and architects was founded in Paris in October 1951, with a manifesto issued in 1953. The Paris-based Vézelay was an active member of Le Groupe Espace, who were inspired

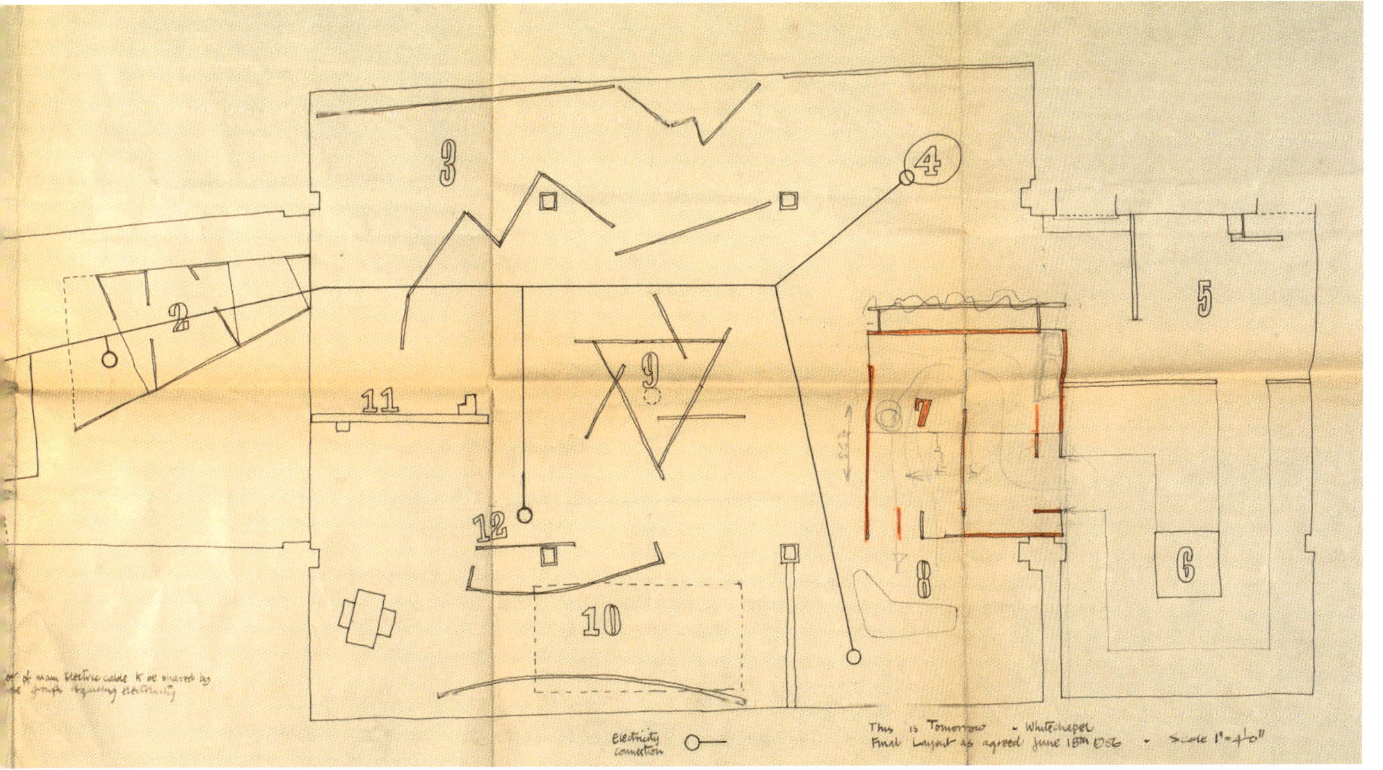

by the pre-war movements of Constructivism and Neo-Plasticism. Robert Adams (1917–1984), Kenneth Martin and Victor Pasmore briefly agreed to join the venture before disagreements set in and they resigned en masse.[16] At the meeting in Heath's studio, Reyner Banham had initially taken the lead but stepped aside to allow the architect Theo Crosby (1925–1994) to become principal organiser.[17] The architect, Colin St John Wilson (1922–2007) suggested dividing the gallery equally amongst groups consisting of an architect, a painter and a sculptor.[18] A statement of aims for the exhibition was agreed: 'to demonstrate various ways in which architects, painters, sculptors and other plastic artists can collaborate in the creation of coherent works of art'.[19] By October 1955, arrangements progressed and Edward Wright (1912–1988) was commissioned to design a catalogue to which Alloway wrote the main introduction.[20] By June 1956, Colin St John Wilson and fellow architect Peter Carter (1927–2017) had surveyed the gallery and drawn up final plans to accommodate everyone. The exhibition occupied the entire ground floor of the Whitechapel Gallery. This included the lobby, where the first two groups were placed and therefore seen on entering and departing the gallery. A suggested route bearing left led the spectator into the main gallery space where the majority (eight) of the groups were situated. At the rear of the gallery, the final two groups (5 and 6) shared a narrow space.[21]

Adrian Heath was part of group 11 and collaborated with the architect John Weeks (who was also in group 9). Heath included his 1951 painting, *Growth of Forms*, now in the Sainsbury Centre collection. The composition of this tall painting was organised on an orthogonal horizontal-vertical grid: a complex construction of juxtaposed squares of different sizes. The colours in gradations of olive green, ochre, greys and rust brown create a harmonious arrangement. *Growth of Forms* was illustrated in the exhibition catalogue with the accompanying text:

A particular area has been broken down into a series of small rectangles. The successive changes

made in the disposition of these neutral shapes in order to achieve a rhythm of area have resulted in their various tones and textures.[22]

The painting took its title from D'Arcy Wentworth Thompson's (1860–1948) book *On Growth and Form*, published in 1917 with a second edition in 1942.[23] This book inspired a generation of artists and was one of the principal sources that unite a broad selection of artists, not simply those strictly engaged with abstraction or constructed art. Many artists, including Heath, were attracted to Thompson's description of how nature grows as in shells or horns and the occurrence of fractals.[24] Heath comments in a statement in the catalogue for *Nine Abstract Artists*: 'Ultimately can a final form be achieved in a painting any more than it is in a natural growth such as a tree or a flower? Both are shaped by the continuous play of opposing forces'.[25] Although Heath no longer worked from the appearance of nature, he was attracted to the fundamental geometry of nature at a molecular level and as is often revealed in shape and pattern.

Heath and Weeks collaborated on the construction of a free-standing concrete block wall, with a description and line drawing appearing in the catalogue. It was situated perpendicular to the entrance and thus assisted the visitor to circumnavigate the gallery. This structure directly related to Heath's painting where he applied his method of using root rectangles to create harmonious proportions in a golden rectangle. The wall was more improvised than the drawing suggests. The concrete blocks were slotted together as supplied and thus were more expressive, giving the completed composition a raw Art Brut appearance. The statement by Heath and Weeks in the catalogue concludes: 'The use of common building materials – concrete block – is intended to demonstrate how an aesthetic intention can be expressed in the most humble materials'.[26] The wall's raw appearance aligns itself with the aims of architects Alison Smithson (1928–1993) and Peter Smithson (1923–2003) and the New Brutalist agenda of truth to materials as proclaimed by Reyner Banham

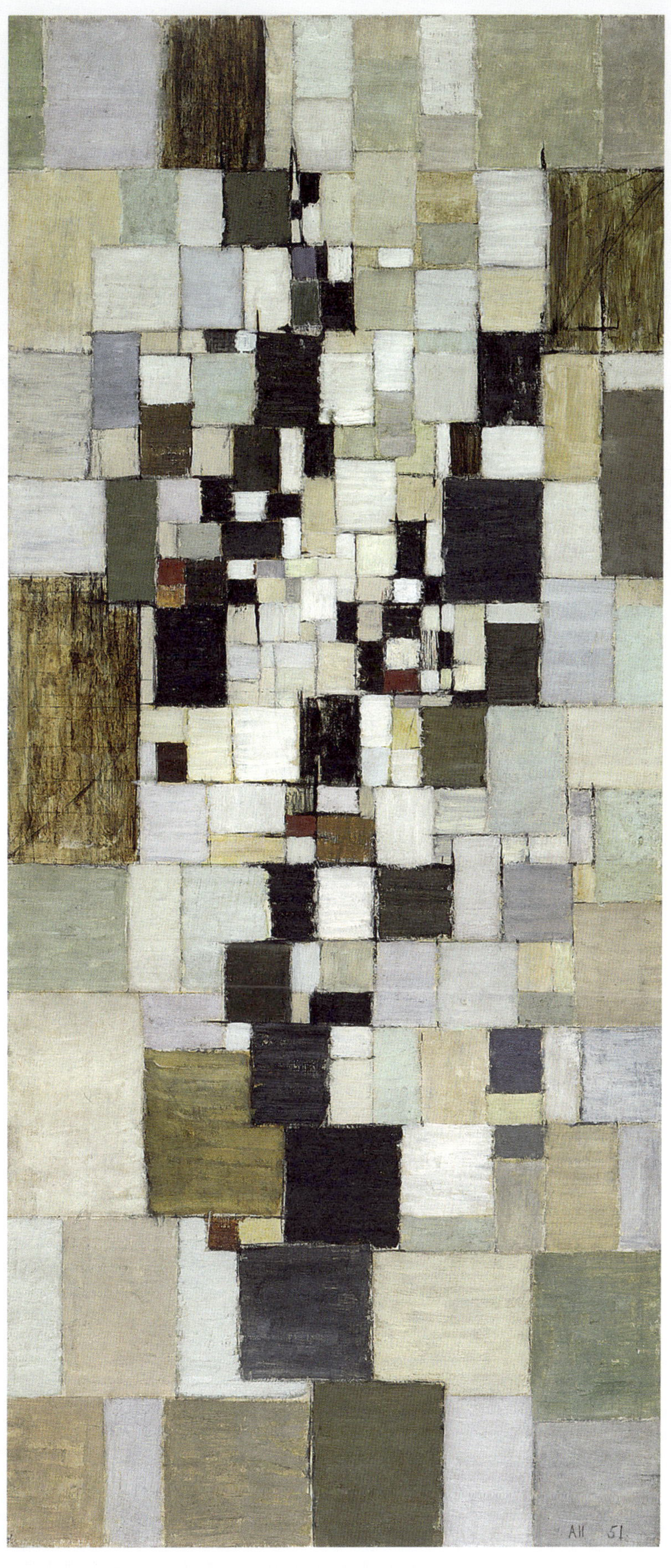

→ Adrian Heath
Growth of Forms
1951
Oil on canvas
Sainsbury Centre

in the previous year.[27] Interestingly, in 1958 the architect Trevor Dannatt used free-standing concrete block walls as part of his innovative design of the Jackson Pollock (1912–1956) exhibition, also at the Whitechapel Gallery.

Victor Pasmore formed group 7 with the architect Ernö Goldfinger (1902–1987) and sculptor Helen Phillips (1913–1995). Goldfinger was a Hungarian architect who came to England in the 1930s and would go on to become a prominent exponent of Brutalist architecture. For *This is Tomorrow*, Goldfinger created an open-plan modular pavilion constructed from interlocking orthogonal screens to create a series of four open cubes. This acknowledged the influence of Le Corbusier (1887–1965), who had published the hugely influential *Le Modulor* in 1948 and *Modulor II* in 1955. The structure was supported by a framework to brace the screens from above and was painted in black in contrast to the white wall. There was a strong reference to Dutch De Stijl from the mid-1920s: Theo van Doesburg and Cornelis van Eesteren's (1897–1988) Maison d'Artiste and Maison Particuliére and Gerrit Rietveld's (1888–1964) Schröder House in Utrecht. The spirit of De Stijl was exposed in the catalogue statement: 'the sculptor's function is to activate a space determined by the architect. The primary requisite is to attain a complete whole. The harmony depends on an affinity between the elements'. It goes on to warn of the dangers of individual forms of expression and 'conflict of individual interests. Only if architecture, painting and sculpture are concerned with the same function, is proper collaboration possible'.[28] Notably, on one of the exterior sides of the screens was a wall- mounted sculpture by Helen Phillips. She had produced an extensive series of geometric constructions in wire which explored ideas of modular growth proposed by the American architectural theorist Buckminster Fuller (1895–1983) and D'Arcy Wentworth Thompson.

Pasmore had become the principal figure in the post-war generation of British abstract art after his dramatic shift towards abstraction in the late 1940s. The Paul Klee exhibition at the National Gallery, London in 1945–46 and the first publication in English of Klee's essay 'Modern art'

(1924) had a profound impact on Pasmore's painting.[29] By the end of 1951 he was experimenting with constructed reliefs. In June 1952, in the publication *Broadsheet No.2*, Pasmore offered his own statement on abstract and constructed art: 'In this new phase of art, the object is invested in the material with which the artist works... he must be prepared to make use of the resources of modern technology and adjust himself to an age when machine-craft is taking the place of handy-craft'.[30]

In Pasmore's exhibition at the Redfern Gallery in May 1952, he exhibited eight reliefs. He was guided towards making reliefs, a hybrid art form between painting and sculpture, by the American artist Charles Biederman (1906–2004). He published two important books (*Art as the Evolution of Visual Knowledge*, 1948 and *Letter on the New Art*, 1951) where he describes his own constructed art. Biederman had been making constructed art since 1937 and saw abstraction as the final accomplishment of art in its relationship with nature. He saw this paradigm shift in terms of a progression: 'Our task is to lead in building the new culture to which Europeans gave birth, Like the very first artists we also stand at the beginning of a new epoch of human art'.[31] He believed in the alliance of the two cultures: 'art and science are the two major means by which man formulates and reformulates his changing developing interpretation of reality'.[32]

Victor Pasmore showed two wall-based constructed reliefs in *This is Tomorrow*. They each occupied a single cube of Goldfinger's modular structure. The reliefs were constructed of the same machine-formed materials as the structure itself:[33] the first was a square-format orthogonal arrangement of horizontal planes on a solid white-painted base; the second, an arrangement of vertical forms fixed to a transparent Perspex sheet. The latter is very similar to *Transparent Black Relief Construction* (1956–57) in the Sainsbury Centre collection. The relief included in *This is Tomorrow* is also an arrangement of vertical forms over a transparent sheet of Perspex, but set in front of a black-painted board. Pasmore assembled prefabricated planes of painted wood which he arranged as projecting elements either side of a central axis. He recalled the development from his early experiments with collage into relief, when he explained how he was 'constructing a picture like a carpenter constructs a box with wood, saw and hammer and nails'. He went on to state:

> Hence collage developed into relief. Beginning from a standpoint of the rectangular picture plane, this meant projecting analogous sections of its surface forwards into actual space, thus producing an orthogonal structure equivalent to that of architecture. Did not naturalistic tradition use perspective in order to produce an illusion of space and solidity? This suggested that the surface format of a painting could not provide the conditions necessary for complete independence unless combined with sculpture or architecture. In response to this, therefore, I continued with the development of relief projection.[34]

Pasmore's engagement with architecture began in 1955, when he was appointed Consulting Director of Urban Design by the Peterlee Development Corporation (PDC). His work at Peterlee can be considered as producing something of a constructionist environment, and the Apollo Pavilion was the most iconic element. This large-scale non-functional building was a constructed sculpture. Pasmore had begun designs in 1963, although the structure was not completed until 1969, the year the space flight landed humans on the moon, hence its evocative name.

Group 2 consisted of artists Richard Hamilton, John McHale (1917–1985) and architect John Voelcker (1927–1972). In 1951 Hamilton had organised an exhibition at the ICA called *On Growth and Form*. This exhibition, inspired by D'Arcy Wentworth Thompson, was opened by Le Corbusier. For *This is Tomorrow*, the group created a brash and noisy multi-sensory environment later heralded as the emergence of Pop Art. Influenced by popular culture, notably from America and post-war consumerism, the group succinctly reflected the sense of commercialisation. The group also included, although unacknowledged, Terry Hamilton (b.1962) and Magda Cordell (1921–2008), who helped with planning and building the exhibit.[35] For example, they painted the Op Art dazzle panel optical illusion corridor which formed part of their space.[36] The group included source material from art, advertising, mass communication, popular culture, film, science fiction and popular music. They also included Robbie the Robot, a prop from the science fiction film *Forbidden Planet*. The appearance of the robot, just as the film went on general release in the UK, caught the imagination of Pathé News.[37] There was a large Cinemascope collaged mural. The abstract painter Mary Webb later recalled her fascination with technicolour films demonstrating how pop culture affected abstract artists too.[38] There was common ground in responding to the new situation, as artists and society responded to rapid advances in science and technology, commercialism and consumer society. Marshall McLuhan (1911–1980) became

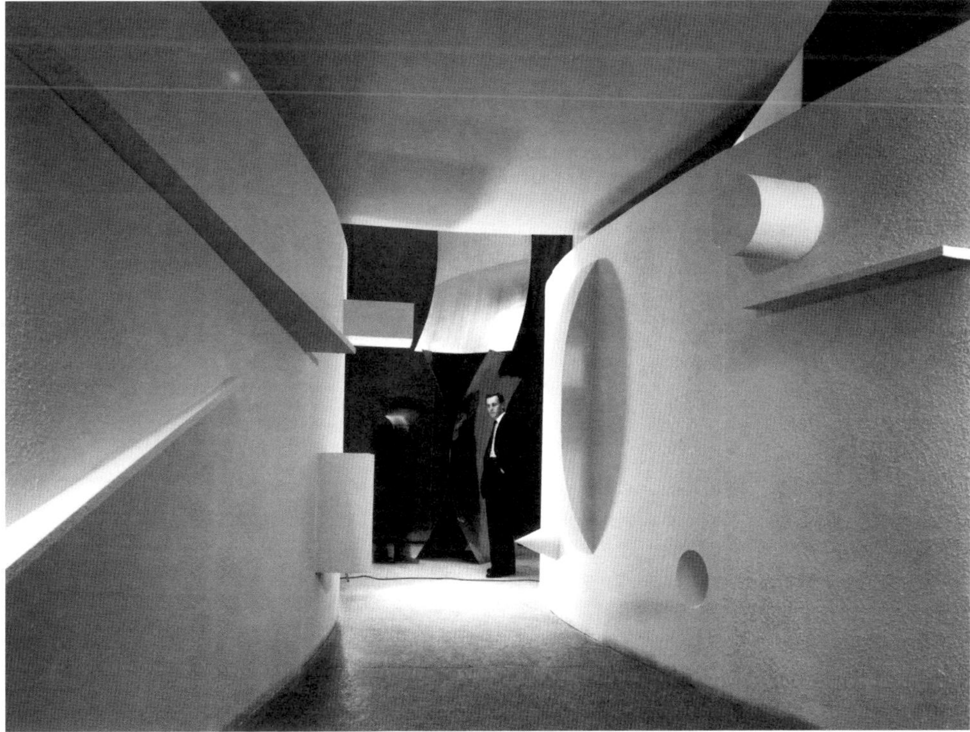

→ Group 10 installation at *This is Tomorrow*.

an important theorist of the new culture: 'Nobody yet knows the language inherent in the new technological culture; we are all deaf blind mutes in terms of the new situation. Our most impressive words and thoughts betray us referring to the previous existent, not to the present'.[39] John McHale supplied much of the archival material for group 2. This included source material for Hamilton's collage, *Just what is it that makes today's home so different, so appealing?* (1956). This now famous collage was reproduced in the catalogue, but not shown in the actual exhibition.[40] McHale, working mainly in collage but also making constructed art, had been drawn to the Constructivists and was included in the exhibition *Artist versus Machine* in 1954 at the Building Centre in London, alongside Anthony Hill, John Ernest (1922–1994) and the Martins.

Hamilton was too eclectic to stay within any constructivist orthodoxy, and like Paolozzi and Turnbull, he could stray between seemingly polar opposites. Shortly after *This is Tomorrow*, in 1957, Hamilton collaborated with Pasmore and Alloway on the project *an Exhibit*. This exhibition was held at the Hatton Gallery in Newcastle and travelled to the ICA in London in 1958. Then came *an Exhibit II* at the Hatton Gallery in 1959. These projects can be seen as a direct result of the experimentation evident in *This is Tomorrow*. *Exhibit* consisted of an immersive multi-sensory installation in which the spectator was expected to enter, experience and participate. This constructed art environment was not preconceived before work started on site, taking form 'with a series of empirical decisions and further improvisation'.[41] The structure was made from an arrangement of suspended rectangular plastic sheets in red, grey, black and white, creating a multi-dimensional (exploded) suspended construction. Alloway regarded constructed art as playful expression and this relates to his reference to Dutch historian and cultural theorist Johan Huizinga (1872–1945) in his catalogue text for *This is Tomorrow*. Huizinga's book, *Homo Ludens* of 1938, published in English in 1944, discusses the importance of the play element in culture and society. Alloway reflects on how specialisation in the arts and the use of art language can

interfere with the visitor's reception of a work of art: 'In *This is Tomorrow* the visitor is exposed to space effects, play and signs, in a range of materials and structures, which taken together, make of art and architecture a many-channelled activity...'[42] Hamilton and Pasmore joined the teaching staff at Newcastle in 1953 and 1954 respectively and jointly established the pedagogical Basic Design course, inspired by the Bauhaus. The spread of Basic Design was assisted by the exhibition at the ICA in 1959 called *The Developing Process*, organised by Pasmore and Hamilton with the assistance of Harry Thubron (1915–1985) and Tom Hudson (1922–1997) from Leeds College of Art.[43]

Group 10 consisted of artist Robert Adams in collaboration with architects Peter Carter and Colin St John Wilson and structural engineer Frank Newby (1926–2001). In one of the more coherent and successful collaborations, the resulting structure was a fusion of architecture and sculptural form. The leading critic Neville Wallis writing in the *Observer* noted: 'a genuine synthesis of sculpture and architecture – directing one's gaze to a towering construction of curved planes by Robert Adams'.[44] The structure consisted of curved wall sections and a fin-like curved roof section, creating a passageway. The wall sections were incorporated relief forms, such as rectilinear blocks, cylinders and circular voids. Adams also contributed a dramatic free-standing sculpture consisting of a series of stacked concave aluminium sheets. Adams was already one of the most important British sculptors of his generation, having shown at the celebrated group exhibition of British artists at the Venice Biennale of 1952 and would exhibit there again in 1962 with a retrospective exhibition.

Group 9 consisted of Kenneth Martin, Mary Martin and architect John Weeks. The Martins were key exponents of abstraction and constructed art in post-war Britain. They often exhibited together, but worked independently. Kenneth was principally concerned with painting and mobiles, where he explored chance and order. Mary focused on the constructed relief and the permutations associated with structures, rotations and the golden ratio.

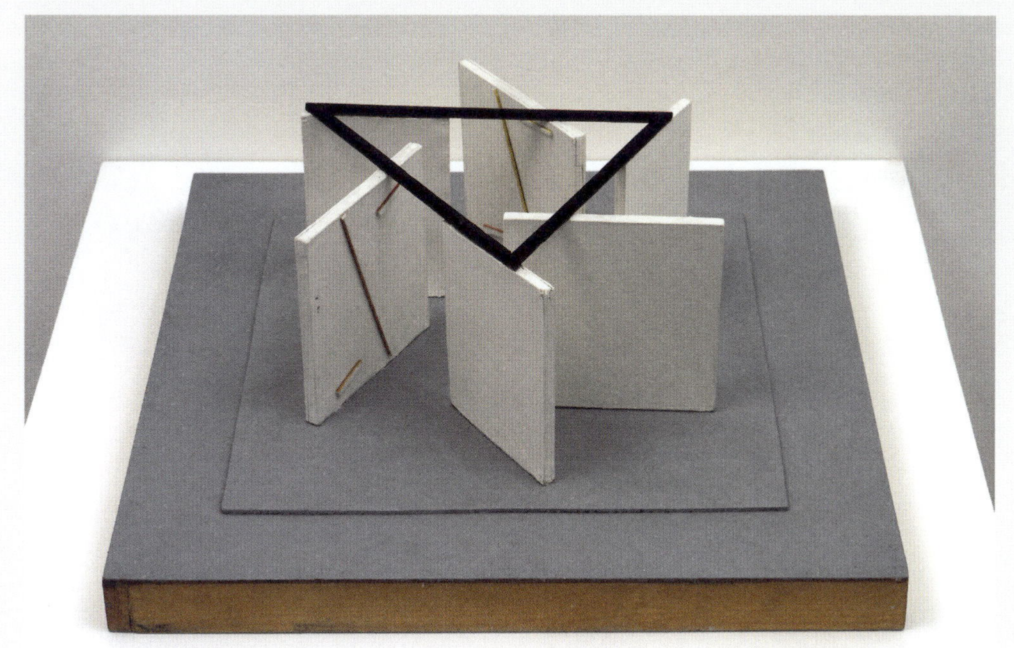

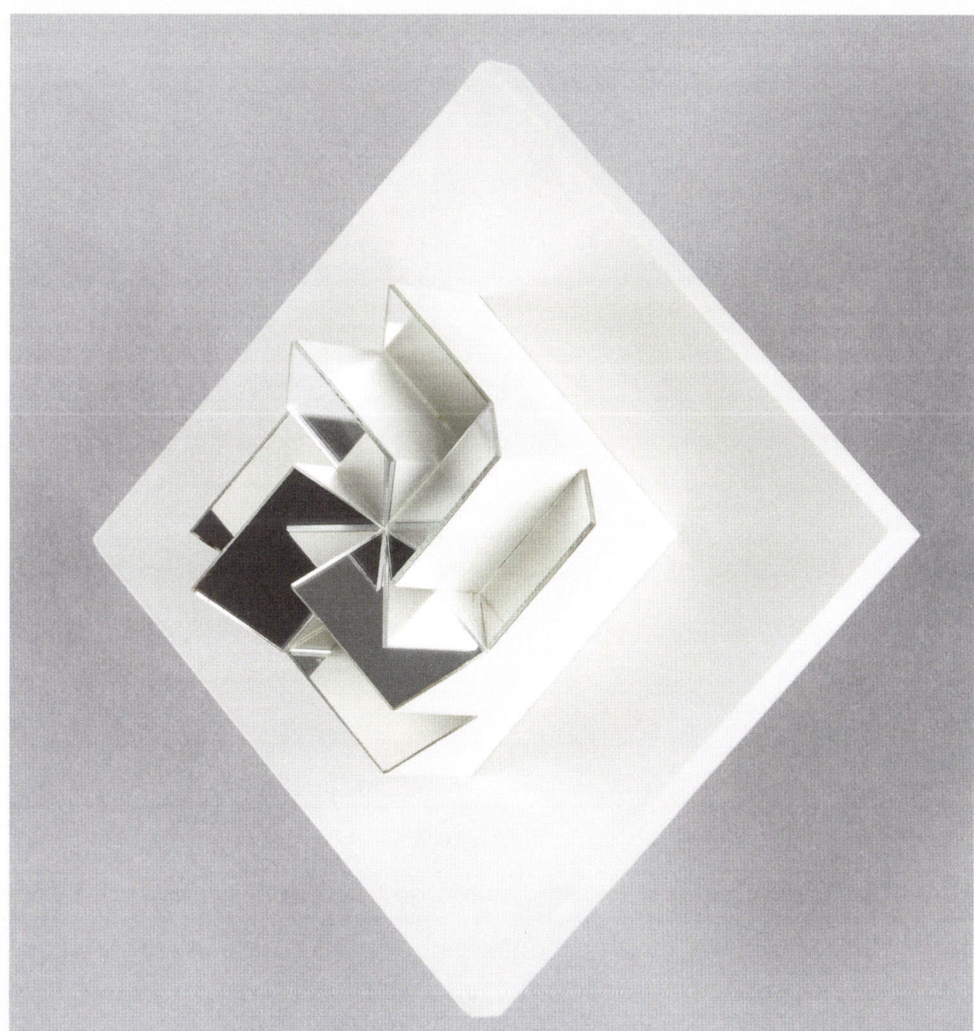

↑ Maquette by Mary Martin and John Weeks for *This is Tomorrow*.

→ **Mary Martin**
Rotation
1968
Polystyrene and mirror glass
Sainsbury Centre

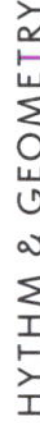

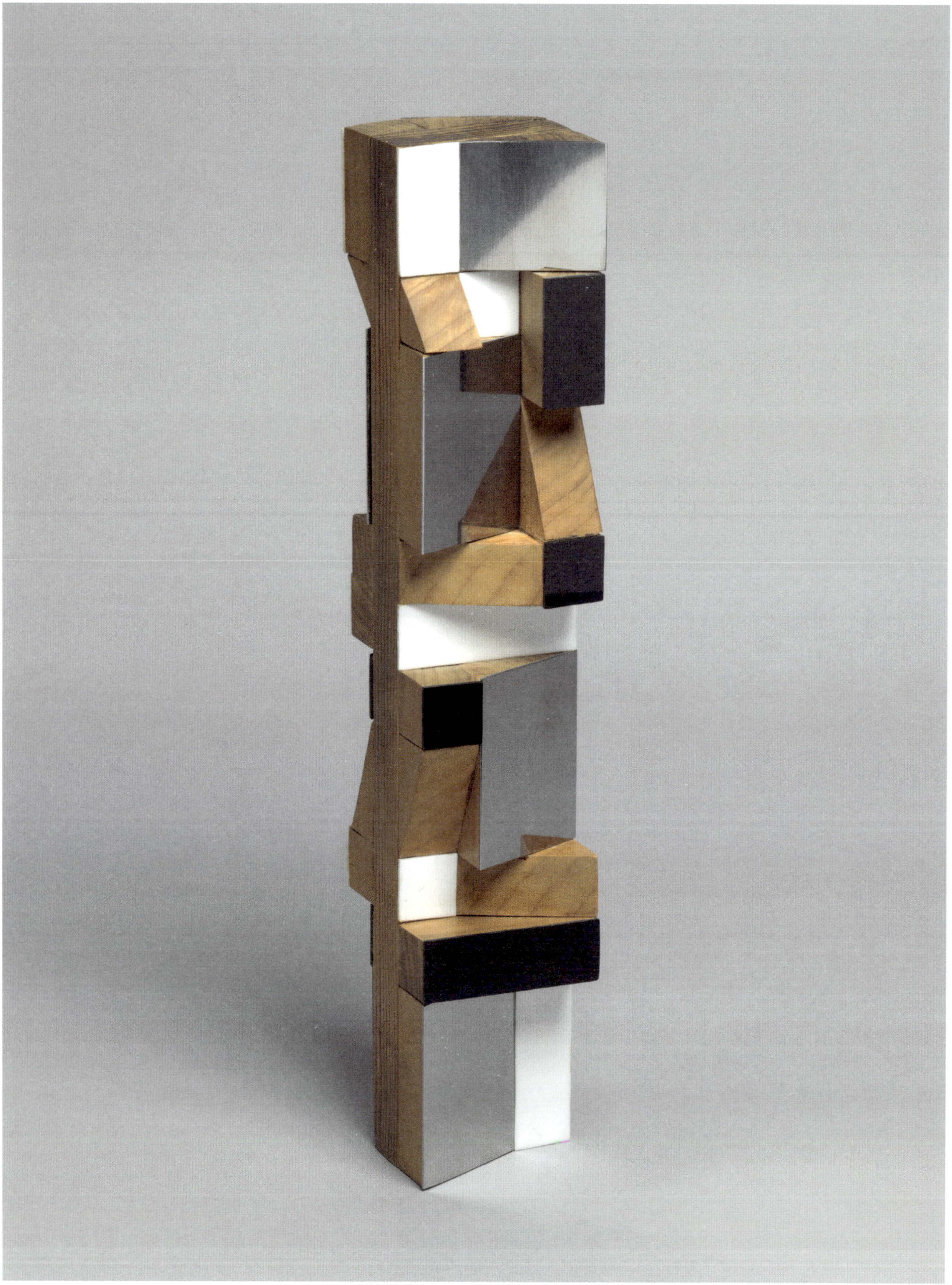

Although working to a strict geometric order, her relief works always retained a handmade quality creating a greater visual stimulation than any precision engineering. In the aftermath of the exhibition, Mary Martin made a wall relief, *Waterfall* (1957), for the Musgrave Park Hospital in Belfast designed by John Weeks. She had begun making reliefs in 1951. She explored three main themes: of spiral movement, climbing forms and expanding forms. They were determined by precise mathematical models such as the golden section or the Fibonacci sequence. She explained the importance of them being handmade:

> I make my reliefs myself because I could not possibly direct another person to make what I do not yet know. This is in spite of the fact that I start with a drawing, often suggested by a mathematical idea, which I carry forward to a precise concept of shape and form. Yet, if I were to hand it over to someone else to make, the result might be decorative, since there may be alterations before it becomes an expressive form. That is the difference between decoration and the work of art. The mechanics of construction are part and parcel of the feeling. Form and construction must be one.[45]

For *This is Tomorrow*, Mary Martin and John Weeks created a space divided by five white screens that were positioned by rotating a square. The screens were fixed from above by a black-painted triangular brace. The screens varied in width so that three were almost square, while the others were less wide with proportions determined by root triangles. In the catalogue it is illustrated with six walls, but one was removed to allow greater access. The space contained a suspended mobile by Kenneth Martin, *Screw Mobile with Cylinder* (1956), which is now in the Arts Council collection. The mobile, either motion or static, added a dynamism to the space, casting its shadow dramatically across the white screens. The space around simultaneously became as important as the work itself. The critic in *The Times* commented,

'the mobile of Mr Kenneth Martin, set in its framework of screens, a group in which the lines of the mobile and the surface of the screens unfold to a perfect and refined order'.[46]

All three collaborators wrote statements for the catalogue: Mary Martin wanted to express the joint aesthetic approach as equal partners, noting it could not have been made without all three, but adding enigmatically that not all three were present at every stage. She goes on to reflect on the principle of collaboration between artists and architects and wonders if each constituent part is any less for the partnership. 'Does it lead to the destruction of the work of art, the artist, or of the architect?' She goes on to state, 'if there is sympathy and the circumstances are good, collaboration can produce not only unity but an enhancement of the parts'.[47] Weeks' statement focused on the materials: 'the walls of 4" bellrock panels – chosen for rigidity and uniformity of surface. And they could be obtained in any size without visible joints'.[48] Kenneth Martin commented upon the effects of the mobile in space. He reminds readers:

> the mobile is an object representing no other object (concrete). It exists in its own right neither penetrating nor being absorbed into the architecture. Nevertheless it is an inherent part of the concept. The constructive artist is concerned with the physical nature of this work and the representation of the physical. His interest in materials and structures relate him to the architect and the engineer from whom he can learn. Form and function go together. Material can inspire – concept dictate material – material qualify concept. In this work whose function is purely aesthetic, mobile, relief, and architecture have been created through movement and are fused together by the coordinated development of the same basic principles. The whole form of the work is the result of the simplest actions, it is the building by simple events of an expressive whole.[49]

← Mary Martin
Climbing Form
1957
Plywood, Perspex and steel
Sainsbury Centre

Kenneth Martin adopted abstraction in 1948–49 and mobiles in 1951. His first attempts were the 'mobile reflectors' in which geometrical plates were suspended and balanced from rods. In 1953 he made his first 'screw mobiles', and one of the earliest, *Screw Mobile* (1953), is in the Sainsbury Centre collection. The geometry resulting in spiral structures is naturally occurrent in shells; it was discussed at length in the chapter on 'The Equiangular Spiral' in D'Arcy Thompson's *On Growth and Form*, which Martin is known to have consulted.[50] In his manuscript 'On the Development of the Mobile' of June 1955, Martin states:

> I attempted to render the revolution of an ellipse by means of brass rod. I divided the ellipse horizontally at regular intervals, ruled lines and then cut rods the length of the lines. I set these horizontal rods at regular intervals and at regular angles along and around a vertical brass rod. The result was an elementary helix.[51]

He found a supplier of brass strips produced in increments of 1/16ths and with these gauges he was able to build sequences based on the Fibonacci system (1,1,2,3,4,8,13,21…) He was taught to braze metal by Robert Adams.[52] *Screw Mobile with Cylinder* (1956, Arts Council collection) was shown in *This is Tomorrow*, suspended by newly available nylon thread, strong but almost invisible. In a separately published essay in 1956, Martin expanded on his statement in the catalogue: 'While maintaining itself as a discrete entity, as a work of art complete in itself, it can be part of an expressive architecture. It can enliven our consciousness of environment moving as it does in our space and casting moving shadow'.[53]

Like the work of other Constructivists, Kenneth Martin wanted his mobiles to create harmony with scientific and engineering disciplines. His use of helices for the *Screw Mobiles* in 1953 coincided with the proposed model of a double helix for the molecular structure of DNA (deoxyribonucleic acid), published by James Watson and Francis Crick in Nature in April of that year. As he suggested in the *'concrete object' in 'An Art of Environment'*: 'Its form need no longer be solid or rectangular. It can expand into and pierce space; open space and light can enter into it. It need no longer be still but can move, linking space with time'.[54] In this process, colour, the last illusionistic device of the painter, was replaced by reflection. Light, space and movement were now recognised as 'concrete' materials for art. Alexander Calder, who had made the form his own in the preceding decades, had an exhibition at the Lefevre Gallery, London in 1951. Anthony Hill had written enthusiastically about him in *Broadsheet No. 1*, 1951, asserting the importance of mobiles 'in demonstrating the possibilities of volume suspended in space''.[55] In the inter-war years, mobiles and kinetic works had also been explored by Russian Constructivist artists Alexander Rodchenko (1891–1956), Naum Gabo (1890–1977) and Georges Vantongerloo (1886–1965).

Group 5 consisted of Anthony Hill, John Ernest and Denis Williams. It was the only team not to include an architect. In the exhibition catalogue Hill wrote a statement simply called 'The Future':

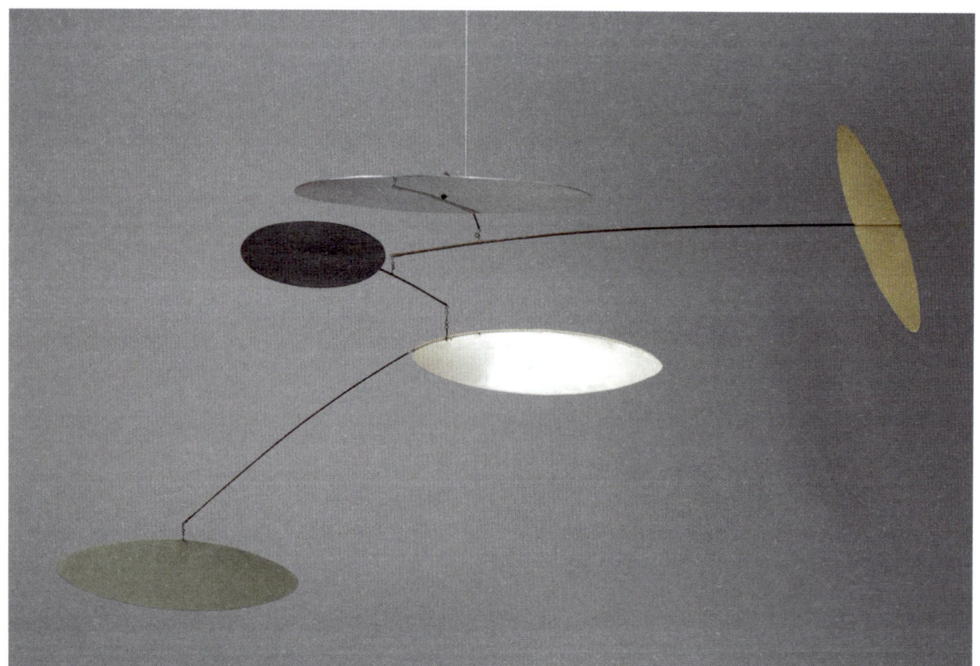

← Kenneth Martin
Mobile Reflector, Elliptic Motif
1955
Steel, duralumin and aluminium
Sainsbury Centre

→ Kenneth Martin
Screw Mobile
1953
Brass and mild steel
Sainsbury Centre

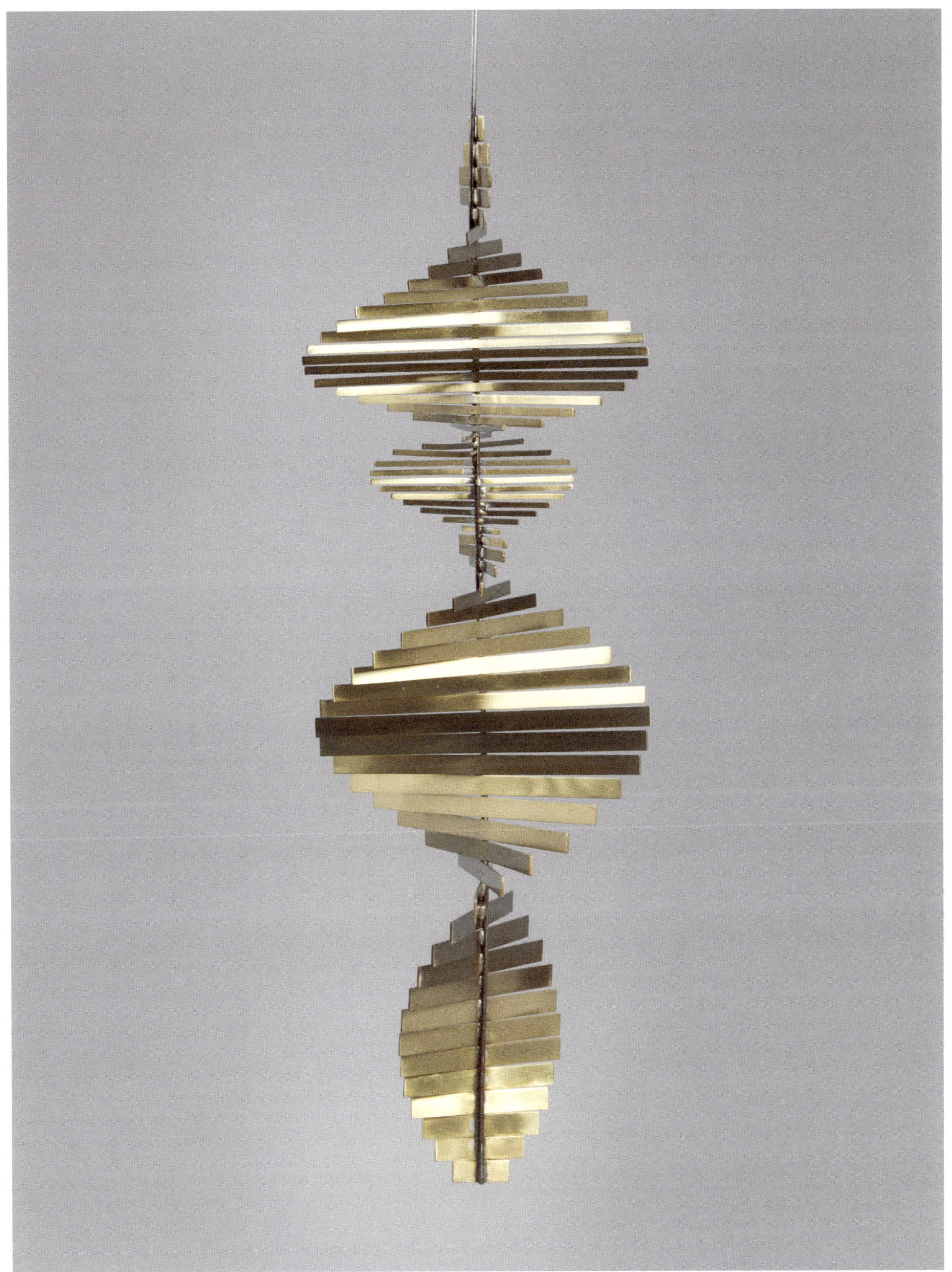

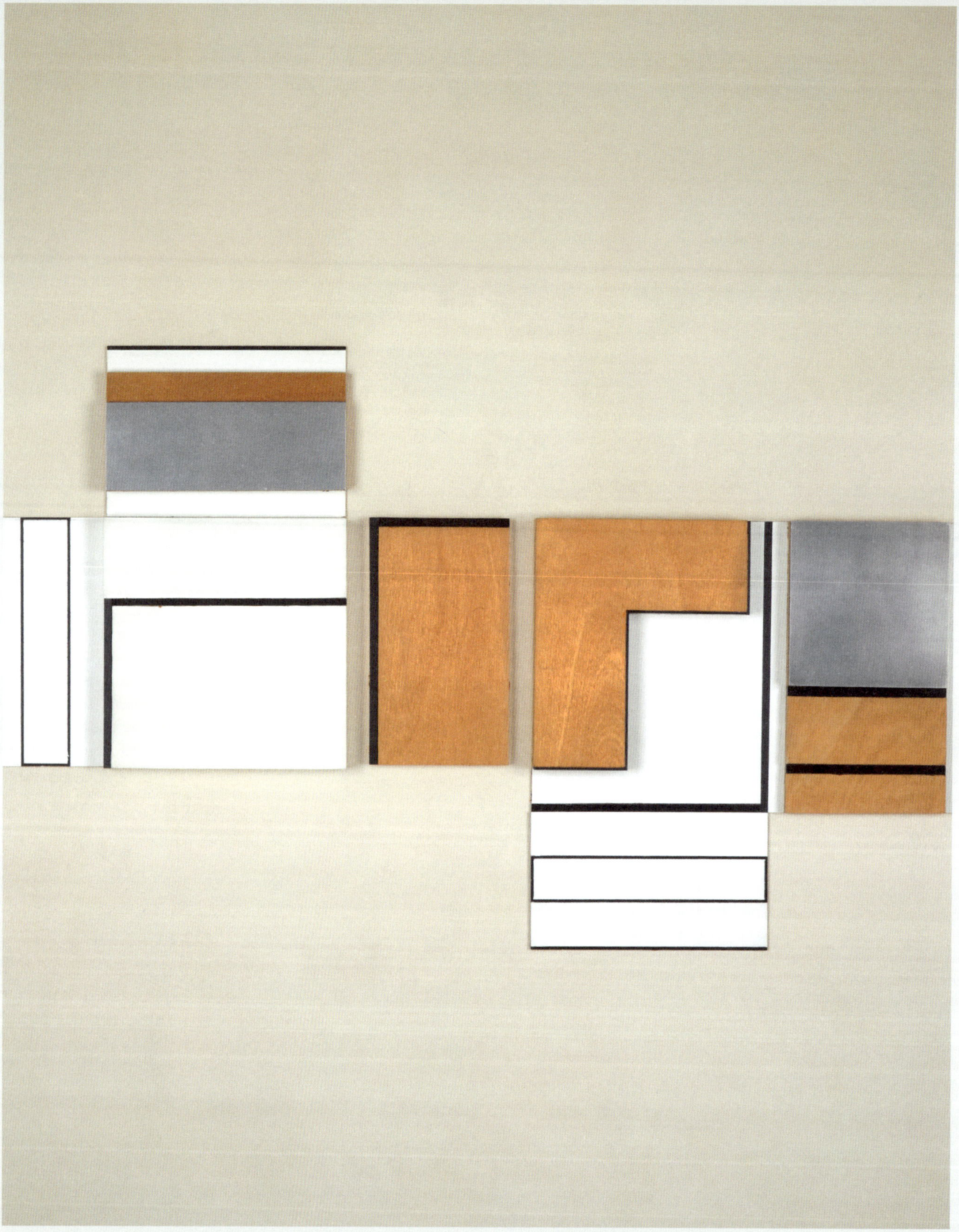

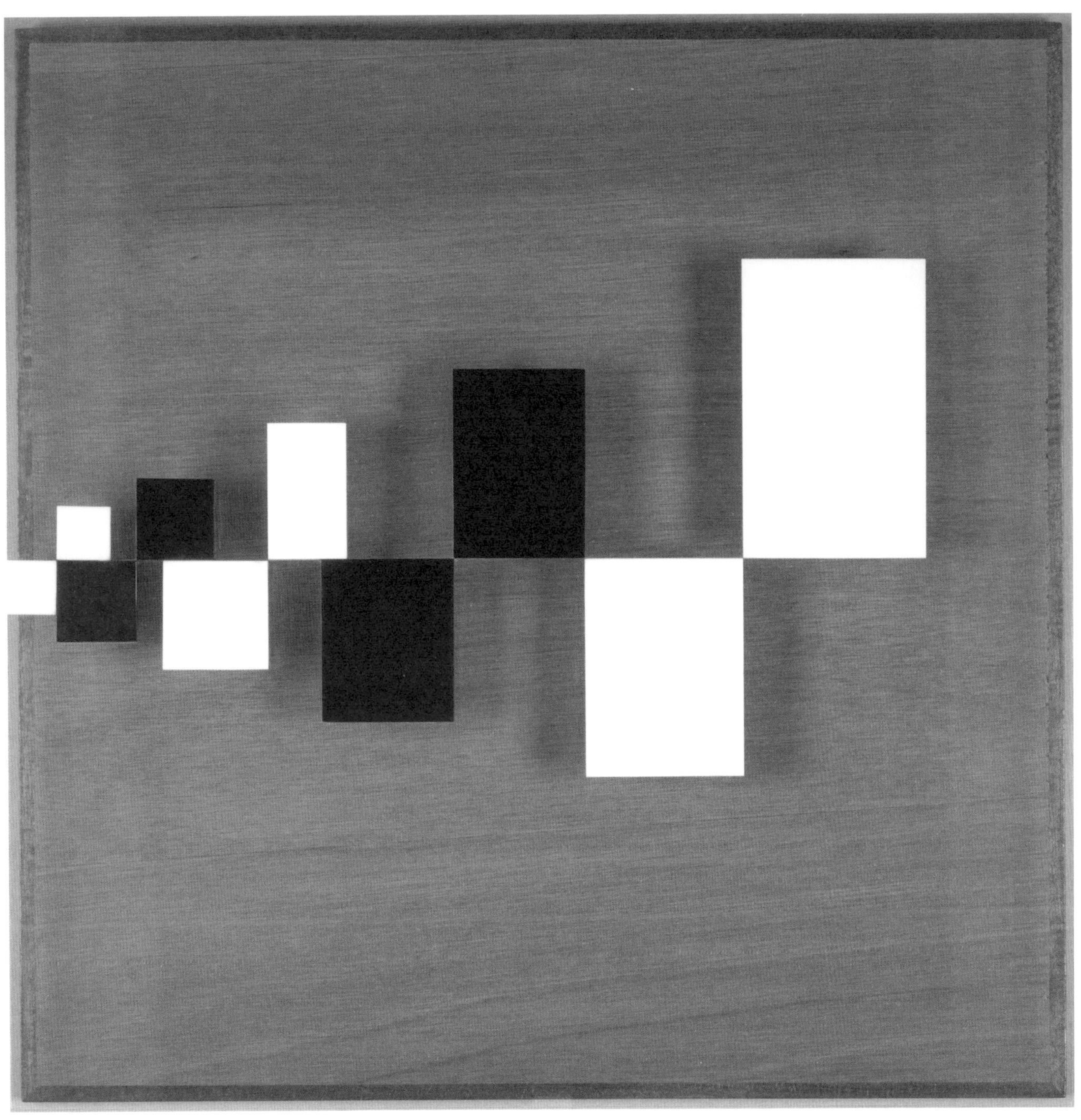

← John Ernest
Linear Relief II
1964
Wood, aluminium and Perspex
Sainsbury Centre

↑ Anthony Hill
Progression of Rectangles,
Version II
1954–59
Wood, Perspex and brass
Sainsbury Centre

Constructed art is an independent art form and will be valued for its merits as art, and not because of some alliance with architecture. Like many forms of art, it contains aspects of architecture in itself, but these have been heightened to a degree hitherto impossible.[56]

Hill and Ernest both showed reliefs and constructions. Hill's relief was illustrated in the exhibition catalogue, but sadly no longer exists.[57] It was made from Perspex, aluminium angle and styrene sheet, and a similar variation is in the Sainsbury Centre collection thanks to the Morris bequest. This surviving relief, *Progression of Rectangles, Version II* (1959), was not in *This is Tomorrow* but is a consequent version. The composition consists of a sequence of rectangles that expand from left to right along a central horizontal axis. The rectangles of black and white plastic are mounted flat onto a plane of transparent Perspex, which itself is held by distancing pegs on a solid wooden panel. Also for the exhibition *This is Tomorrow*, Hill made a series of white cellular cubes composed of polystyrene window louvres. Hill was a mathematician as well as a dissident, creating an alter ego called Achill Redo, through which he could explore his interest in Dada and the relationship between Constructivism and Dadaism.

John Ernest's relief was made from duralumin, plywood and vinyl sheet.[58] Ernest was also a mathematician, as well as a dextrous craftsman creating work by hand and with great precision. In 1954, he also exhibited in *Artist versus Machine* at the Building Centre in London, a venue that aimed to promote architecture and new construction materials and techniques. He also collaborated with scientists, for example he worked with the Nobel prize-winning chemist John Kendrew, creating visual representations of his discoveries. He made two constructions for the exhibition. One of these, *Tower (Vertical Construction)*, 1955, was illustrated in the exhibition catalogue. At 6 feet tall, it was made of rectangular planes of aluminium as well as black, grey and clear plastic sheet slotted in spiral formation onto metal rods.[59]

I wanted to make things which were almost entirely composed of empty space. We only become aware of space when there are things in it, but I tried to make the things in it as immaterial as possible using thin rod and sheet material, and sometimes transparent material. [60]

Ernest's second construction was smaller and orthogonal, incorporating red planes.[61] Denis Williams contributed a square painting composed of smaller squares, each of a different size. Unfortunately, the painting is not recorded in photographs of the exhibition. As the only Black artist in the exhibition, this is a sad omission as it has tended to obscure his inclusion and contribution to the project. In the exhibition catalogue, two pages from Williams' journal were reproduced. His handwritten text makes a theoretical exploration of the square, which he calls 'The Square Articulate', stating 'The square considered as the simplest comprehensible unit of space'.[62] Williams had won a two-year British Council scholarship to travel from his home in Guyana in 1946 to attend the Camberwell School of Art in London, where Pasmore was teaching at the time. Williams was also an accomplished writer: one of his most celebrated works, *Human World* (1950), examines how the artist's practice engaged with anti-colonial resistance and modernist discourse surrounding abstraction. In December 1950, Williams had an exhibition at Gimpel Fils, one of the most important galleries showing modern art in London of the period. He also taught at the Central School of Art and the Slade. He left London in 1957 to take up a teaching post in Fine Arts and Art History at the Technical Institute of African Studies, Khartoum (1957–62). He then moved to Nigeria and lectured in African Studies at the University of Ife and at the University of Lagos. At both universities he edited journals in African Studies and started museum collections of African artefacts. In 1967 he returned to Guyana where he farmed, continued to paint, pursued research into the prehistoric cultures of Guyana, established the first formal, national school of art, and contributed tirelessly to the role of art in the project of nation-building until his death in 1998.[63]

Group 5 were looking back as well as forward, as Williams and Hill were well versed in the history of Constructivism. In the exhibition, they included a summary of the pioneering work by the Russian Constructivists, the Supremacists and the Dutch De Stijl. They printed and displayed excerpts from the *Realist Manifesto* (1920) and made reconstructions of three key works of Soviet art: Kasimir Malevich's (1879–1935) paintings, *Black square and red square on white* (1915), *White square on white* (1918) and Rodchenko's *Black on black* (1918), made by Denis Williams.[64] In the catalogue they are described as 'replicas and translations'. A replica of a sculpture by Naum Gabo and a painting by Piet Mondrian referred to in the catalogue did not appear in the actual exhibition.[65] Group 5 included a series of short texts in the catalogue, including the following statements:

The New Architecture and the New Art. Never before in history had architecture been so influenced by painting...both de Stijl and Constructivism were to be assimilated by what was to become known as 'modern architecture' (Philip C. Johnson... 'Mies Van Der Rohe', M.M.A., 1947)

The New art has just begun. Constructed art, which began with New-Plasticism and Constructivism, is still at a very early stage. It is not, as the status quo holds it to be, merely a past phase wherein the idea of a logically pursued, non-mimetic art made its only possible contribution as an influence on architecture and design.[66]

Group 1 consisted of William Turnbull, Theo Crosby, Germano Facetti (1926–2006) and Edward Wright. Like Paolozzi and to a lesser degree Adams, Turnbull was too eclectic to be defined too closely with evangelical Constructivism. However, his colour field paintings of the late 1950s and his later constructed sculpture place him in the orbit of abstraction and constructed art. His artist statement in the exhibition catalogue was

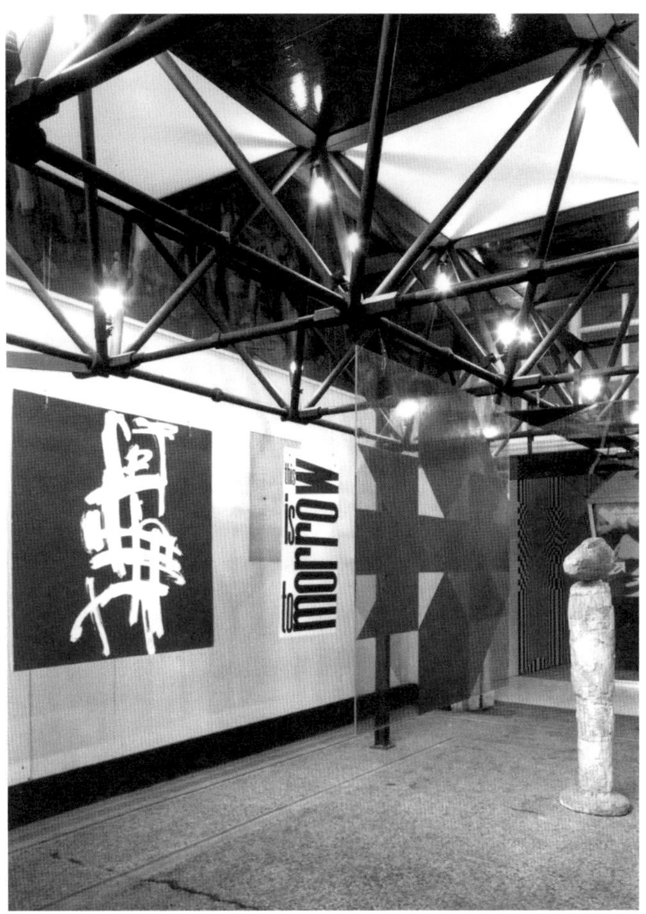

more provocative: 'Sculpture used to look "modern"; now we make objects that might have been dug up at any time during the past forty thousand years'.[67] Turnbull's totemic sculpture, *Sungazer* (1956), dominated the space. Group 1 occupied the entrance vestibule of the Whitechapel, and Theo Crosby created a space-frame structure across the ceiling. Germano Facetti and Edward Wright, both graphic designers, contributed wall panels consisting of images and lettering.

The artists Nigel Henderson and Eduardo Paolozzi and architects Alison and Peter Smithson formed group 6.

↑ Group 1 (Theo Crosby, William Turnbull, Edward Wright and Germano Facetti) installation at *This is Tomorrow*.

Under the title *Patio and Pavilion*, they created an environment that had a post-apocalyptic aesthetic, comprising a makeshift shelter with adjoining yard patio, with decorated flooring obscured by sand. The Smithsons provided the space and shelter, whilst Henderson and Paolozzi assembled both objects and imagery to fill the space titled 'The fundamental necessities of the human habitat in a series of symbols'.[68] As we have seen, Paolozzi was too eclectic to be defined too closely with the Constructivists, but his wide-ranging activities meant that at times he exhibited alongside them, for example in *Artist versus Machine*. This show was organised by Victor Pasmore, Kenneth Martin and Robert Adams together with John Weeks. The exhibition featured works by Robert Adams, John Ernest, Adrian Heath, Anthony Hill, Kenneth Martin, Mary Martin, John McHale, Eduardo Paolozzi, Victor Pasmore and Jean Spencer (1942–1998), among others. The show promoted the use of industrial materials and techniques, advocating that art should engage with technology, science and architecture.

The exhibition *This is Tomorrow* questioned the autonomous role of the artist: how far could collaboration reduce the perceived role of the artist working in isolation? As various forms of machine-made materials and processes were adopted, there was also the question about the unique mark of the individual artist. However, the personality of the practitioner continually found a way to express itself. Constructivism was an orthodoxy and aimed to be analytical rather than expressive, but the cult of personality continued. There was also a debate concerning whether constructed art was merely another style or aesthetic, rather than something more radical, political and transformative of society, in the same way that Reyner Banham had asked the question 'Is New Brutalism ethic or aesthetic?'.[69] The more purist practitioners certainly believed with zeal that it was more than just another style. They set out to establish a set of principles and new logic based on scientific and mathematical principles, the laws of nature and the physical reality of matter. In 1929–30, Van Doesburg in

De Stijl had made an attempt to redefine the various practices under a common denominator, which he called Concrete Art.[70] This had followed the Soviet experiment in art, Malevich's *0.10* exhibition (1915) held in Petrograd (now Saint Petersburg). The theories and practices of Constructivism were formulated in 'The Realistic Manifesto' written by Naum Gabo and Antoine Pevsner (1886–1962), published in 1920; Mondrian's 'Neoplasticism' (1917); and in Germany by artists associated with the Bauhaus from 1919 to 1933. Concrete Art spread worldwide and transcended borders, although geography was never erased and regional variations emerged, whether in England or Brazil.

The exhibition title *This is Tomorrow* raises the question of what the protagonists saw as the art of the future. As we have seen, the artists working in Constructed art and those formulating a proto-Pop Art were all looking simultaneously backwards as much as forwards. One critic at the time quipped 'this is yesterday', as it was pervaded by nostalgia.[71] Whilst Turnbull looked further back than most, the revolutionary art of Soviet Russia or Dutch De Stijl of the 1920s and '30s still seemed vital and relevant in 1950s Britain. The theorist Reyner Banham was not formally part of one of the groups, but alongside Alloway he contributed an introductory text to the exhibition catalogue. Presented as six verses, it describes the development of Modernism and the synthesis of all the arts. It reads as concrete poetry, as Banham explores the modern movement and the union of architecture, painting and sculpture: from the dream of *Gesamtkunstwerk*, the emergence of Art Nouveau, to the importance of the cube and the space frame. The verses are permeated with his enthusiasm for the 'now', populism and technology: principles that were a guiding force of the Independent Group. Mary Banham (1929–2019), an architectural critic in her own right, reflected on the period: 'while we often disagreed about the detail, the cement that held us together was an overwhelming belief in the future and in technology as the means, along with a certainty that the past was of interest only as a tool for thinking about a brighter

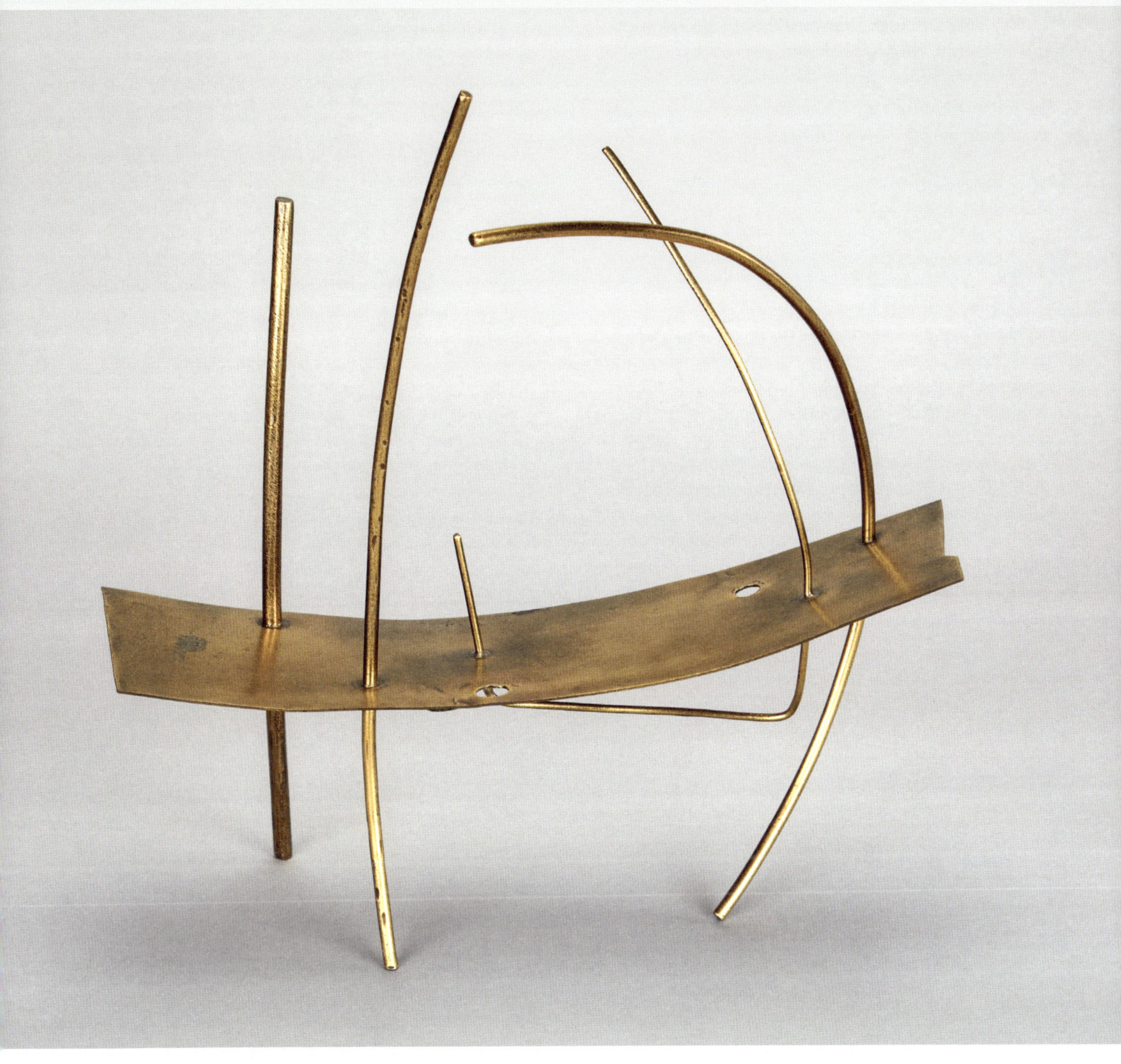

↑ Robert Adams
Pierced Sheet
1951–52
Brass
Sainsbury Centre

future'. She concluded by saying 'the women, all young and some with children, believed most strongly of all'.[72]

Alloway's introduction to the exhibition catalogue was more cautious when he stated:

> An exhibition called This is Tomorrow – devoted to the possibilities of collaboration between architects, painters and sculptors – might appear to be setting up a programme for the future. There are powerful precedents for placing art in a time-perspective that relies on the future to complete it.[73]

The writer and critic David Lewis (1922–2020) also wrote an introductory statement. He called for painting and sculpture to create a 'living harmony' with architecture; that they 'might co-operate with architectural and spatial elements and properties in order to play a dramatic part in an even wider harmonious whole'. He went on to stress 'the need to move towards a wider and fundamentally different kind of inclusiveness... the artist-architect relationship must imply creative participation between different individuals. The role of architecture is important not merely to be "up-to-date", and "technically efficient"'.[74]

The idea of progression in art was being challenged by artists such as Turnbull as well as more broadly, e.g. by Wyndham Lewis (1882–1957) in *The Demon of Progress in the Arts*, published in 1954.[75] Increasingly the position of a linear progression in art, held by many scholars of the period, was evaporating; it looked like the beginning of the end for the myth of progress: that is, that there is a perceptible progress in artistic endeavour which can be mapped by a linear progression. This was linked by association to cultural superiority and race science of the colonial period, which demanded that European culture was simply more 'evolved' and therefore intellectually superior to what had come before. With no medical or scientific foundation, this position became increasingly hard to maintain; it was finally dismantled in the post-modern period.

By contrast, the zealot Constructivists were ideological in their belief in the progressiveness of art practice and its transformative and 'improving' potential in society. They were as devout and pious as any follower of a religion. This was a key pillar of philosophical discourse concerning the Modern movement in the development of twentieth-century art.[76] Anthony Hill wrote a statement in the catalogue

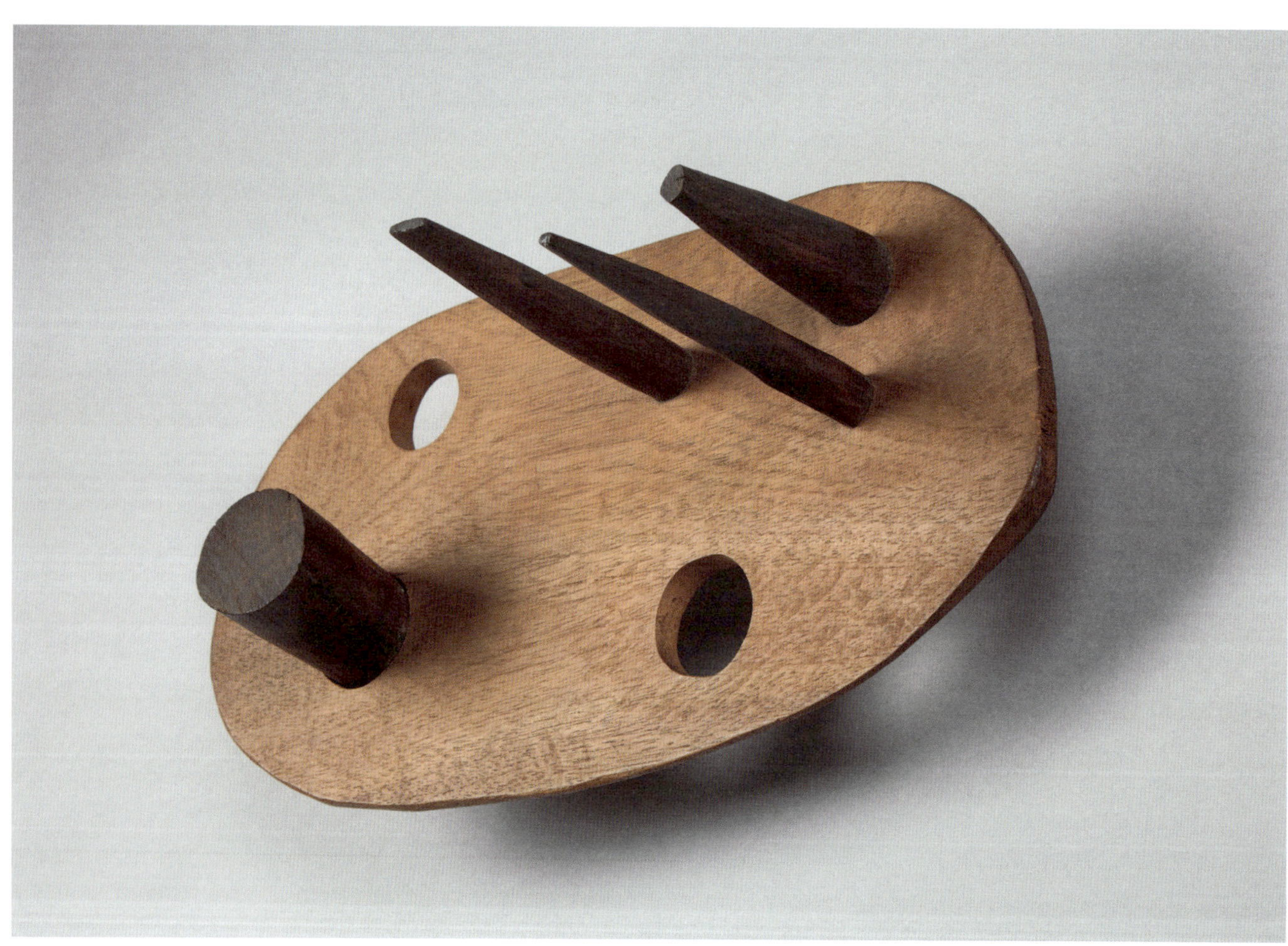

simply called 'Future', where he states: 'Constructed art is an independent art form and will be valued for its merits as art, and not because of some alliance with architecture'.[77] But in actual fact he was still looking back to the revolutionary art of Soviet Russia. There was a growing sense of art's role in mainstream society and the growing forum of popular culture, notably the increasing importance of cinema and pop music. Their irreverence was underscored by the infamous appearance of Robby the Robot from the film *Forbidden Planet*. Science fiction had become an increasingly important genre in the post-war world. Among the visitors to the exhibition was the twenty-six-year-old J. G. Ballard (1930–2009).[78] The exhibition encouraged the intersection between art and other disciplines such as cybernetics, the hybrid post-war science of communication, advertising, systems research, learning theory, communications theory and computer technology. This more complex picture is expressed in the aftermath of the exhibition and its legacy in the intersection of art and technology.

The divergence of art practice during the period saw abstract and constructed art splinter into more forms. Tachism, the dominant painting movement in France of the 1950s, was challenged by the New York painters and the emergence of Abstract Expressionism. In 1956, *Modern Art in the United States* came to the Tate Gallery. The Jackson Pollock exhibition at the Whitechapel Gallery in 1958 was followed in 1959 by the much-celebrated exhibition *The New American Painting*. The influence of America was still in its ascendency. The important exhibition *Situation* attempted to counter this with a survey of recent abstract British painting. Held at the RBA (Royal Society of British Artists) galleries, London in September 1960, it included large-scale abstract paintings by William Turnbull, Gillian Ayres (1930–2018), John Hoyland (1934–2011) and Richard Smith (1931–2016). A year earlier, in 1959, Smith had worked with Ralph Rumney (1934–2002) and Robyn Denny (1930–2014) on *Place*, an experimental exhibition at the ICA, which had drawn inspiration from *This is Tomorrow*, in which canvases were positioned on the floor to create a labyrinthine environment.

Victor Pasmore showed at *Documenta II* in Kassel in 1959 and *Documenta III* in 1964. As his international profile grew, Pasmore had solo exhibitions in London, New York and Rome. He represented Britain at the Venice Biennale in 1960 and in the 1965 São Paulo Biennale, and the same year was honoured by a retrospective exhibition at the Tate Gallery. Anthony Hill had a solo show at the ICA in 1958, showing eight constructed reliefs. In 1962, Hill was included in a group show at Galerie Denise René, Paris titled *Art Abstrait Constructif International*.[79] Robert Adams had a solo show at the Galerie Parnass, Wuppertal, West Germany in 1957. In the same year he was commissioned to create his magnificent relief for the new Municipal Theatre at Gelsenkirchen, completed in 1959. In 1962 came his retrospective at the British Pavilion of the XXXI Venice Biennale. The now legendary exhibition *Konkrete Kunst: jahre entwicklung* was held in Zurich, 1960. This major survey of the last 50 years of Constructivism included a number of artists who had been in *This is Tomorrow*. The artist Max Bill (1908–1994), the exhibition organiser, proposed that Constructivism was still an evolving and 'developing' practice. As well as showing the pioneers such as Hans Arp (1886–1966), Giacomo Balla (1871–1958), Wassily Kandinsky (1866–1944), Paul Klee, František Kupka (1871–1957), Malevich, László Moholy-Nagy (1895–1946), Mondrian and Sophie Taeuber-Arp (1889–1943), he also included Pasmore, Kenneth and Mary Martin and Anthony Hill.

In 1961, another project organised by Theo Crosby continued the conversation between artists and architects that started in *This is Tomorrow*. The Sixth International Union of Architects was held at the South Bank in London in a pavilion designed by Crosby. It incorporated two mobiles by Kenneth Martin and a series of relief panels by Mary Martin and Anthony Hill. There was also a 42-foot steel scaffold tower designed by John Ernest outside the entrance.[80] In 1962, the exhibition *Experiment in Constructie* was held at the Stedelijk Museum, Amsterdam with relief works by Mary Martin, Anthony Hill and John Ernest. The exhibition toured to Zurich and was curated

← Robert Adams
Pierced Relief
1952
Mahogany
Sainsbury Centre

by Joost Baljeu (1925–1991), the Dutch artist and editor of the journal *Structure*. In 1963, the Arts Council assembled a major exhibition called *Construction England*. The exhibition was formulated in its first iteration in 1961 at the Drian Galleries in London. This group show featured Pasmore, the Martins, Hill, Ernest, Willams and McHale. It was then reconfigured by the ICA and travelled to the USA in 1961–62 as a show titled British Constructivist Art.[81] On its return it was toured by the Arts Council as *Construction England* and went on an eight-venue tour across Britain through 1963. The artists Williams and McHale were no longer included, having both left the UK.

In the exhibition booklet there was an introductory text by Alan Bowness (1928–2021), who at the time was an academic at the Courtauld Institute but in 1979 became director of the Tate Gallery. Bowness's text expressed succinctly the characteristic of constructed art as a purely twentieth-century art form: 'its makers must necessarily be forward-looking'.[82] He goes on to make reference to the materials, also 'new' and associated with technology rather than with art.[83] Bowness summarised by reflecting on the previous decade or so since Pasmore had made his first construction in 1951. The 1963 exhibition marks a highpoint in constructed art in England. As the decade progressed, the hermetic position of many of the purist Constructivists from wider forms of abstraction and constructed art would place them at odds with expanding variations in abstract sculpture and painting. The territory was continuing to change with artists such as Anthony Caro (1924–2013) and the New Generation sculptors and painters, Op Art in Britain and Minimalism in the USA. These related and emerging scenes served to overshadow the aims of the post-war generation of artists interested in a highly theorised orthodox version of abstraction and constructed art. In Paris in 1960 even Le Groupe Espace was superseded by Le Groupe Mesure, and by 1963 this too was in danger of expiring due to the emerging scene.[84]

The exhibition *This is Tomorrow* has had an enduring legacy that its contributors could not have imagined. In 2019, the Whitechapel Art Gallery decided to revisit the exhibition with *Is This Tomorrow?* This time architects and artists were asked to address issues such as the depletion of natural resources, migration, technology and spirituality. The collaborative projects took the form of environments, models, structures and systems, incorporating artworks, objects, film and graphics, such as Rana Begum and Marina Tabassum Architects' *Phoenix Will Rise* (2019). This coincided with the opening of the Museum of Tomorrow in Rio de Janeiro (2015) and the Museum of the Future in Dubai (2020). Once again, artists and architects are engaged in futurology, exploring how society can best prepare and respond to things to come. □

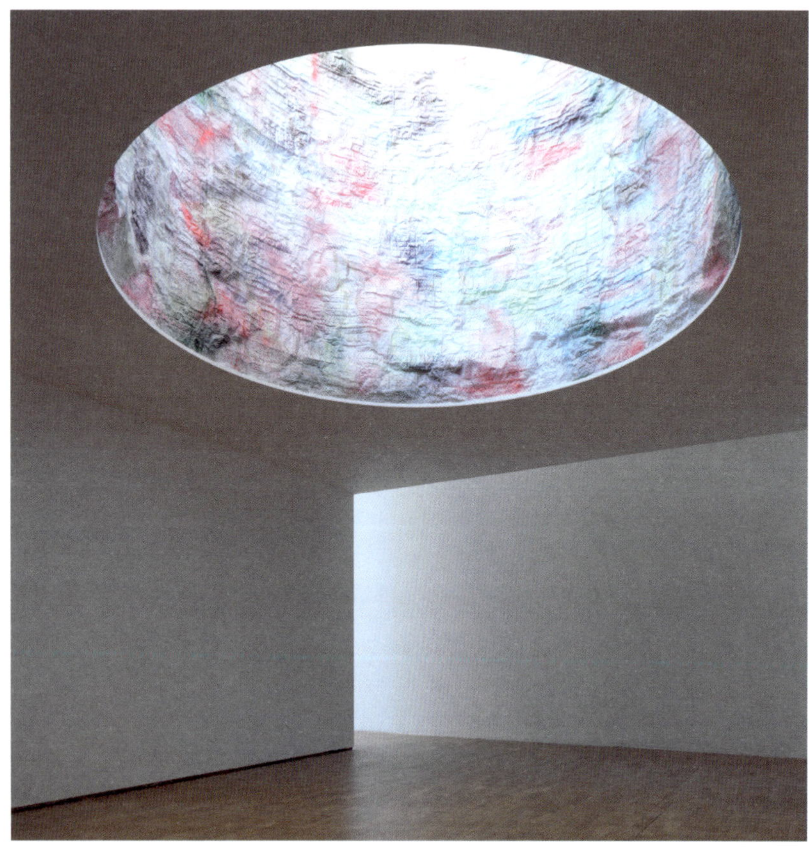

← Rana Begum and Marina Tabassum Architects, *Phoenix Will Rise*, 2019 at *Is This Tomorrow?* at the Whitechapel Gallery, 2019.

ENDNOTES

1   C. P. Snow, *Two Cultures: And a Second Look. An Expanded Version of the Two Cultures and the Scientific Revolution* (Cambridge: Cambridge University Press, 1964), p.50.

2   Gladys Fabre and Doris Wintgens Hötte (eds), *Van Doesburg and the International Avant-garde* (London: Tate Publishing, 2009), p.6.

3   The Independent Group: David Robbins (ed.), *Post-war Britain and the Aesthetics of Plenty* (Cambridge, Massachusetts and London: M.I.T. Press, 1990), p.135.

4   https://www.britishpathe.com/video/this-is-tomorrow-aka-this-is-tomorrow, accessed 2 April 2021.

5   Reyner Banham, *New Brutalism: Ethic or Aesthetic* (New York: Reinhold, 1966), p.64.

6   Reyner Banham, 'The new brutalism' (1955), reprinted in Reyner Banham, *A Critic Writes: Essays* (Los Angeles and London: Berkeley, 1996).

7   Kenneth Martin used the term Constructionists in 'An Art of Environment' in *Broadsheet No. 2*, 1952, but stopped using it c.1964. As explained in Alastair Grieve, *Anthony Hill* (London: Arts Council, 1983), p.5.

8   Ann Massey, *The Independent Group: Modernism and mass culture in Britain* (Manchester: Manchester University Press, 1995), p.25. The first use of the term Independent Group was in November 1952. There was never an agreed list of artists associated with the group.

9   David Thistlewood in Robbins, 1990, p.213.

10 Alastair Grieve, *Constructed Abstract Art in England: A Neglected Avant-Garde* (New Haven and London: Yale University Press, 2005), p.13

11 Kenneth Martin, 'Abstract Art', in *Broadsheet No. 1*, 1951.

12 Grieve, 2005, pp.17–27.

13 Lawrence Alloway, *Nine Abstract Artists* (London: Tiranti, 1954).

14 Ibid., pp.1–2.

15 Grieve, 2005, p.35.

16 Grieve, 2005, pp.35–6. In 1926, the British artist Marjorie Watson-Williams moved to Paris, where she adopted the name 'Paule Vézelay'. By the early 1930s she had become an active member of the Parisian avant-garde. The artists of Le Groupe Espace were influenced by the pre-war movements of Constructivism and Neo-Plasticism. The failure to link with the London-based Constructionists led to another exhibition held at the Royal Festival Hall exhibition in 1955. As well as Vézelay, artists included Vera Spencer, Ithel Colquhoun, Sonia Delaunay and Jean Arp.

17 Grieve, 2005, p.36.

18 Jeremy Millar, 'This is Tomorrow', *The Whitechapel Art Gallery Centenary Review*, 2001, p.68.

19 Alastair Grieve, 'This Is Tomorrow, a remarkable exhibition born of contention', *Burlington Magazine*, April 1994, p.227.

20 Lawrence Alloway, Reyner Banham and David Lewis, *This is Tomorrow* (London: Whitechapel Art Gallery, 1956).

21 Graham Whitham in Robbins, 1990, p.134.

22 Alloway, Banham and Lewis, 1956, unpaginated.

23 D'Arcy Wentworth Thompson, *On Growth and Form*, originally published in 1917 (Cambridge and New York: Cambridge University Press and Macmillan, 1942, 2nd edn).

24 Grieve, 2005, p.180.

25 Adrian Heath artist statement in Alloway, 1954, p.26.

26 Statement by Heath and Weeks, Alloway, Banham and Lewis, 1956, unpaginated.

27 Banham, 1955.

28 Alloway, Banham and Lewis, 1956, unpaginated.

29 Herbert Read, *Paul Klee on Modern Art*, 1945.

30 Neil Walker (ed.), *Towards a New Reality* (London: Lund Humphries, 2016), essay by Alastair Grieve quoted, p.61.

31 *Structurist*, No. 5, quote by Biederman, 1948, p.8.

32 Ibid., p.13.

33 Alan Bowness, *Victor Pasmore: A catalogue raisonné of the paintings, constructions and graphics, 1926–1979* (New York: Rizzoli, 1980). I have been unable to determine precisely which constructed reliefs Pasmore showed in *This is Tomorrow*. Although there are very similar variations illustrated in the catalogue raisonné, none match precisely.

34 Ibid., pp.100–106.

35 Whitham in Robbins, 1990, p.139.

36 Magda Cordell McHale, 'Retrospective Statement', in Robbins, 1990, p.190.

37 Pathé made at least two newsreels featuring the exhibition, https://theo-inglis. medium.com/yesterdays-tomorrow-is-not-today-jg-ballard-and-this-is-tomorrow, accessed 2 April 2021.

38 Author interview with Mary Webb, 30 December 2020. Mary was taught at Newcastle 1958–63 by Victor Pasmore and Richard Hamilton.

39 Marshal McLuhan, *Structurist*, No.5, 1965, p.7.

40 Cordell McHale in Robbins, 1990, p.190.

41 *An Exhibit*, exhibition pamphlet, ICA, 1958, unpaginated.

42 Lawrence Alloway, 'Introduction', in Alloway, Banham and Lewis, 1956, unpaginated.

43 *The Developing Process*, exhibition catalogue for the ICA, 1959 (Kings College, University of Durham, 1959).

44 Neville Wallis, 'At the galleries', *Observer*, 1956.

45 Mary Martin, *Mary Martin*, exhibition catalogue (London: Tate Publishing, 1984), p.28.

46 Grieve, 2005, p.40.

47 Statement by Mary Martin in Alloway, Banham and Lewis, 1956, unpaginated.

48 Statement by John Weeks in Alloway, Banham and Lewis, 1956, unpaginated.

49 Statement by Kenneth Martin in Alloway, Banham and Lewis, 1956, unpaginated.

50 https://www.tate.org.uk/art/artworks/martin-small-screw-mobile-t00552, Tate Collection online, catalogue entry for *Small Screw Mobile* (1953) by Matthew Gale, October 1997, accessed 30 July 2020.

51 Grieve, 2005, p.138.

52 Ibid.

53 Ibid., p.142.

54 Kenneth Martin, 'An Art of Environment', *Broadsheet No. 2* (London, 1952), unpaginated.

55 Anthony Hill, 'Mobiles and Alexander Calder', *Broadsheet No. 1*, 1951.

56 Statement by Anthony Hill in Alloway, Banham and Lewis, 1956, unpaginated.

57 Grieve 1994, p.230.

58 Grieve, 2005, p.37.

59 Long thought destroyed (Grieve, 1994, p.230). In fact it re-emerged sixty years later (2015) in the Studio International Exhibition at Raven Row, London (now in the Catherine Petitgas collection).

60 Grieve, 1994, p.230.

61 Ibid. According to Grieve, not the one illustrated in the *This is Tomorrow* catalogue.

62 Reproduced handwritten notes by Denis Williams in Alloway, Banham and Lewis, 1956, unpaginated.

63 https://www.peepaltreepress.com/books/art-denis-williams, artist, art historian, archaeologist, anthropologist, biographer and novelist, accessed 3 April 2021.

64 Grieve, 1994, p.230.

65 Alloway, Banham and Lewis, 1956, unpaginated; the painting dated 1935 is not named.

66 Alloway, Banham and Lewis, 1956, unpaginated.

67 Statement by William Turnbull in Alloway, Banham and Lewis, 1956, unpaginated.

68 Alloway, Banham and Lewis, 1956, unpaginated, stated description of the *Patio and Pavilion*.

69 Banham, 1966.

70 Gladys Fabre and Doris Wintgens Hötte (eds), *Van Doesburg and the International Avant-garde* (London: Tate Publishing, 2009). The manifesto appeared in the magazine, by now called *Art Concret*, in April 1930.

71 Basil Taylor, 'Yesterday, Certainly: Tomorrow, Perhaps', *Spectator*, 17 August 1956.

72 Mary Banham, 'Retrospective Statements', in Robbins, 1990, p.188.

73 Alloway in Alloway, Banham and Lewis, 1956, unpaginated.

74 David Lewis, 'Introduction', in Alloway, Banham and Lewis, 1956, unpaginated.

75 Wyndham Lewis, *The Demon of Progress in the Arts* (London: Methuen, 1954).

76 Paul Greenhalgh, *The Modern Ideal* (London: V&A, 2005), p.104.

77 Statement by Anthony Hill in Alloway, Banham and Lewis, 1956, unpaginated.

78 J. G. Ballard, *Miracles of Life* (London: Harper Collins, 2008), p.188.

79 *Anthony Hill: A retrospective exhibition* (London: Arts Council, 1983), p.72.

80 Sam Gathercole, 'The Lost Cause of British Constructionism: A Two-Act Tragedy', *British Art Studies*, issue 18, November 2020, p.15, https://www.britishartstudies.ac.uk/issues/issue-index/issue-18/the-lost-cause-of-british-constructionism, accessed 4 April 2021.

81 Grieve, 2005, p.52.

82 Alan Bowness, *Construction England* (London: Arts Council of Great Britain, 1963), unpaginated.

83 Ibid.

84 Brandon Taylor, *After Constructivism* (New Haven and London: Yale University Press, 2014), p.174.

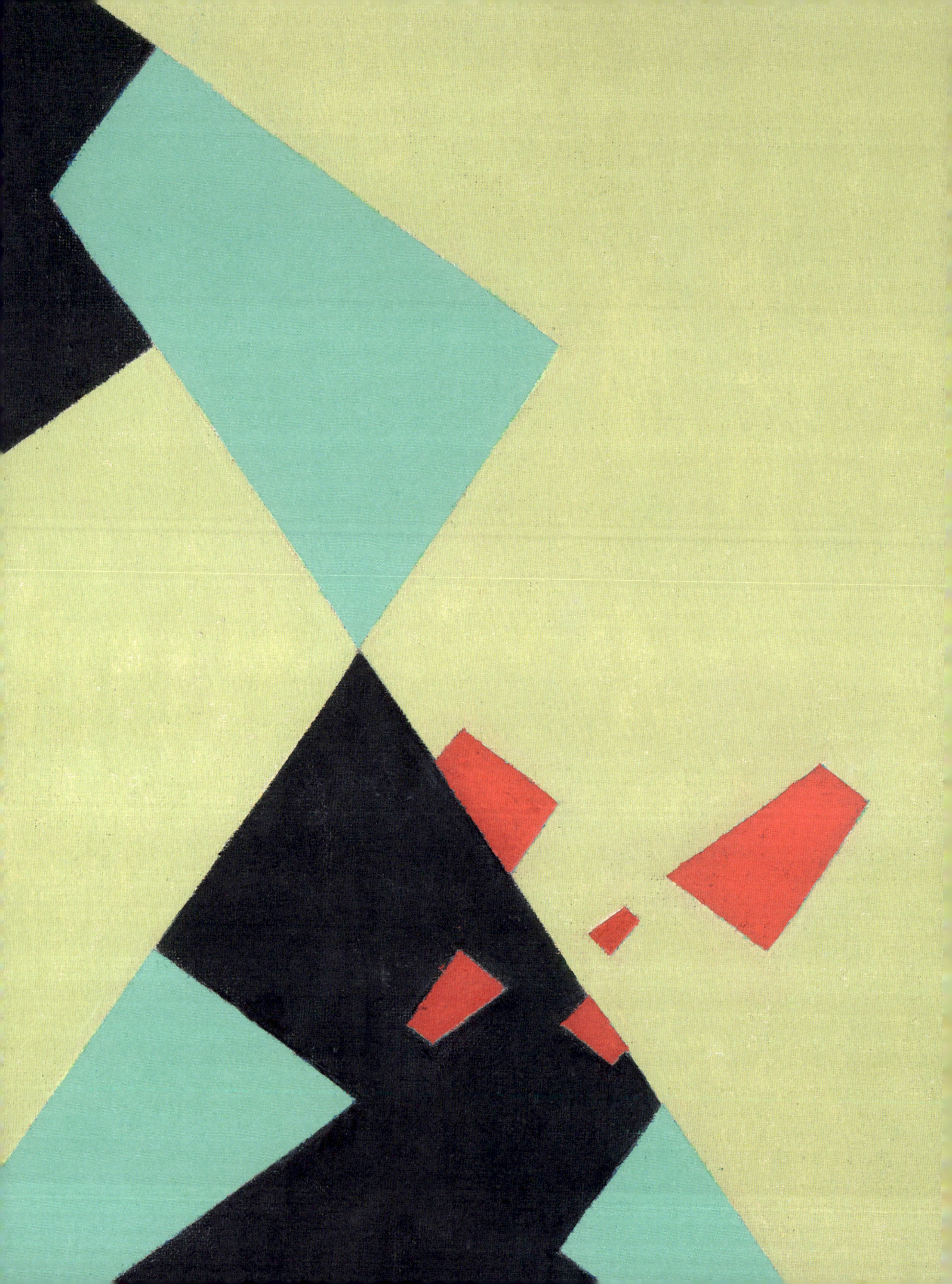

construction's other

— for Jeffrey Steele, 1931–2021 —

Andrew Bick

We call Concrete Art those works of art which originate on the basis of means and laws of their own, without external reliance on phenomena or any transformation of them, in other words, without undergoing a process of abstraction. Concrete painting and sculpture are the formulation of what is optically perceptible. Their means of formulation are colours, space, light, and movement.

Max Bill (St Gallen: Erker-Verlag, 1971), quoted in Lawrence Alloway on Max Bill, Albright Knox Art Gallery, 1974

THIS STATEMENT BY MAX BILL (1908–1994) offers an eloquent summary of his principles of art, design, curation and architecture, as founded in Theo van Doesburg's (1883–1931) original *Manifesto for Concrete Art* in 1930. As with other post-war developments, such as the Brazilian concrete and neo-concrete artist groupings based around São Paulo and Rio de Janeiro respectively, the language of the Swiss concrete artists was clear and concise. Despite the eloquence of figures such as Anthony Hill (1930–2020) and Jeffrey Steele (1931–2021), no such equivalent public recognition of the terminology exists for Constructionism and Systems in the UK. Perhaps this is part of a widely acknowledged British struggle to understand all aspects of non-figurative art; or perhaps it is because artists as diverse as Hill and Steele embodied an innate acknowledgement of the contradictory nature of van Doesburg's original position, which meant that the conceptual journey of their work did not pause to consider public communication or the idea of wide audience engagement as a significant measure of art's value, but focused on the complexity inherent in the search for a clear position.

British artists followed a consistent line of enquiry, formed not just from the thinking of Max Bill and Richard Paul Lohse (1902–1988) in Switzerland, but also from the influence of the theories and Constructionist work of Charles Biederman (1906–2004), a unique figure in American art, and counterparts such as Joost Baljeu (1925–1991) and those grouped around the magazine *Structure* in Holland.[1] These are contexts that assume the British artists' internationalism, and are therefore the norm for groupings who enjoyed greater exposure in mainland Europe than in the UK itself. The important and now considerably augmented collection at the Sainsbury Centre that is the subject of *Rhythm and Geometry* demonstrates this equivalence in the work of the British artists: an equal level of quality and commitment to a set of concerns measurable against the international practice and theory of key times in late Modernism. It also suggests that there is a more complex sequence of ongoing parallels existing between concrete and neo-concrete, Constructionism

← Natalie Dower
Square Root Two Spirals Nine Moves
2015
Oil on linen
Sainsbury Centre

→ Max Bill
Silkscreen in 4 colours
1970
Screenprint on paper
Sainsbury Centre

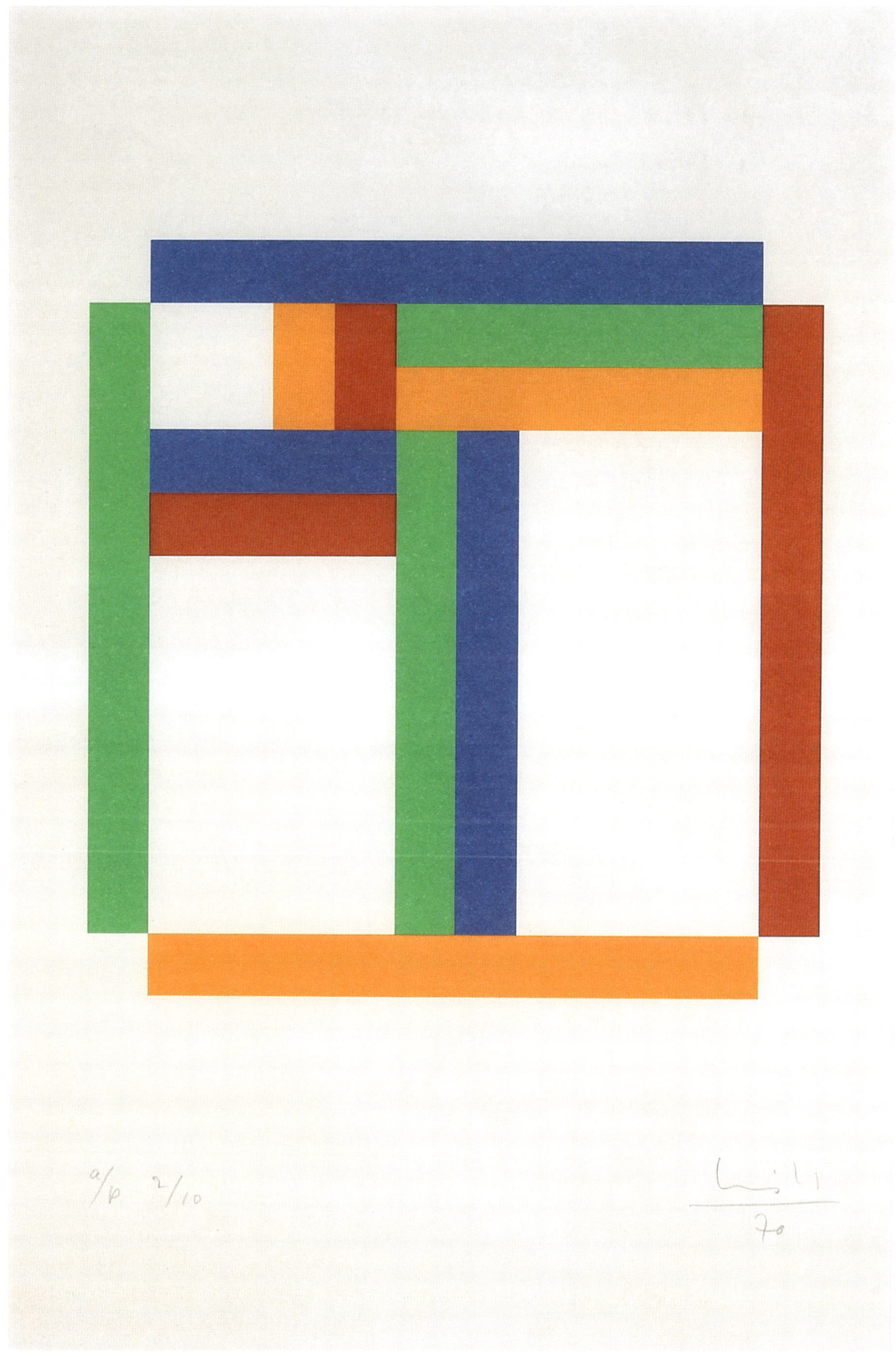
a/p 2/10
70

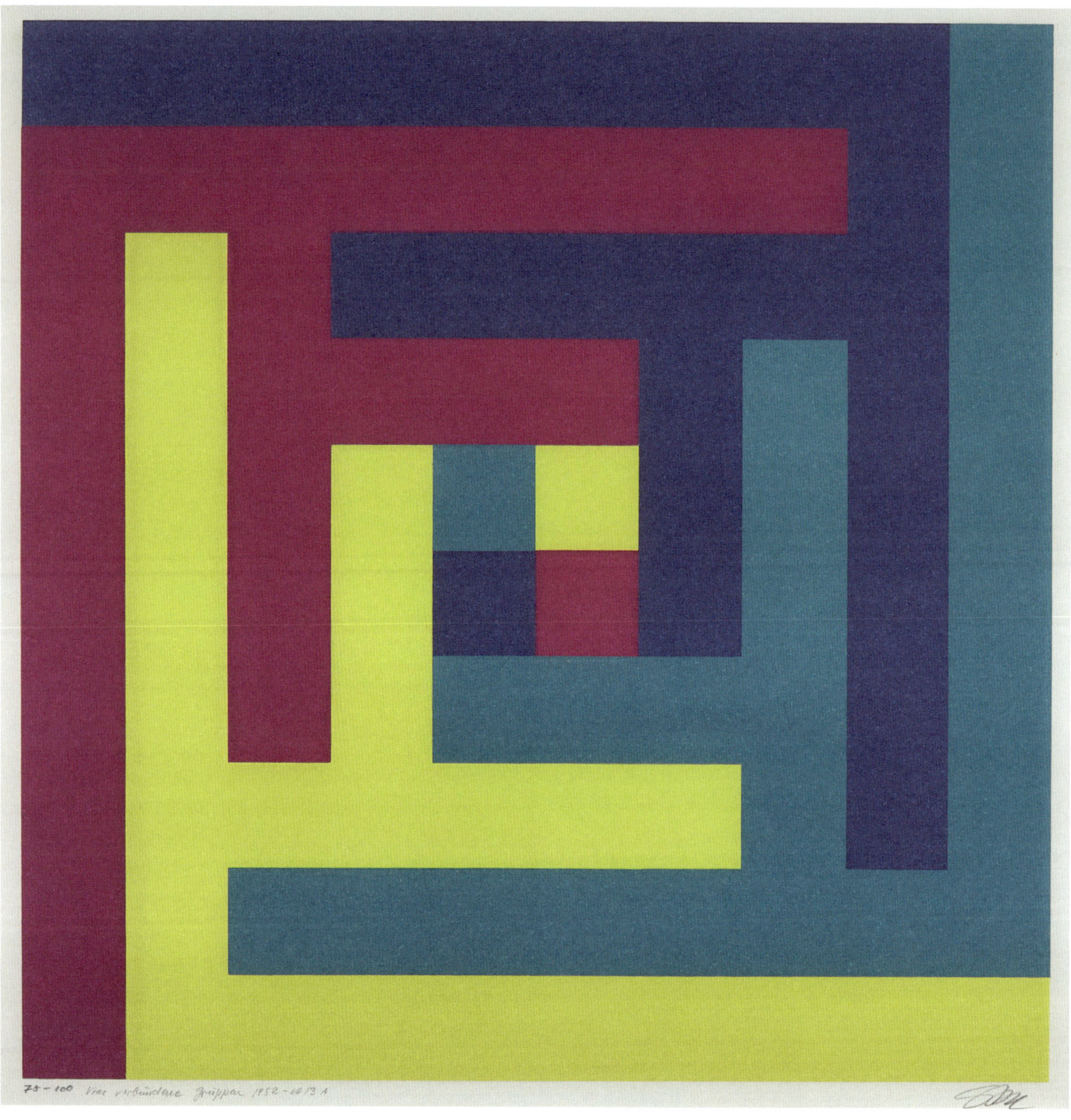

↑ **Richard Paul Lohse**
Four coloured groups
c.1952–66
Silkscreen on paper
Sainsbury Centre

→ **John Ernest**
Relief: Triangular Motif II
1959
Formica, aluminium, wood and
hardboard
Sainsbury Centre

and Systems, concrete poetry, conceptualism and contemporary practices that demands a reappraisal of these qualities after Modernism. Also, using the concrete/constructive approach as a lens through which to examine the contemporary allows for new forms of practice in which both ideas and materials have an effective presence.

Alastair Grieve's *Constructed Abstract Art in England, A Neglected Avant-Garde* examines the work of six of the founding Constructionists who are at the core of the collection, now augmented by the Joyce and Michael Morris bequest.[2] Grieve notes in his introduction the fluidity of terminology: Abstract art, Concrete, Construction, Constructionist, that surrounded this group of artists. He also cites Lawrence Alloway's (1926–1990) prescient comment in 1953 that 'the vocabulary of so-called "abstract" art is in an appalling condition'.[3] The struggle for an effective language for communication is, in Grieve's view, one of the key reasons for neglect. The word neglect is itself questionable, however, since a

significant number of collectors, critics and writers have remained dedicated to the work of Constructionism and Systems. Nevertheless, a review of the language and thought structures that surround these artists and their successors, as much as their art, is timely. The lively and detailed conversation that in various forms these artists continued to hold with academics, curators and writers indicates a living entity of thought and artistic practice, rather than a closed subject, historically overlooked.

That conversation, between artistic generations and thinkers and activists in other fields, is the clearest measure available to us of a cohesive body of work and its successions and variations. It can be traced through a series of catalogues and commentaries, and as a broader piece of research through private correspondence and records of dialogues and encounters in art schools. Such conversations rarely become part of a public or popular context, but their continuity through successive generations is a more accurate measure of

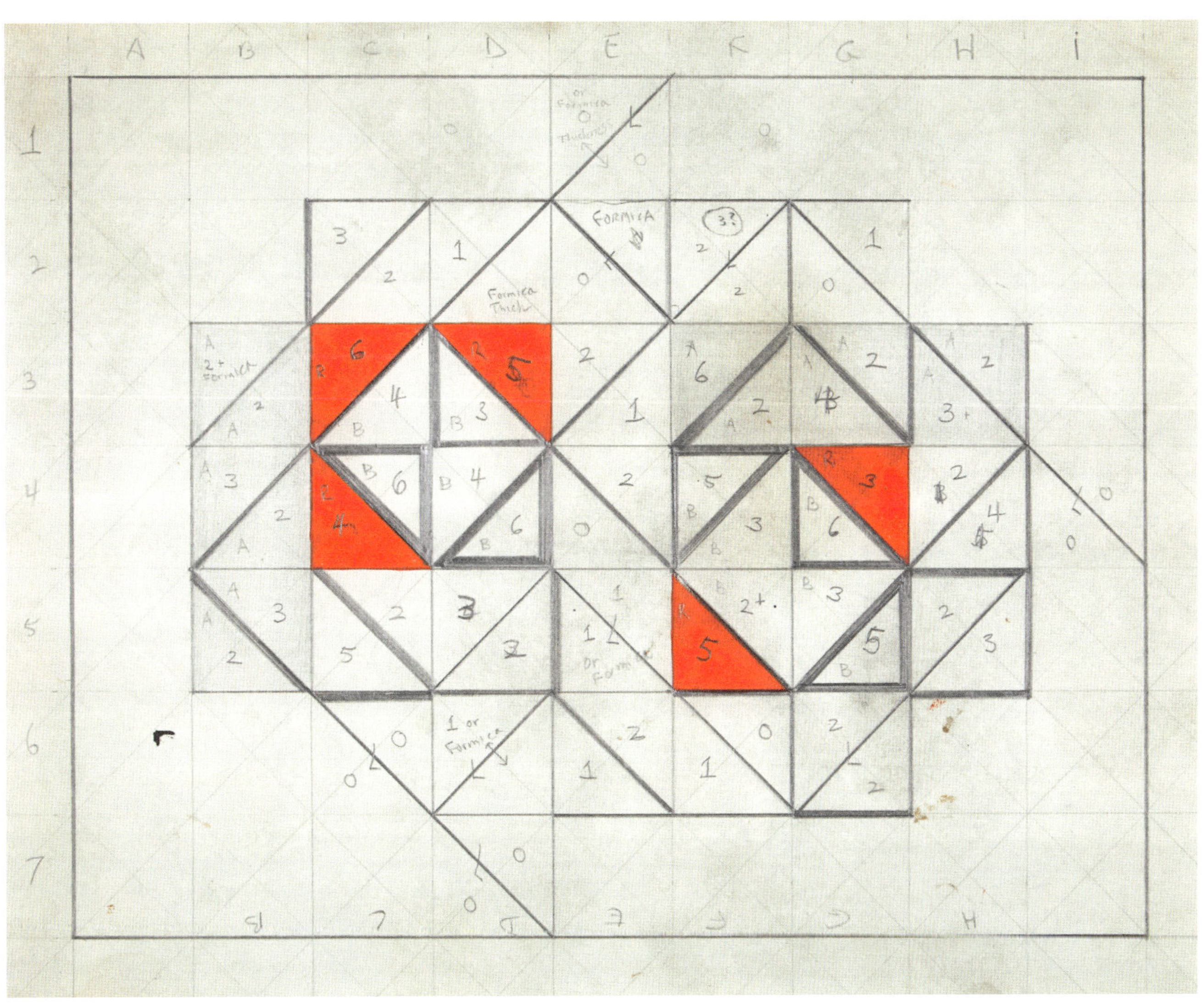

development than can be found in the trends of any given time. This essay therefore offers a sense of how Constructionism and Systems might not only be re-appraised, but also be considered as a relevant address through art practice to the contemporary context.

The key figures in the Constructive element of British art, and their roles in teaching successive students, form a thread that starts with Victor Pasmore (1908–1998) and Richard Hamilton (1922–2011) at Newcastle University, continues with Noel Forster (1932–2007), who worked at Chelsea School of Art with Roger Ackling (1947–2014), John Carter (b.1942), Anthony Hill and Trevor Sutton (b.1948), and arrives at contemporary artists such as Rana Begum (b.1977). Mary Webb (b.1942) was also taught by Pasmore at Newcastle, and although remaining detached from both the Constructionists and Systems as groupings, she was aware as a first-year student of the work of fellow alumnus Noel Forster, who at that point was finishing a postgraduate Hatton Fellowship.[4] Forster too remained independent of all organised groups, but did attend some of the meetings of *Exhibiting Space*, the transdisciplinary forum organised by Ray Thomson and Trevor Clarke (b.1949), students of Jeffrey Steele, in Thomson's Whitechapel Studio from 1984. This latter grouping also included contributions from Jean Spencer (1942–1998) and Richard Bell (b.1955), such as the latter's important collaboration with Nicole Charlett (b.1957) on *Colour Presentations*, a touring exhibition of 1986. This then makes the connection back to Jean Spencer, who along with Malcom Hughes (1920–1997) also supported and

took part in *Exhibiting Space* projects. Jean Spencer was Slade Secretary (an academic role in this context), a tutor to students 1988–98 and Reader in Fine Art from 1995. Begum was a Slade MA student much later than Spencer's time there, but did connect with Gary Woodley who had also worked with Spencer and John Ernest (1922–1994). The latter had been Spencer's tutor at Corsham College of Art. Similarly, Goldsmiths connected Peter Lowe (b.1938) and Susan Tebby (b.1944) to Kenneth Martin (1905–1984) as his students. Tebby's participation with Natalie Dower (b.1931), Nicole Charlett and Jean Spencer in *Countervail* at Mappin Art Gallery (1992) and Mead Gallery (1993) makes links to a younger generation, including Judith Dean (b.1965) and Jane Wilbraham (b.1967). *Countervail* was developed from a dialogical relationship with sociologist Elizabeth Chaplin as part of the process of generating the exhibition project. In her text for the *Countervail* publication, titled *Working On: Working With: Working For*, Chaplin points out that 'working **with** [her emphasis] the Systematic Constructive artist Malcolm Hughes arose in 1984'.[5] The point of all these interconnections (and there are others) is the many dialogues around practice that they undoubtedly denote, but specifically the connectivity through conversation across generations that is a symptom of the generative nature of the principles formed around concrete, Constructionist and Systems-based art. This is, in effect, construction's other.

Two significant exhibitions that sit either side of the end of the 1970s and start of the 1980s serve to characterise aspects of the specifically English debate

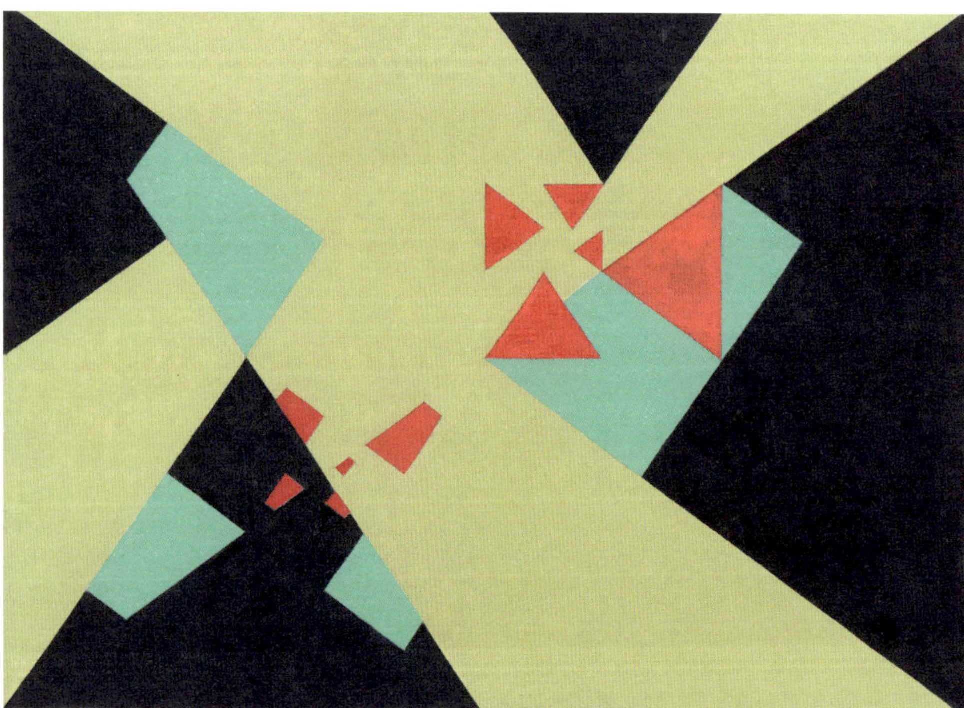

← Natalie Dower
Square Root Two Spirals Nine
Moves
2015
Oil on linen
Sainsbury Centre

→ Michael Kidner
Intersection
1992
Fibreglass, rubber, paint, metal,
elastic and wood
Sainsbury Centre

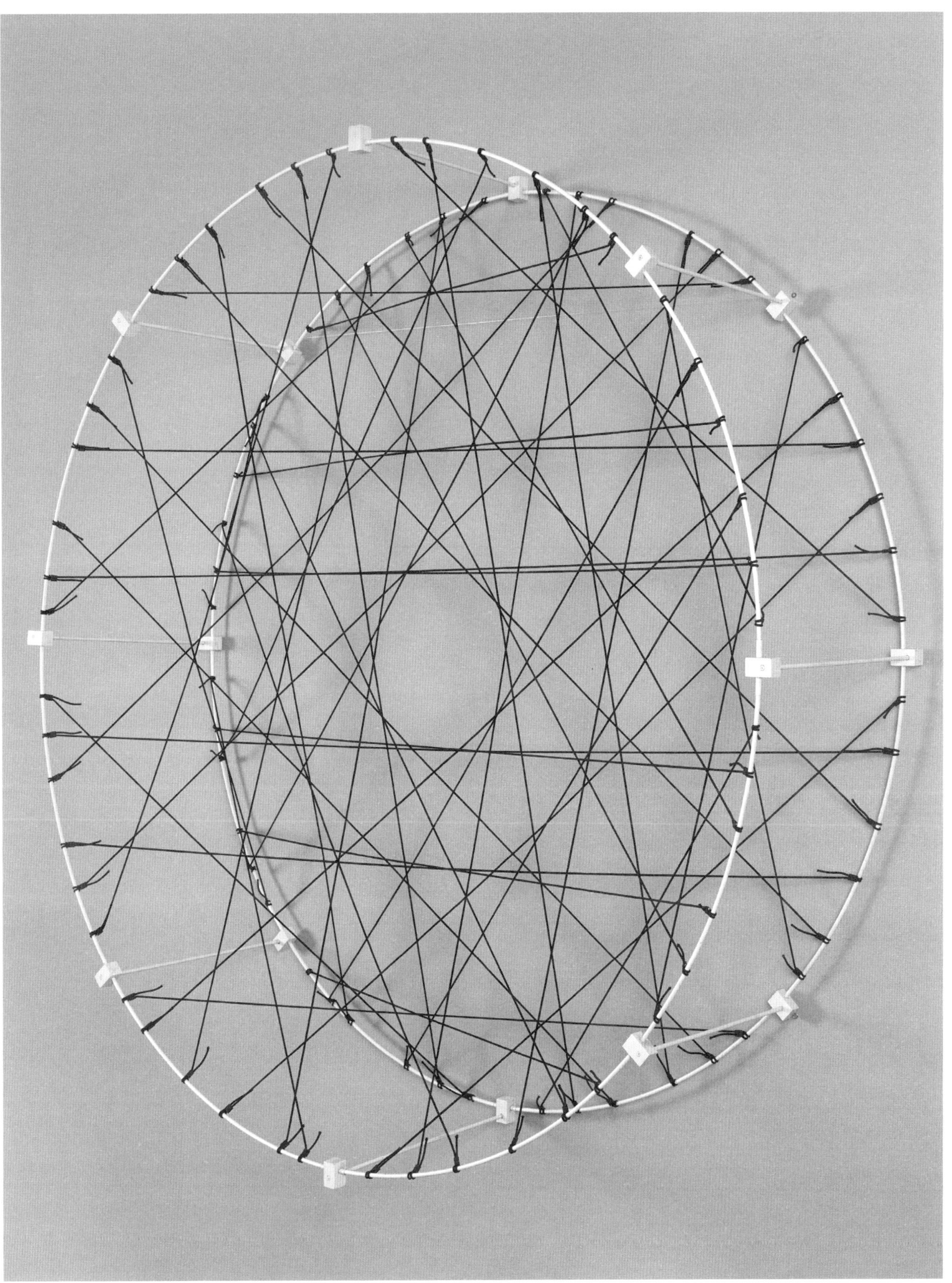

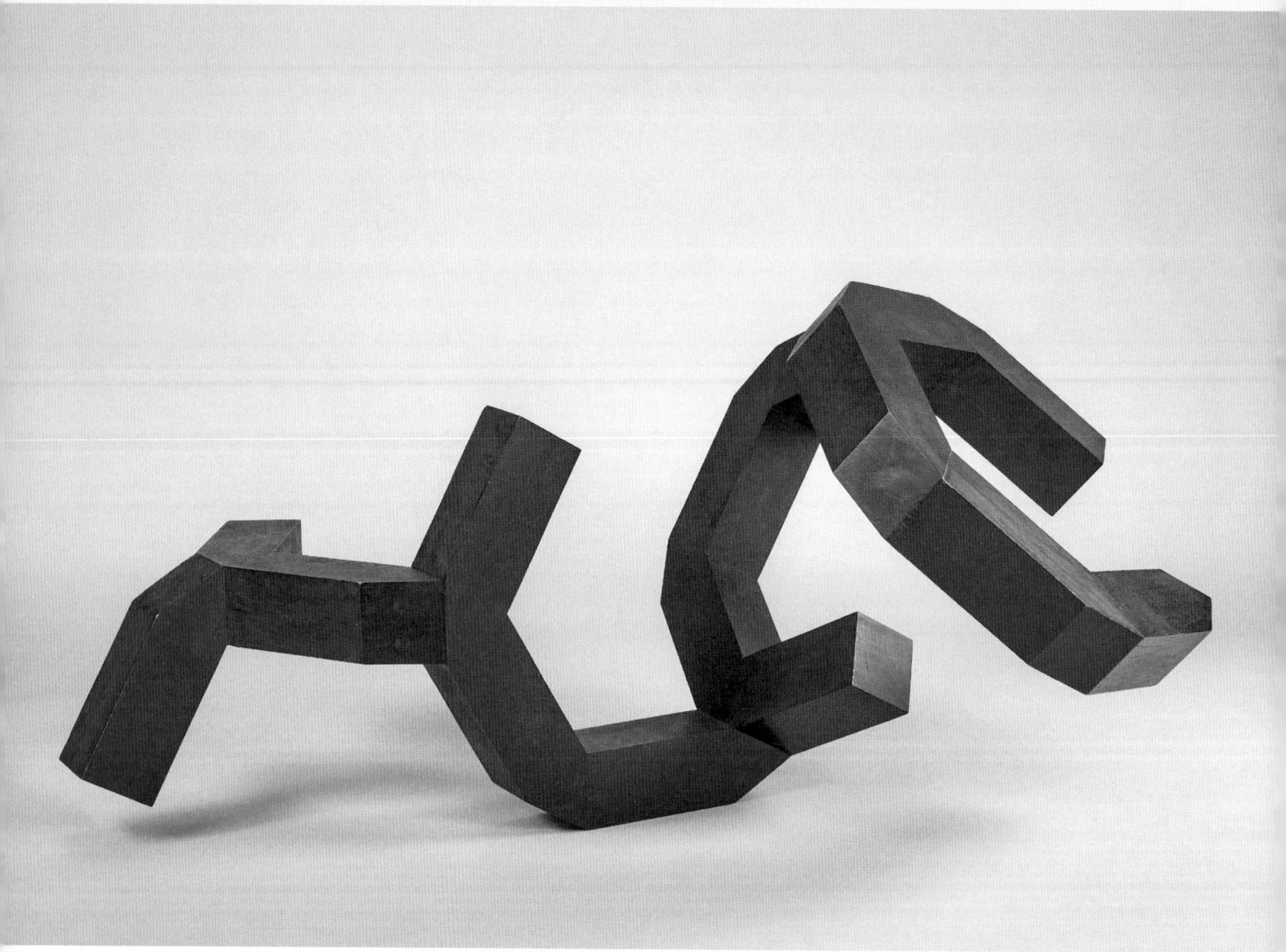

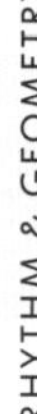

↑ **Norman Dilworth**
1, 2, 3, 4, 5
1999
Stained wood
Sainsbury Centre

around the questions of concrete and constructive art; and in both, the curator and art historian Stephen Bann (b.1942) is a consistently engaged and significant figure. Both exhibitions, in their commonalities as much as their distinctions, serve to emphasise the differences between a localised debate in the UK and its extreme disconnect; at times, paradoxically, the participating British artists defined a more particularly international approach to practice than their international counterparts. What this suggests is that the periodic choking of discourse is a particular and localised problem in Britain, and that the art in question travels more successfully than home language and reception might imply. The introductions to these two exhibitions demonstrate the point: *Constructive Context* (Arts Council, selected by Stephen Bann, 1978) and *Pier + Ocean* (Hayward Gallery, Gerhard von Graevenitz, 1980).

Constructive Context was an Arts Council collection touring exhibition and a survey of British artists working within this tendency in the 1970s, organised by Stephen Bann. In effect it was a theorisation of the field of constructed art in the UK, developed from previous writing such as his book *Experimental Painting: construction, abstraction, destruction, reduction*,[6] and the edited volume *The Tradition of Constructivism within the series The Documents of 20th-Century Art*.[7] Among the participants from *Constructive Context*, Norman Dilworth (b.1931), John Ernest, Anthony Hill, Malcolm Hughes, Michael Kidner (1917–2009), Peter Lowe, Kenneth Martin and Jean Spencer are all represented in the collection at the Sainsbury Centre. Bann points out how much the exhibition was devised in participation with the artists; his introduction states:

> Indeed the idea of tradition, with its natural assumption of formal vocabulary handed down from one generation to another, fits well with the conception of an exhibition like this, in which the wide spectrum of ages rightly suggests that the younger participants have learned a great deal from their elders…But the common elements which we can discover among them belong to the present

rather than some ideal point of origin in the past. They also suggest an option on the future, in that the currents of investigation which are being pursued break continually into new and exciting territory.[8]

Norman Dilworth assisted Gerhard von Graevenitz (1934–1983) in the organisation of *Pier + Ocean* at the Hayward Gallery in the summer of 1980, then at the Kröller-Müller Museum, Otterlo, Netherlands. Correspondence in *Art Monthly* at that time indicated a level of friction between critics, particularly Stephen Bann,[9] who strongly supported the group of British artists who had been meeting for two years to discuss this exhibition without being able to agree on a format and selection of artists. Von Graevenitz then took on the planning of the exhibition, joined by Norman Dilworth, and pushed it towards a more diverse and global look at affinities. Von Graevenitz' final selection included conceptualism, minimalism and Arte Povera as part of the exhibition, as well as video works by artists such as Bas Jan Ader (1942–1975) and photography by William Wegman. Nevertheless, at the heart of the exhibition were works by Richard Paul Lohse and Joost Baljeu sitting in relation to the works of Norman Dilworth, Anthony Hill, Peter Lowe and Kenneth Martin. The subtitle, *Construction in the art of the seventies*, was qualified by von Graevenitz in his introduction, pointedly emphasising the plurality of the Constructive paradigm; an indicative selection of key words from this short text includes flux, formlessness, permeability, shift.

Bann had seen the potential of this exhibition to link the obvious reference to Mondrian and early Modernism with a more detailed analysis of Constructionism. In a series of correspondences and a review in *Art Monthly*, Bann voiced his criticism of what he regarded as a watering down of the original principles of the project. It was plain that von Graevenitz and Dilworth saw a linkage with the works of Daniel Buren (b.1938), Jan Dibbets (b.1941), Richard Paul Lohse, Walter de Maria (1935–2013), Mario Mertz (1925–2003), Richard Tuttle (b.1941), Fred Sandback (1943–2003) and Joel Shapiro (b.1941), to name a few more of the divergent inclusions, as about 'a shift in the concept of space'. Dilworth himself viewed *Pier + Ocean* as generous and inclusive, opening new ways forward;[10] whereas Jeffrey Steele and several of his fellow Systems artists saw the final exhibition as a form of censorship, which had excluded their work and foreclosed real political debate.

Arguably, it was the progressive disenfranchisement of Bann's context, as he describes it, in the 1978 exhibition, rather than the exclusion of certain artists, notably Michael Kidner, Jeffrey Steele and Gillian Wise (1936–2020), that was the root of Bann's critical response to *Pier + Ocean*. Steele's statement from the 1972 Systems catalogue, quoted in Bann's introduction to *Constructive Context*, is useful, however, both in its lambent turn of phrase and its forward-looking conceptualisation:

Combinations of elements of a kind which neither nature nor any other human activity can produce, and which for that reason are sometimes intrinsically very simple, act as messengers between the known and the unknown. But the message is a syntactic and not a semantic one. The process can be compared to trying to communicate by signals with an intelligence on another planet with whom we have no common experience and therefore nothing to communicate <u>about</u>. This must be the hidden, unconscious part of ourselves which has been variously postulated by art, mythology, philosophy, science – a system whose better understanding may contribute to our survival as a species.[11]

Clearly Steele understands that space for ambiguity must exist at the heart of a systematic art process, but is unflinching in his argument that this has a rational basis. Perhaps useful here is one other sentence from von Graevenitz in the *Pier + Ocean* catalogue: 'It should be pointed out that this exhibition constitutes a construction

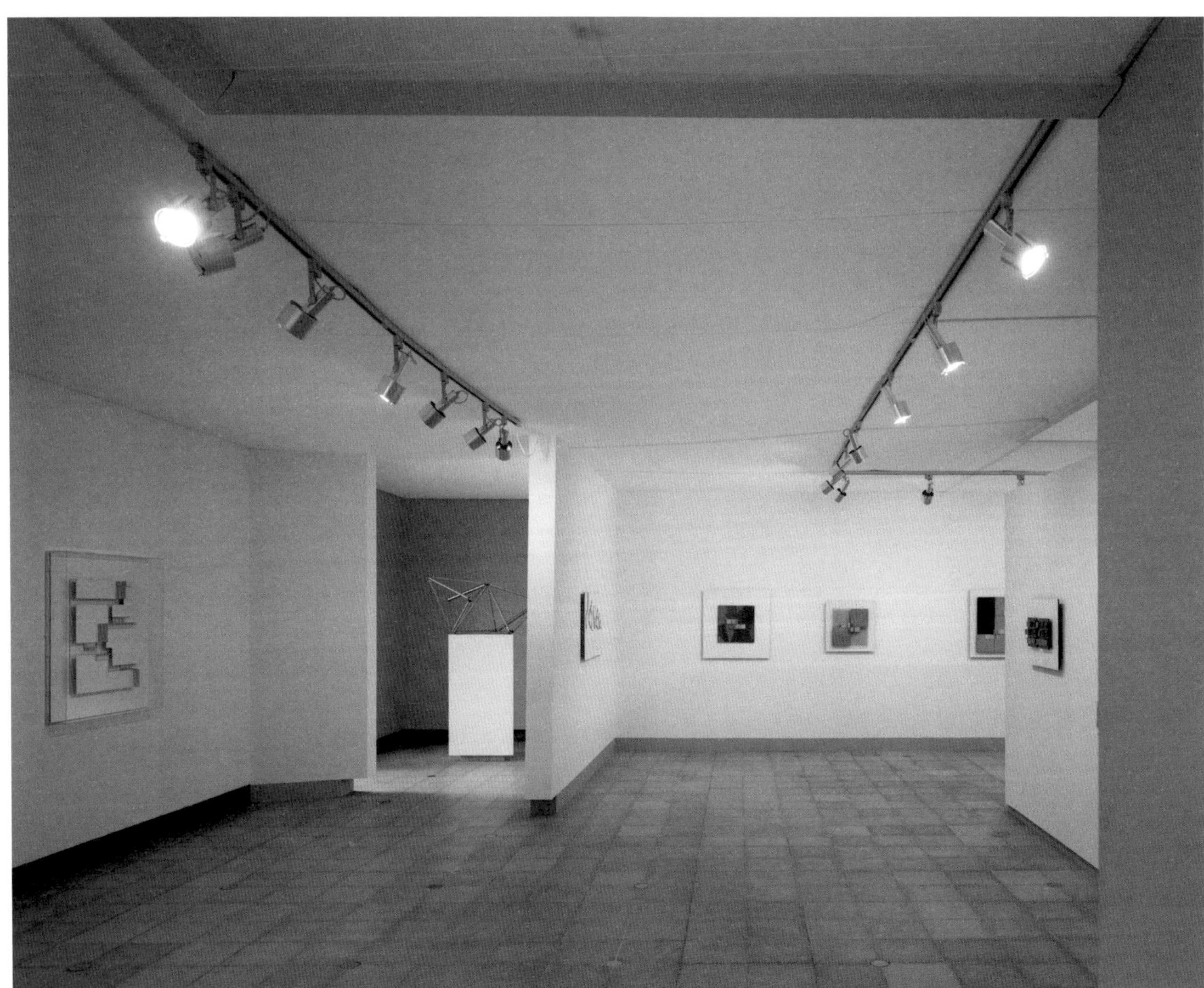

in its own right'.[12] This reads as a shrewd insertion of the idea of construction's ability both to dissolve form and to take on new forms; that the concrete/constructive is founded in principle rather than style. It is ultimately a more ambiguous understanding of the parameters of construction, and therefore a more enduring model of working than either von Graevenitz or Bann could reasonably have estimated in the early 1980s.

The connections between Bann, Dilworth and Steele pre- and post-*Constructive Context* are of course more compelling than any immediate differences in the aftermath of *Pier + Ocean*. Aside from private arguments, the differences often boil down to who was or was not included in various key exhibitions, and indicate a general diminution of opportunity as the public funding of art exhibitions in the 1980s and '90s moved to echo the Royal Academy's 'blockbuster' model, serving audience numbers and markets more than ideas.

Norman Dilworth moved from the UK to Holland and then on to France out of frustration with the limitations afforded him to develop his artistic position in the UK. Undoubtedly the localised fall-out of his support for von Graevenitz over *Pier + Ocean* left him disillusioned with the scenario in Britain, but he was also drawn to the more open possibilities of living and working in Holland, where the second staging of the exhibition at the Kröller-Müller Museum was an unqualified critical success.[13] Perhaps this direction was predicted in Bann's introduction to *Constructive Context*, where he distinguishes Dilworth as part of a 'European context', noting that 'a relevant parallel is with some of the sculptural work of the immensely wide-ranging Swiss concrete artist Max Bill'. As an intriguing postscript to the arguments around the exhibition, a letter dated 5 April 1980 and signed by Dilworth, Lowe and Steele stated 'we regard Max Bill's inclusion as indispensable. What are his reasons for not wishing to take part?'[14] With the benefit of hindsight, when reading the various statements and positions as well as discussing them retrospectively with figures such as Jeffrey Steele, what stands out is what they have in common.

Bann not only laid the theoretical platform for the British Constructionist and Systems artists through his writing and editing in the 1970s, but was also a significant figure within the parallel world of concrete poetry. Writing much later (1989) in the retrospective survey book *The Coracle* (Coracle Press Gallery 1975-1987), Bann states in 'Coracle's Concrete Thinking':

> There have, unquestionably, been reorientations in the geo-political field of contemporary art over this period and *CORACLE* has changed in accordance with them. But it is not a question of anything so simple as a shift from critical to constructive attitudes, from an American to European perspective. *CORACLE* has been in the vanguard in what might be termed a shift towards concrete thinking. Its very duality of function, both as a publisher of books and planner of exhibitions, has given it an exemplary role in this process.[15]

What is interesting in Bann's text is the repeated use of the terms concrete and constructive, taken in the context of his previous writing, curating and research and his editing of the most comprehensive anthology of concrete poetry in English.[16] What is also important in Bann's argument is the idea of the concrete being taken on as a methodology in newer art forms, in the case of *Coracle* through publishing and 'planning exhibitions'. A significant insight that adds to the emphasis on dialogue between Constructionist and Systems artists in this essay is the observation of parallel activities of artists' publishing and the artist/curator, both functioning in ways that are concrete. There are further interesting connections: Bann corresponded closely with Ian Hamilton Finlay (1925–2006), working with him on many exhibitions and publications. *Concrete Poetry at the Brighton ('67) festival*, an edition of Finlay's little magazine *Poor. Old. Tired. Horse.*, emerged from their work on the exhibition itself.[17] Two editions previously, *Poor. Old. Tired. Horse.* was titled *Charles Biederman: An Art Credo* (1967), thus looping

← Anthony Hill exhibition at the Hayward Gallery, London, 1983.

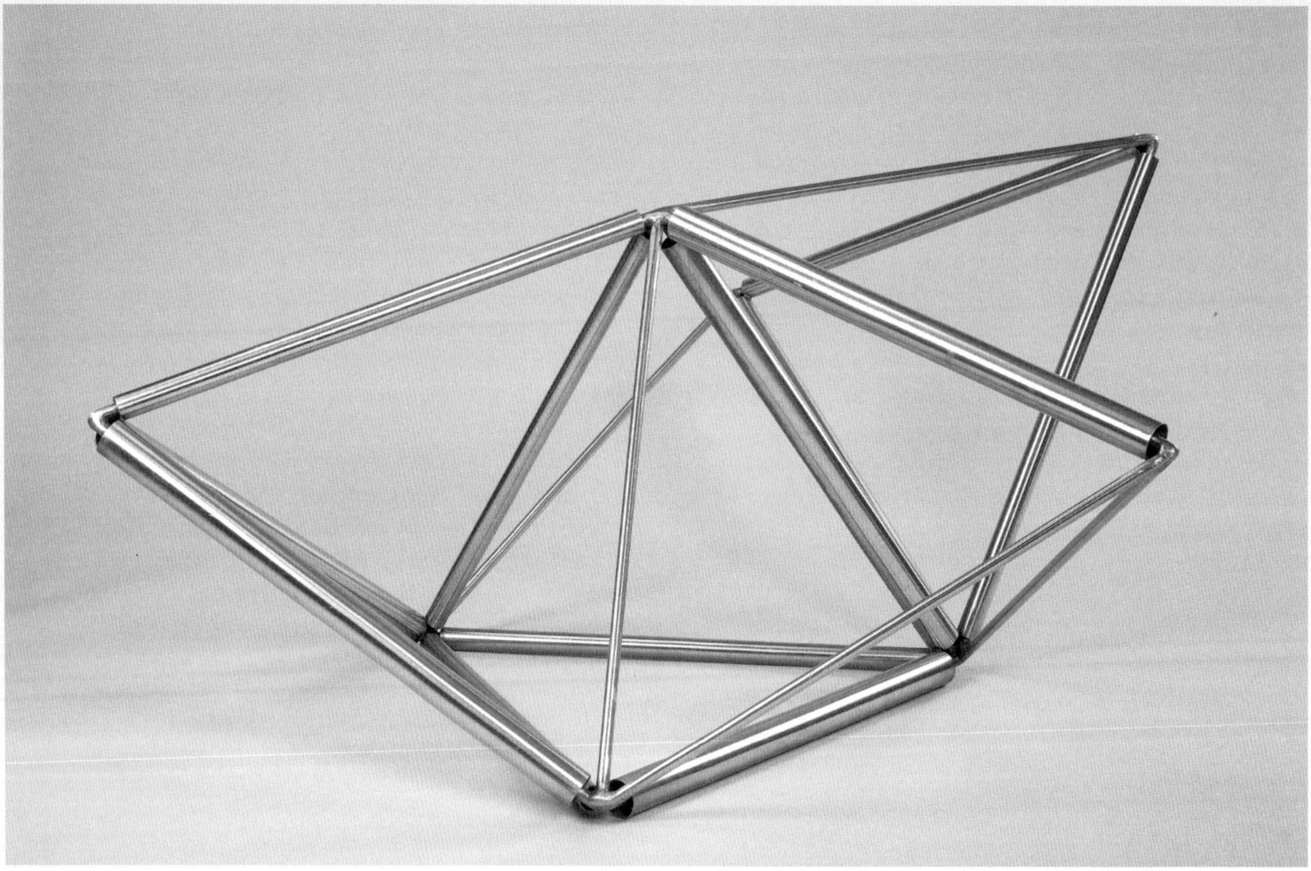

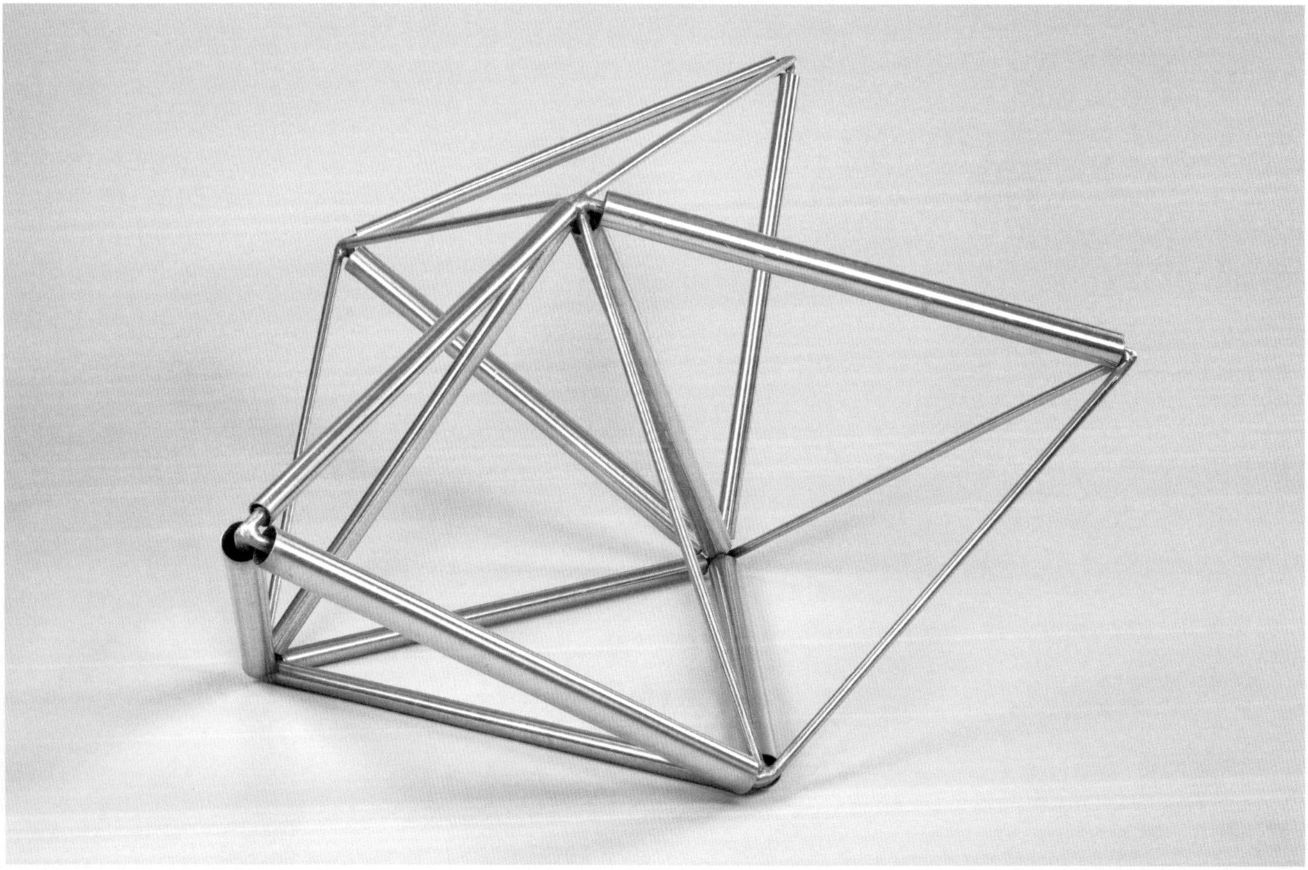

back to Biederman as the model for the Constructionist artists.[18] Bann's 1989 references, including to 'planning exhibitions', also echo von Graevenitz's notion that the 'exhibition constitutes a construction in its own right'.[19]

Anthony Hill's retrospective exhibition at the Hayward Gallery in 1983 was a summation of the Constructionist work that he had largely stopped making from 1976 onwards. Hill's exhibition, loved by those who saw it but not widely attended, is still enthusiastically spoken of by many, notably writer and curator Andrew Wilson and former student of Hill, designer Mark Thompson. The exhibition nevertheless fell into a lacuna that can only be described as the gap between the expectations of Constructionism in the 1960s–1970s and then its presence in the 1980s as a slow fading of the kind of discourses around public space and spatial/rational art forms that Hill and his peers had grasped so acutely. Hill had worked with architects at least as far back as his involvement in the Sixth Congress of the International Union of Architects (IUA), 3–7 July 1961, on the South Bank, London. Wilson's contribution to a survey exhibition of Hill's work cites various of Hill's own statements on the construction/architecture paradigm:

The functional aspect of constructional reliefs as a type of architectonic idea can be recognised in Hill's elaboration of the possibility for 'constructional articulation' to play a 'role in space articulation, particularly interior space, on an environmental scale', such as in the IUA building. Similarly, he has described the constructed relief as a 'chamber architecture' in which its physical space works within a larger environmental space... Hill has additionally suggested that the mathematical thematic can itself be thought of as an 'inner architecture'. [20]

An essay by Sam Gathercole, which concerns itself with the end of the Constructionist ideal in British art, makes the case for a decline in social and political currency for the Constructivist artists based on diminished levels of social engagement as the decades since the 1960s moved on.

The work occupied a position of depersonalised resistance to the bucolic, individualistic romanticism that prevailed in much post-war British art. It stood— figuratively and, where and when possible, literally— alongside emergent forms of modern architecture in developing what the art critic Lawrence Alloway termed 'an aesthetic of the typical'. This linked, in turn, with certain discourses of the Welfare State: the assertive but quiet manners of constructionism chimed with those of the New Humanism of the 1950s. New publics were being shaped through new institutional and infrastructural frameworks, and through and by new social spaces. Beyond the 1950s, however, constructionism's manners were regarded as complicit in a more problematic culture and politics. The society produced by the Welfare State was vital in floating the possibility of a more egalitarian society constituted through new distributions of power and new forms of agency, but the energies it released developed into a range of fault lines in the 1960s. [21]

Neave Brown could be considered as the archetype of a brand of municipal architect who saw space and light as a public service.[22] Hill's exhibition in partnership with Neave Brown's spatial design occurred at a moment when the question of what and who such elevated art forms were for, and their social and intellectual imperatives, seemed remote from the predominant arguments of the new Thatcherite individualism. Gathercole's analysis goes on to delineate the ways that, in his words, '*constructionism* was stymied by emerging discourses', but ends with the suggestion that any sense of failure would derive from the way that contexts and discourses framed its position within international art. Here, I argue, lies the discrepancy. Internationalism was embedded in the code of conduct for artists such as Hill from the beginning of their practice. At the point of internal hiatus in arts and politics that coincided with Hill's 1983 Hayward Gallery exhibition, those of the original Constructionist artists who could leave

← Anthony Hill
Co-Structure, Version 3, Hommage
à Roberto Frucht
1970–75
Welded stainless steel
Sainsbury Centre

simply moved away. By the early 1980s Norman Dilworth was already living in Holland and then later France, remaining in close dialogue with Gerhard von Graevenitz until the latter's tragic death, and later involved in long-standing friendship with François Morellet (1926–2016).

Gillian Wise, ever the internationalist, lived in Paris and Leningrad (St Petersburg) and held scholarships in the US at MIT, Harvard and University of California. Her work offers modes of looking/making/remaking across a diverse oeuvre that has been fractured and scattered through personal circumstances. It nevertheless has a cogency that relates specifically to her reinventions of space across two- and three-dimensional media, moving between relief construction and sculpture, drawing, printmaking and painting.

The grainy image reproduced here was taken from Wise's pages in the Amos Anderson's Kunstmuseum exhibition catalogue *SYSTEMI • SYSTEM, An exhibition of syntactic art from Britain* (Helsinki, 1969), showing a maquette constructed from six panels of Perspex, one opaque and five transparent, with elasticated cord threaded through small drilled holes arranged on a cubed grid between the layers. This evolved as a signature mode of construction for Wise through the 1970s. The reproduction shows a very early example of work classically represented by the relief construction in the Sainsbury Centre collection, *Relief, Six Fold Progression on Two Planes* (1968–69). The cord and its reflections weaving between the layers of Perspex is suggestive of a more ephemeral kind of space than is typical in relief construction of this period. The interplay of light, shadow, reflective surface and thus implied understanding of the viewer's movement around the object produce configurations that exceed normal imagined permutations of a grid. A similar work,

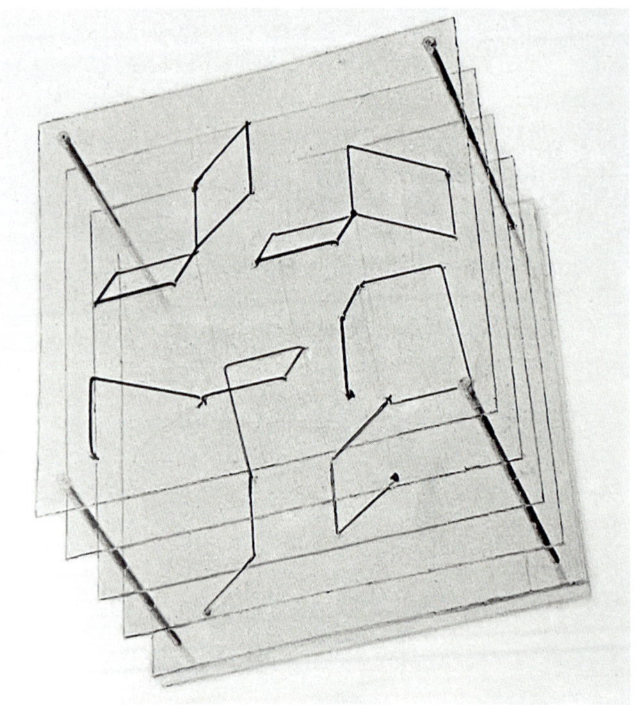

reproduced in a colour slide photograph dated Charlotte St Studio, 1969, appears in Wise's self-published *20 Small Works & the Alice Walls at the Barbican*.[23] Her caption in this small book describes this as 'part of a series of structures – a continuous single line over two or more levels within a square format' and goes on to connect it to the Helsinki work and her time on a British Council graduate exchange year to Leningrad Beaux Arts.

Also now added to the Sainsbury Centre collection as part of a sequence of screen prints is *Net 3, Tiré à* (1975), a neat encapsulation of Wise's spatial and

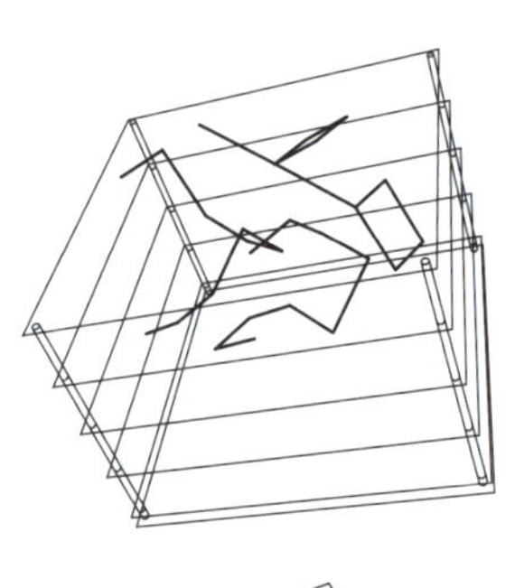
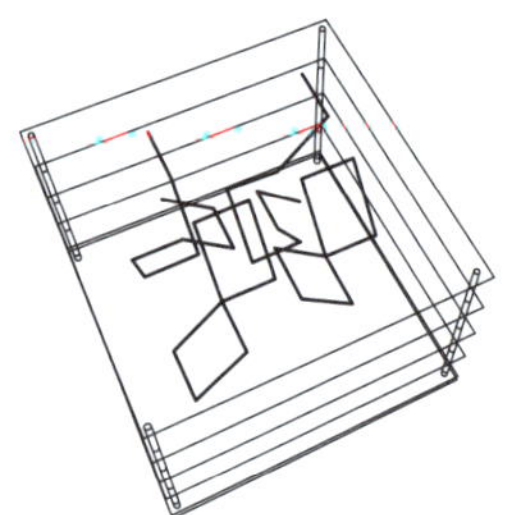
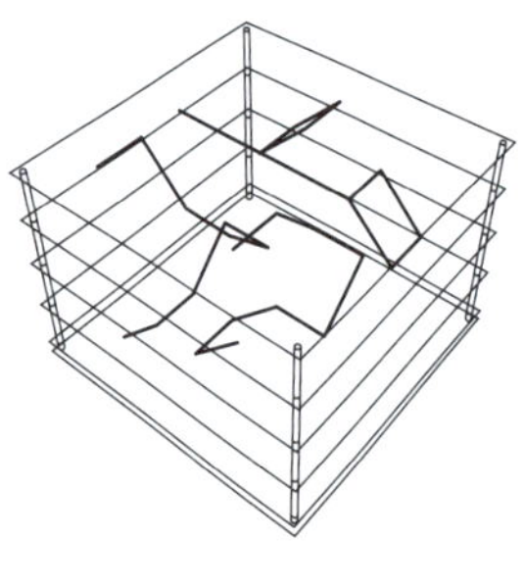
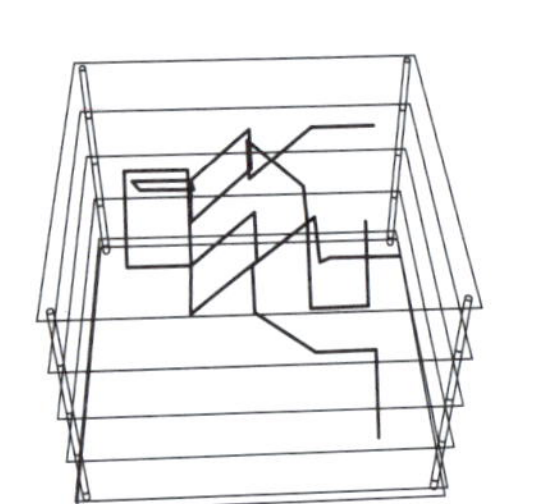
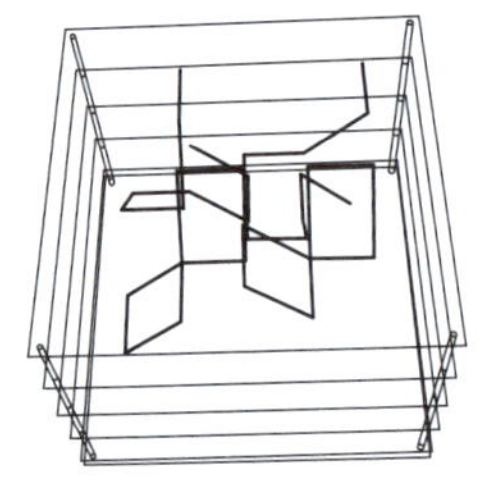
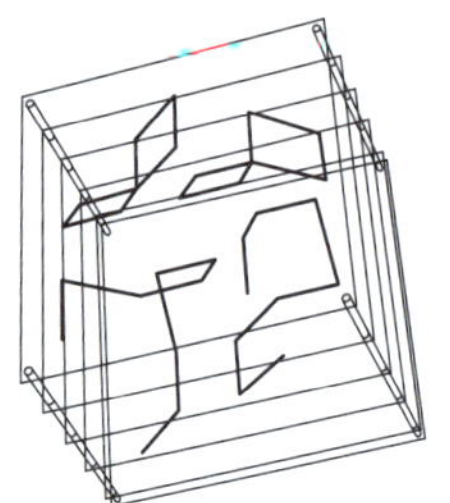

↑ **Gillian Wise** maquette from the catalogue of *SYSTEMI • SYSTEM, An exhibition of syntactic art from Britain*, 1969.

← Digital reconstructions of a Gillian Wise structure from 1969. Andrew Bick with Ben Deakin and Anna Lytridou.

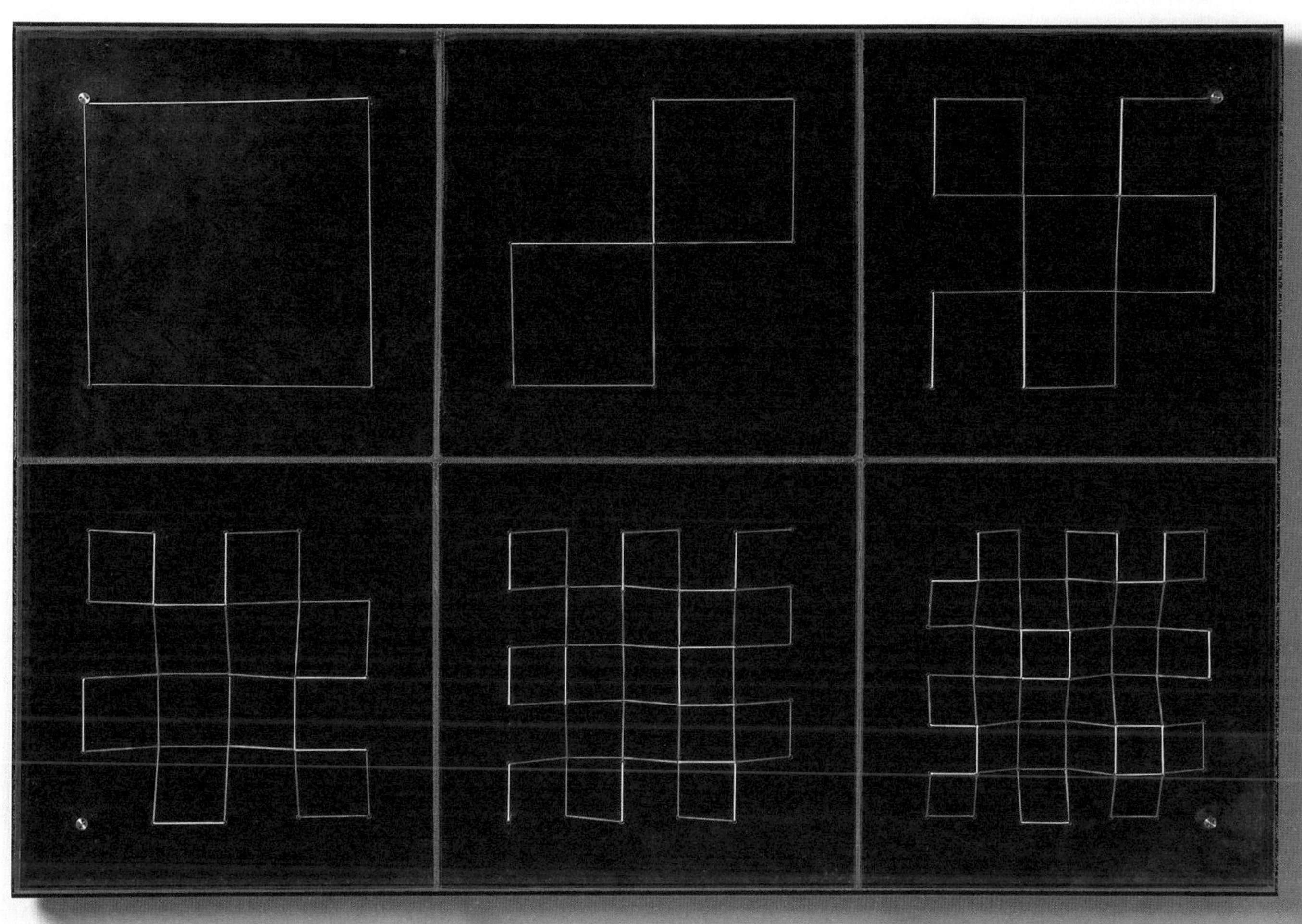

↑ Gillian Wise
Relief: Sixfold progression on two
planes
1968–69
Perspex, elastic, metal pegs and
hardboard
Sainsbury Centre

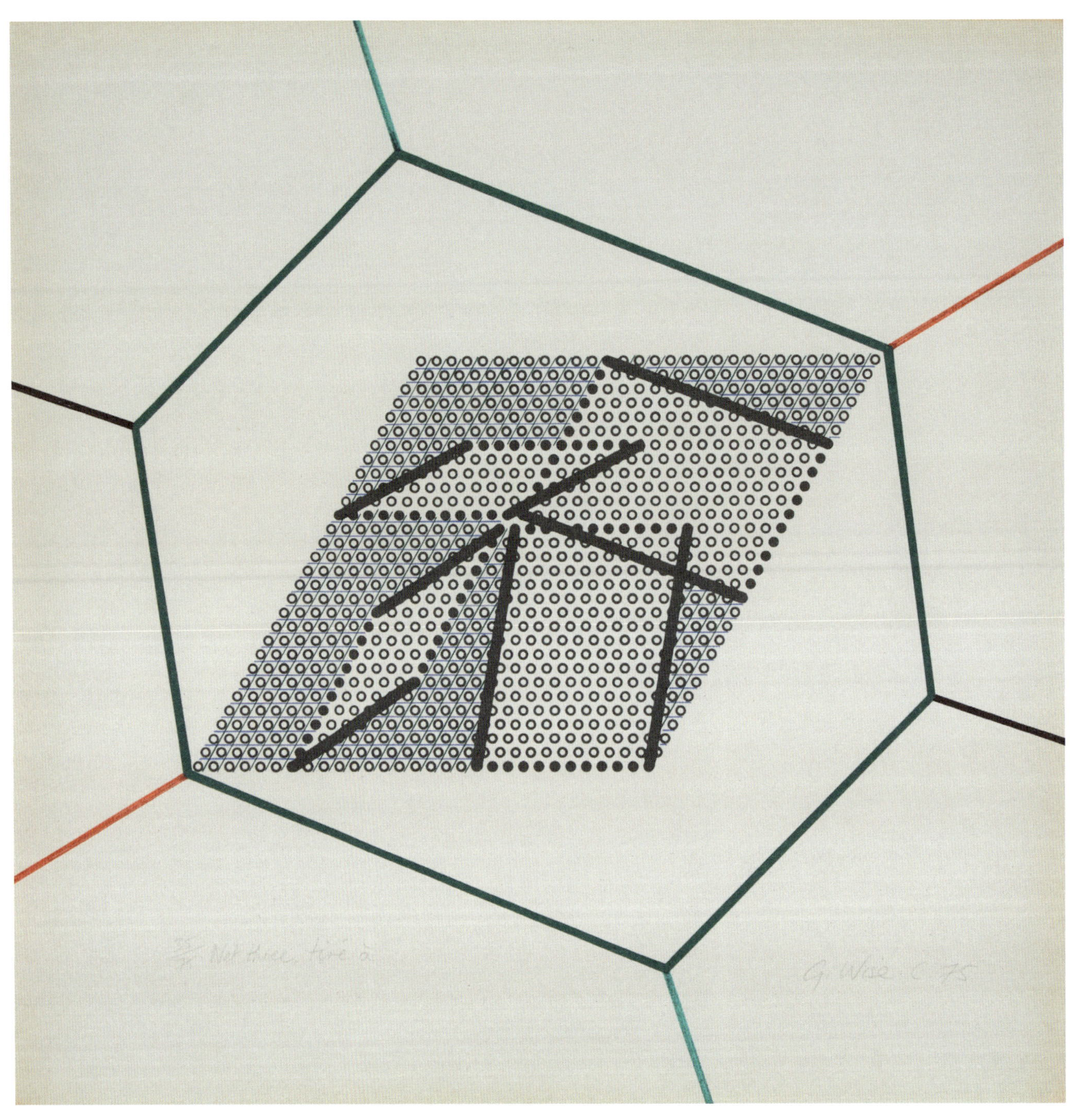

↑ **Gillian Wise**
Net 3, Tiré à
1975
Screenprint on paper
Sainsbury Centre

→ **Tess Jaray**
Tamlin
1971–72
Acrylic on canvas
Sainsbury Centre

graphic inventiveness. Wise's self-published catalogue, *Drawn from structures: 6 themes 1967–76*, contains a small black and white reproduction of an acrylic painting on an acrylic sheet, using an identical composition to this print along with a captioned sketch of the same image showing notations of what Wise describes as 'eye movement path'. Current experiments in reconstructing aspects of this sequence of works have informed the understanding of Wise's approach to this text. The images illustrated were generated using Adobe Illustration and SketchUp software, to give some indication in two dimensions of what occurs visually with these structures as the eye and body travel around them.

The reason for their inclusion is simply to demonstrate how rich an optical imagination Wise was able to develop between the dates of the original structure and the screen print (1969–75), yet without recourse to contemporary computer software as a tool. As such this offers a useful paradigm for the generative capacity that is a key aspect of Wise's work. Through physical means, clear Perspex, drilled holes and elasticated cord, the square becomes a rotated and distorted form, seen through as many different angles

as the eye can take in as the viewer moves around the construction. The continuous line within the structure becomes visually unmoored: beginning and end uncapturable from any fixed viewpoint. In the 1969 photograph, reprised as print and prototypical drawing, what occurs is a process of a squared grid taking flight, cubes in line form generating an unpredictability that seems equivalent to motion capture filming, which is the visualisation of permutations the naked eye cannot imagine.

Of the significant participants in the later Systems group, Jeffrey Steele (1931–2021) is worth citing: he was the key theorist, as much as artist, of developments that underpinned *Constructive Context*; and thanks to his open engagement with artists in mainland Europe, these developments represented a resolutely internationalist approach. From Steele's pages from the catalogue for *Constructive Context*:

...the meaning of a given system is identical with its social use. The abandonment of the idealist position leaves us with no possibility

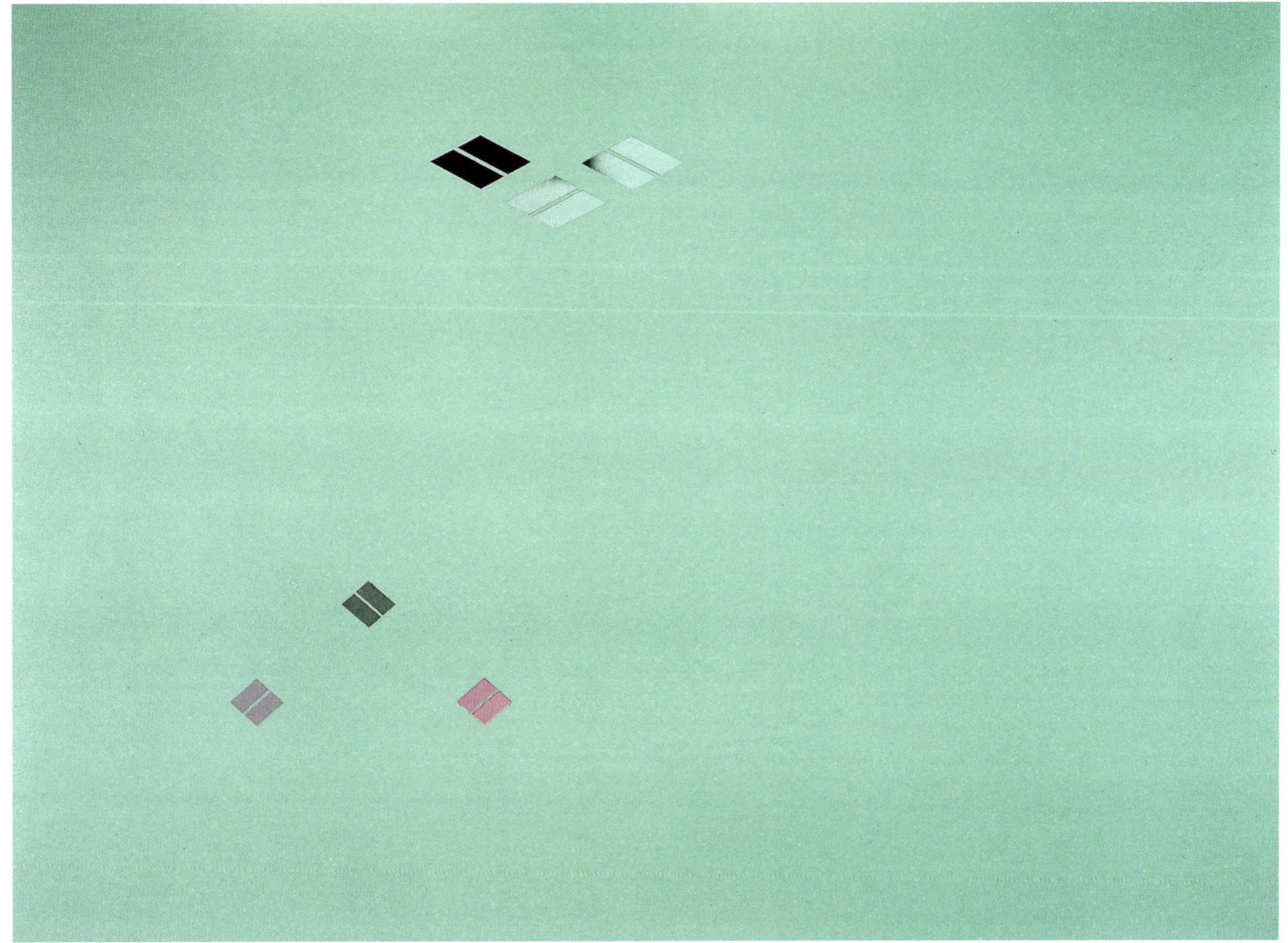

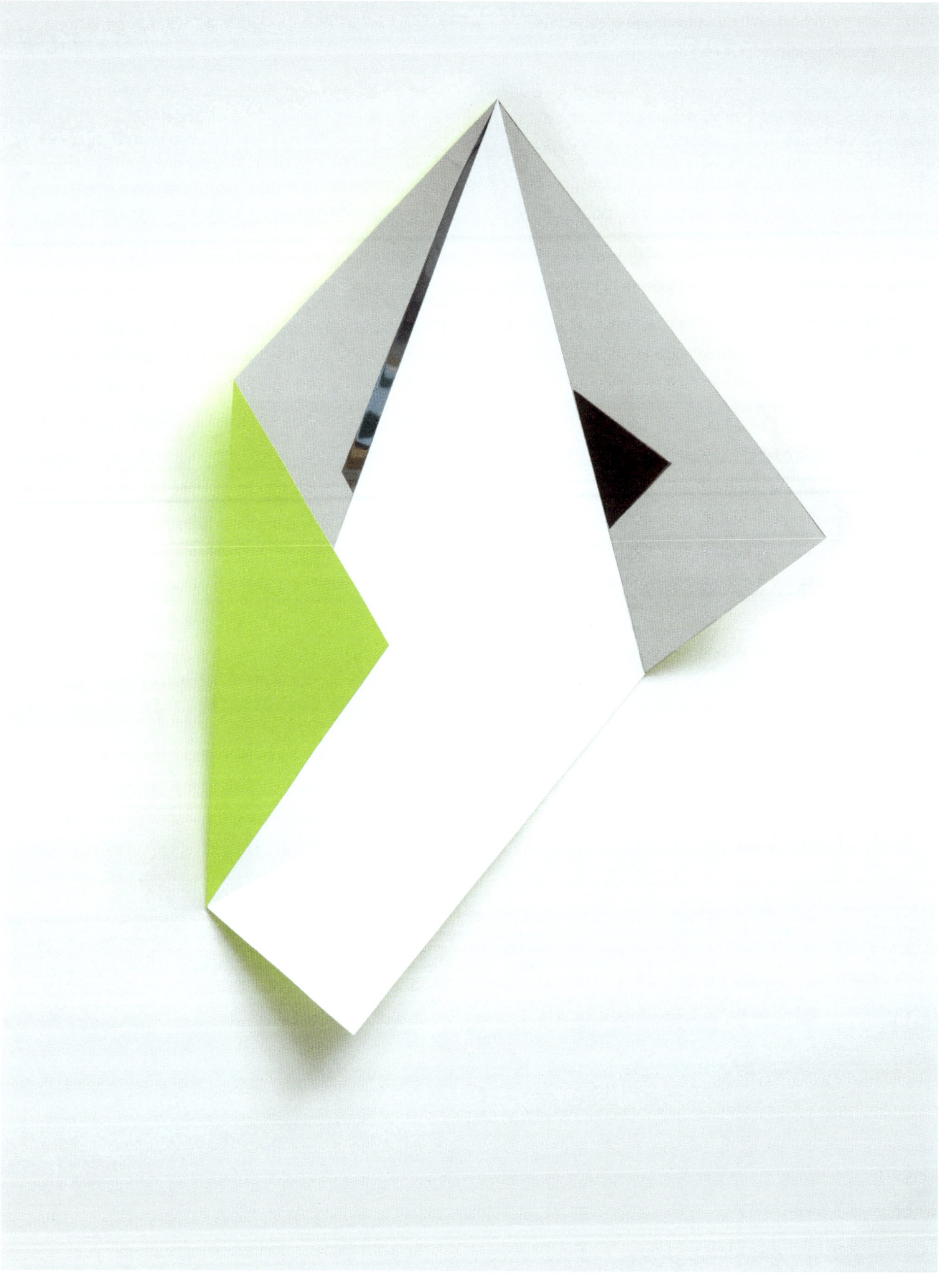

of locating the significance of a work of art outside the political context of its construction, diffusion, conservation, destruction.

...Between a given work and a given environment, the elements from which both are constructed and their properties, there subsists pairs of corresponding factors which combine at the level of practical human-sensuous activity, without change to either but in a mutually revealing way. Since prevailing economic and political conditions have tended to derange the relations between systematic and constructive art and its proper architectural object, this particular function remains symbolic and the present social use of this art is mainly critical and didactic.[24]

Steele's statements pre-empt the criticism levelled at these artists in Gathercole's *British Art Studies* essay. Indeed, a revision of these sentiments was expressed in an interview with artist Katrina Blannin (b.1963) for *Turps Banana Magazine*, issue 11, part of which was used as caption for the painting *Third Syntagmatic ('Tsunami'), (Sg VIII I)*, 1965, in the exhibition *Adventures of the Black Square* (Whitechapel Art Gallery, 2016). The whole quote reads as follows:

... but the way I rationalise it at the moment, from a socialist's point of view still, is that these are ideas about society, in fact a social economic order, that can't come about under a capitalist order. There is

no way of telling what kind of architecture socialism would produce – in terms of a utopia. This is still on the other side of the river – ha – beyond the revolution! This was the great fault of the Bauhaus of course. You can't expect to build a little bit of beautiful socialist architecture only for it then to become its opposite; solely the province of a sub-fraction of the capitalist class and this alongside a lot of decaying crumbling tower blocks which just give Modernism a bad reputation. The cosmeticizing process of Constructivism is then deeply, deeply ugly in terms of its social aspirations. This is not to say that it hasn't produced some beautiful art.

For Rana Begum, a path of learning through dialogue can be traced through contact at Chelsea College of Art with artists Roger Ackling, John Carter, Trevor Sutton and in particular Noel Forster.[25] Later, at the Slade School, she was working with Bruce McLean (b.1944), David Hepher (b.1935) and Gary Woodley, and through a visit from former Slade tutor Tess Jaray (b.1937) ended up working with her as a studio assistant. Begum points out the centrality for these artists of direct understanding of material combinations, hapticity and colour sensation, as much as giving priority to the processes of encountering a work of art in real space and time. She also points out that during her time at Chelsea and the Slade, these discussions in front of an artwork were not questions theorised in relation to social and political concerns, nor were there any conscious attempts to connect art being made to current political preoccupations, trends, or a

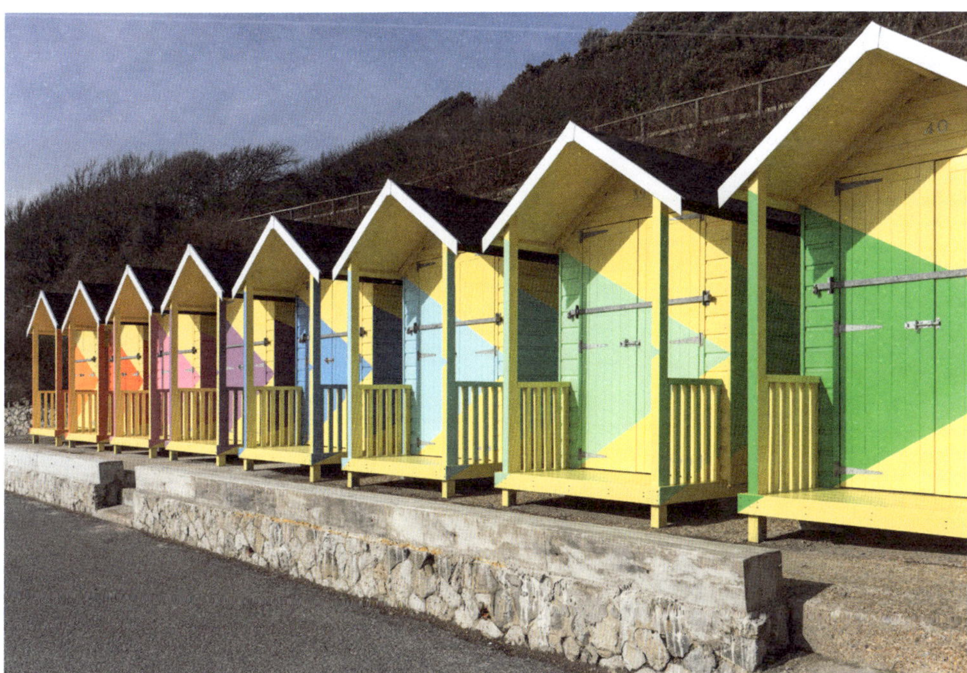

← **Rana Begum**
No. 684, L Fold
2016
Paint on mirror finish stainless steel
Sainsbury Centre

→ **Rana Begum**, No.1054
Arpeggio, 2021 at the Folkestone Triennial.

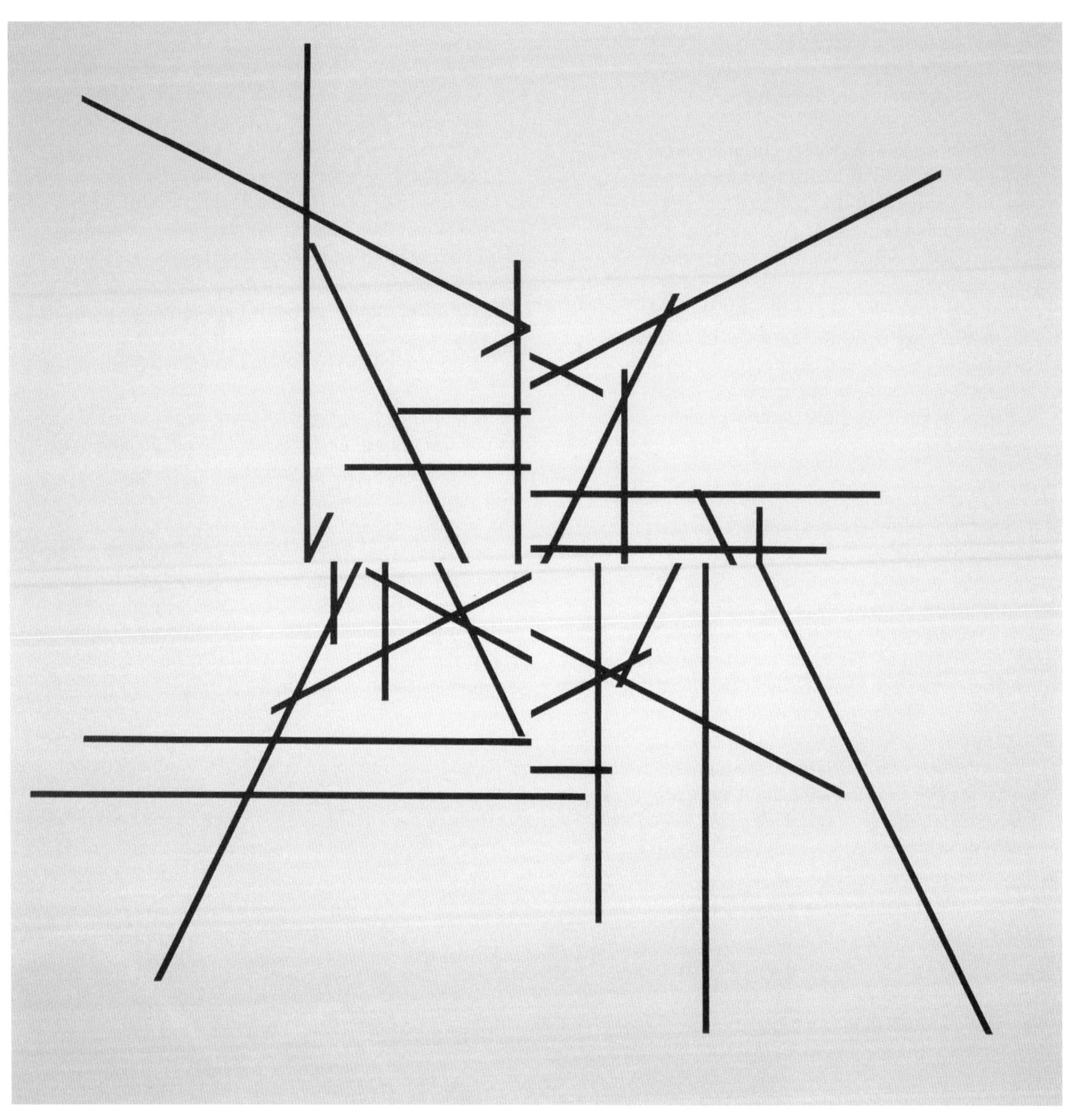

↑ Malcolm Hughes
Rational Concepts
1977
Screenprint on paper
Made for the portfolio introduced
by Richard Paul Lohse.
Sainsbury Centre

sense of the contemporary. Indeed, many of these artist/tutors were deliberate in their refusal to contextualise their practice in relation to such concerns. And yet the experiences of art-making that they mediated re-form in Begum's own work, where the detachment and formality of surface apparent from the very different practices of John Carter, Tess Jaray, Noel Forster, Trevor Sutton and others gets reappraised through her own experience and identity. Seeing their work in this exhibition therefore reaffirms the same set of underpinning principles and might also suggest ways forward from the unease expressed in Jeffrey Steele's conversation with Katrina Blannin quoted on the wall panel for *Adventures of the Black Square*.

Begum's contribution to the 2021 Folkestone Triennial was *No.1054 Arpeggio* (2021); it restores the vernacular architecture of the beach huts while in parallel introducing it to all the paradigms associated with concrete art forms. The fact that this composition sits playfully in a typical English seaside location is indicative of the polyvalent nature of such forms of practice, when given confident and sensitive forms of support. What we are seeing is a set of principles playing out beyond the paradigm of social housing and a state welfare settlement as outlined in Gathercole's essay, but nevertheless offering a pragmatic notion of aesthetics and social space.

A compact analysis of this succession process can be found in Richard Paul Lohse's introductory text to the 1977 Bern exhibition *Rational concepts, 7 English artists*:

It is readily understandable and not without significance that a number of these artists – born around 1930 – are teachers of visual design at state institutions. What the group have in common, from a work ideology point of view, is the tendency to express themselves by graphic, two-dimensional or plastic means.[26]

Earlier in the same text, Lohse singles out Kenneth and Mary Martin (1907–1969) as artists and teachers who devised a model in which 'methodology and systematics in art are not simply a practical tool for achieving a specific outcome but that this same tool is the substance and expression of the age'.[27] This is not to propose a lineage that is free from theoretical engagement and content, but that such things are both slowly absorbed and slowly diffused by such art practices in ways that accept the contradictory nature of the relationship between thought and object.

Part and parcel of the language that surrounds Constructionism and Systems is of course the periodic revival of interest that identifies developments in parallel, seeing such commonalities as a confirmation of enduring concrete principles. The text by Lohse quoted above was also reprinted in *britisch – systematisch* held at Stiftung für konstruktive und konkrete Kunst, Zürich, 1990. The exhibition, at what is now Museum Haus Konstruktiv, brought together the artists Kenneth and Mary Martin, Nicole Charlett, Norman Dilworth, Malcolm Hughes, Michael Kidner, Peter Lowe, Eric Snell (b.1953), Jean Spencer and Jeffrey Steele, with an introduction by Stephen Bann. Bann's words here strike a reflective note, pointing to the activity of *Exhibiting Space* as an indicator that Constructive artists' tendency to work in groups remained dynamic in the UK throughout the 1980s. He goes on to emphasise the role of teaching in the UK art schools, also noting that 'The contraction of the British art schools has meant that this base is no longer as secure as previously…'[28]

Roger Ackling and Anthony Hill both taught at Chelsea School of Art. Ackling engaged with the unpainted landscape, making small objects using lines burned by magnifying rays of sunlight on pieces of found wood, displaying a Zen-like sense of contemplative spirituality. Hill was avowedly atheistic, a mathematical scholar, a neo-Dadaist as much as a Constructionist, and a polemical disruptor of anything he considered pretentious. And yet, placing their works alongside each other does not cause a mutual cancelling out of effect; it would be better described as a 'vibration' of the senses based in the optical values generated by linear, structural wall-mounted objects. The premise in each case might seem to be opposed, but the presence of the artwork, in real space and time, provokes an equivalent heightened sense of looking, of attentiveness. Such a paradigm, of course, leads us to contemporary artworks such as those of Begum, along with all the associated experiences of which she speaks.

We live in a world full of a sense of urgency concerning diversity and inclusivity, of needing to understand the non-binary and post-canonical as a mainstream cause out of which art has reason to exist in the present. The voices and arguments within the groupings of artists of Constructionism and Systems, outlined in this text, demonstrate a capacity to address contemporary thought, as much as their various practices can be proven to be adaptive, fluid and anchored in the social exchanges that form from artist to artist over successive generations. This gift of conversation, of at times fierce argument, is the opposite of obsolescence and amnesia, one in which succession is built through respectful antagonism and in which the protagonists expect the essential qualities of their practice to be burnished through argument.

POSTSCRIPT

When I was preparing a curated exhibition fusing Constructionism and Systems with contemporary artists' work, I decided on the title *Construction and its Shadow*.[29] Jeffrey Steele, ever alert to nuances of language, was reluctant to accept the allusive and possibly melancholic nature of the 'shadow' in the title, although he fully agreed with the thesis, based in Dada and Constructivism, of a dual-sided art practice, typified by Anthony Hill/Achill Redo. *Construction's Other* was Jeffrey's suggestion for a title, and with hindsight it seems lighter and more precise than my own use of words. The extended dialogue he maintained with me, Katrina Blannin and Brandon Taylor among others, until his death, gave us an important connection with one who joins Hill as one of the key thinkers among these artists.[30] Jeffrey looms large over any discourse on Systems, as an artist whose generosity towards other artists and researchers was notable in later life; he is inevitably included in the discourse. This essay is dedicated to him. □

ENDNOTES

1 See Jonneke Jobse, *De Stijl Continued, The Journal Structure (1958–1964)* (Rotterdam: 010 Publishers, 2005).

2 Alastair Grieve, *Constructed Abstract Art in England: A Neglected Avant-Garde* (New Haven and London: Yale University Press, 2005).

3 Ibid., p.12, citing Alloway 'The Limits of Abstract Painting', *Art News and Review* (1953).

4 From a conversation with Mary Webb, 10 July 2021.

5 Chaplin in Tam Giles et al., *Countervail* (Sheffield: Mappin Art Gallery, 1992), p.26.

6 Stephen Bann, *Experimental Painting: construction, abstraction, destruction, reduction* (London: Studio Vista, 1970).

7 Stephen Bann (ed.), *The Tradition of Constructivism* (London: Thames & Hudson, 1974).

8 Stephen Bann, *Constructive Context* (London: Arts Council of Great Britain, 1978), p.5.

9 *Art Monthly* no. 37, June 1980 pp.24–26 (and in subsequent exchanges, including Jeffrey Steele, *Closing the Dossier on P+O*, AM 40, October 1980).

10 In conversation with the writer at the opening of his curated exhibition of Norman Dilworth, Huddersfield Art Gallery, 9 September 2011.

11 Jeffrey Steele, quoted in Bann (1978), p.8.

12 Gerhard von Graevenitz in *Pier + Ocean: Construction in the art of the seventies: an exhibition* (London: Arts Council of Great Britain, 1980), p.6.

13 https://krollermuller.nl/en/timeline/a-collection-must-grow

14 From the archive of Jeffrey Steele, photocopy posted to the author in September 2009 of *Proposals for an Exhibition at the Hayward Gallery 1980*, noted at a meeting on 3 June 1979 and signed Peter Lowe, Norman Dilworth, Jeffrey Steele.

15 Stephen Bann, *Coracle's Concrete Thinking* (London: Coracle Press, 1989), p.53.

16 Stephen Bann (ed.), *Concrete poetry, an international anthology* (London: London Magazine editions, 1967).

17 Ian Hamilton Finlay, *Poor. Old. Tired. Horse.* no. 24 (Stonypath: Wild Hawthorn Books, 1967). See interview between Bann and Gustavo Grandal Montero, https://monoskop.org/images/e/e5/Grandal_Montero_Gustavo_2015_From_Cambridge_to_Brighton_Concrete_Poetry_in_Britain_An_Interview_with_Stephen_Bann.pdf accessed 12 August 2021.

18 Ian Hamilton Finlay, *Poor. Old. Tired. Horse.* no. 22 (Stonypath: Wild Hawthorn Books, 1967).

19 Bann, 1989, p.53; and von Graevenitz, 1980, p.6.

20 Andrew Wilson, *Anthony Hill, works 1954–82* (London: Austin/Desmond Fine Art, 2003), pp.46–47.

21 Sam Gathercole, 'The Lost Cause of British Constructionism: A Two-Act Tragedy', *British Art Studies*, issue 3, 2016, https://www.britishartstudies.ac.uk/issues/issue-index/issue-18/the-lost-cause-of-british-constructionism accessed 5 July 2021).

22 For detail on this, see Mark Swenarton, *Cook's Camden: The Making of Modern Housing* (London: Lund Humphries, 2017).

23 Gillian Wise, *20 Small Works & the Alice Walls at the Barbican* (Paris: Gillian Wise, 2011).

24 Jeffrey Steele statement in Bann, 1978, p.48.

25 Conversation with the author, 30 June 2021.

26 Richard Paul Lohse, *Rational concepts, 7 English artists* (original folio, unbound in box, Bern: Lydia Mergert editions, 1977), reprinted in German and English, pp.13–14, *britisch – systematisch*, Stiftung für konstruktive und konkrete Kunst, Zürich (1990).

27 Ibid., p.14.

28 Stephen Bann, *britisch – systematisch* (Zurich: Stiftung für konstruktive und konkrete Kunst, 1990), p.10.

29 http://webarchive.henry-moore.org/hmi/collections/collections-displays1/previous-displays1/construction-and-its-shadow

30 See Katrina Blannin's interviews with Jeffrey Steele in *Turps Banana* issue 11; and Steele's *An Encounter Between Two Painters* in issue 14.

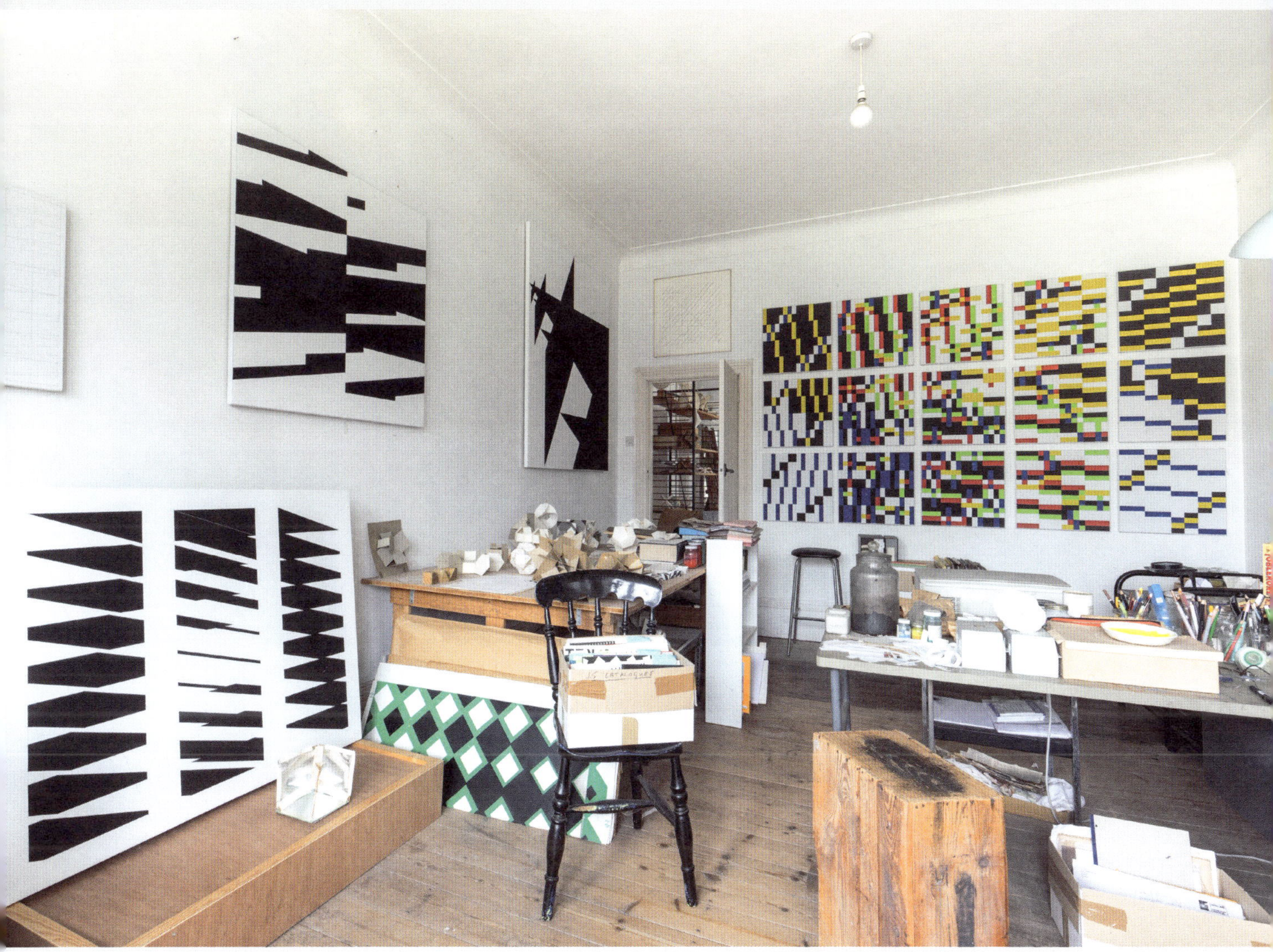

↑ Jeffrey Steele's studio, 2021.
Photograph Ben Deakin.

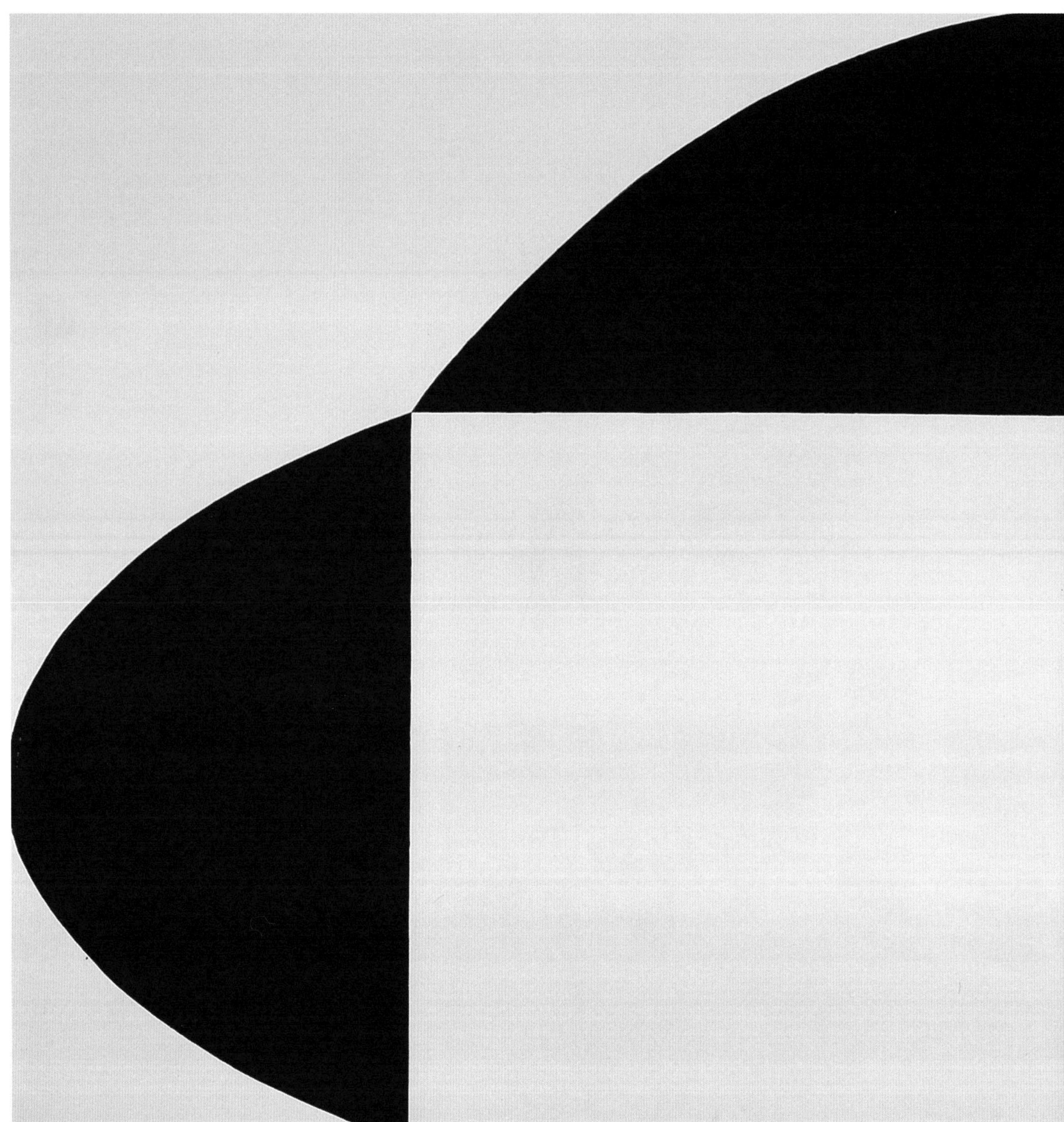

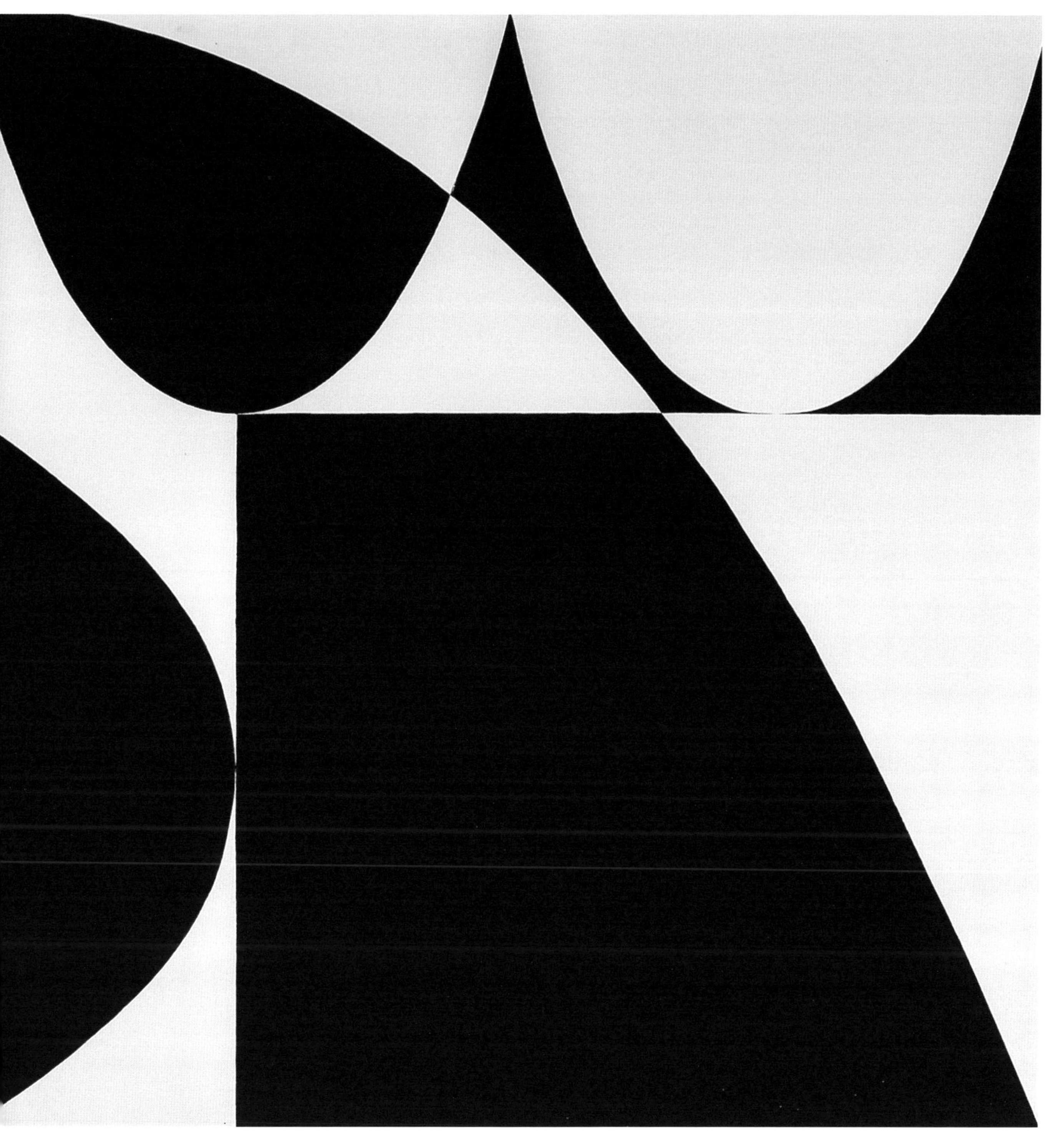

↑ **Anthony Hill**
Catenary Rhythms
1953–54
Reconstructed by Richard Plank,
1982
Paint and ink on board
Sainsbury Centre

Unless otherwise stated, all works are Sainsbury Centre collection.

All dimensions are height x width x depth.

Robert Adams (1917–1984)
Standing Figure
1949
Brass
102.5 x 320 x 205 cm
Donated by Joyce and Michael Morris
31559

Robert Adams
Pierced Sheet
1951–52
Brass
29 x 27.4 x 11 cm
Donated by Joyce and Michael Morris
31555

Robert Adams
Divided Column
1952
Holly (wood)
34.5 x 14.5 x 15 cm
Donated by Joyce and Michael Morris
31548

Robert Adams
Pierced Relief
1952
Mahogany
18 x 33 x 20 cm
Donated by Joyce and Michael Morris
31586

Robert Adams
Conic Form
1952–53
Teak
10 x 11.5 x 13 cm
Donated by Joyce and Michael Morris
31549

Robert Adams
Curved Relief / Pierced Relief
1952–53
Wood
21 x 17.5 x 11.5 cm
Donated by Joyce and Michael Morris
31542

Robert Adams
Counterbalance No. 2
1955
Mahogany
43 x 43 x 22 cm
Donated by Joyce and Michael Morris
31556

Robert Adams
Descending Forms
1955
Engraving on paper
38 x 17 cm unframed
Donated by Joyce and Michael Morris
31621

Robert Adams
Rectangular Forms
1955
Engraving on paper
29.5 x 22.5 cm unframed
Donated by Joyce and Michael Morris
31622

Robert Adams
Horizontal Movement No. 1
1959
Bronzed steel
31 x 50 x 12 cm
Donated by Joyce and Michael Morris
31568

Robert Adams
Emperor Relief
1964
Painted wood
61 x 38 cm
Donated by Joyce and Michael Morris
31603

Robert Adams
Two Curves on a Rectangular Frame
1964
Painted steel
31 x 25.5 x 4.5 cm
Donated by Joyce and Michael Morris
31544

Yaacov Agam (b.1928)
Movement on White
c.1955–66
Perspex, plastic and wood
39 x 39 x 9.2 cm
Donated by Joyce and Michael Morris
31702

Joost Baljeu (1925–1991)
Synthetic Wall Construction
1964
Wood and paint
114 x 60 x 31 cm
Purchased 1969
31154

Wilhelmina Barns-Graham
(1912–2004)
Olive Green Squares on Vermillion
1968
Oil on canvas
90.7 x 121 cm unframed
Presented by the Wilhelmina Barns-Graham Trust with Art Fund support

Rana Begum (b.1977)
No. 670 Mesh Installation
2016
Powder-coated galvanised steel
Dimensions variable
On long loan from the artist

Rana Begum
No. 684, L Fold
2016
Paint on mirror finish stainless steel
148 x 102 x 47 cm
Purchased with support from Arts Council England / V&A Purchase Grant Fund; Art Fund; and the Sainsbury Centre Founding Friends
31532

Richard Bell (b.1955)
Untitled
1990
Screenprint on paper
21 x 29.6 cm unframed
Purchased 1991
31311

Richard Bell
Untitled
1991
Screenprint on paper
29.7 x 21 cm unframed
Purchased 1991
31312

Charles Biederman (1906–2004)
Untitled 3
1936
Gouache on paper
59 x 43 cm unframed
Purchased 1969
31156

Max Bill (1908–1994)
Three Equal Volumes
1969
Perspex
48 x 25 x 25 cm
Purchased 1969
31157

Max Bill
Silkscreen in 4 colours
1970
Screenprint on paper
70 x 49.5 cm
Anonymous gift, 1971
31158

Dominic Boreham (b.1944)
IM 36(2) Po.5, 16.VIII.78
(interference matrix)
1978
Ink on paper
38.5 x 38.5 cm unframed
Purchased 1992
31317

Dominic Boreham
Stos 8/1, 26.V.78
(solid transparent overlay study)
1978
Ink on paper
40 x 39.5 cm unframed
Purchased 1992
31316

list of works

Dominic Boreham
Stos 10/1, 31.V.78
(solid/transparent overlay study)
1978
Ink on paper
71 x 70 cm framed
Given by the artist, 1993
31338

Anthony Caro (1924–2013)
Table Sculpture CCCLXXI
1977
Steel, rusted and varnished
83.2 x 128.2 cm
Given by the artist, 1978
31168

Lynn Chadwick (1914–2003)
Hollow Men
1951
Copper, brass and iron
105 x 33.5 x 20 cm
Donated by Robert and Lisa Sainsbury,
1973
104

Nicole Charlett (b.1957)
(Dis)Placements: Corner Locus
No. 1
1989
Oil on canvas
Each canvas 60 x 40 cm
Purchased 1991
31310

Jocelyn Chewett (1906–1979)
Untitled
1949
Limestone
22 x 12.5 x 14 cm
Given by the artist's family, 1982
31276C

Jocelyn Chewett
Untitled
1950
Limestone
59 x 16.5 x 12.5 cm
Given by the artist's family, 1982
31276B

Jocelyn Chewett
Construction
1965
Painted wood
12 x 6.5 x 6.5 cm
Given by the artist's family, 1982
31276Z

Lubna Chowdhary (b.1964)
'Switch' Series 2: Number 2
2020
Graph paper, adhesive paper and
acrylic
105 x 75 cm unframed
Purchased with support from the Art
Fund, 2021
31711

Lubna Chowdhary
'Switch' Series 2: Number 4
2020
Graph paper, adhesive paper and
acrylic
105 x 75 cm unframed
Purchased with support from the Art
Fund, 2021
31712

Lygia Clark (1920–1988)
LC2
1969
Aluminium
25.4 x 25.4 x 25.4 cm (variable)
Purchased 1970
31169B

Lygia Clark
LC3
1969
Aluminium
25.4 x 25.4 x 25.4 cm (variable)
Purchased 1970
31169C

Harold Cohen (1928–2016)
Untitled computer-generated
drawing
1983
Ink on paper
68.5 x 68.5 cm
Donated by Joyce and Michael Morris
31583

Peter Collingwood (1922–2008)
Macrogauze: EX4, M. 178
c.1978
Linen, steel and aluminium
185 x 88 cm
Donated by Robert and Lisa Sainsbury,
1985
902

Peter Collingwood
Macrogauze: EX2, M. 180
c.1980
Linen, steel and aluminium
154 x 74 cm
Bequeathed by Lady Sainsbury, 2014
900

Robyn Denny (1930–2014)
Six Miniatures III (Green)
1975
Screenprint on paper
71 x 96.5 cm
Formerly in the Picture Loan Scheme
31419

Norman Dilworth (b.1931)
1, 2, 3, 4, 5
1999
Stained wood
50 x 105 x 65 cm
Purchased with support from the V&A
Purchase Fund, 1999
31407

Natalie Dower (b.1931)
Dudeney Oyster No. 2
1985–2019
Oil on wood
27 x 33 x 33 cm
Donated by the artist
31641

Natalie Dower
Blue / Green Dudeney Relief
1989
Oil on wood
20 x 30 cm
Donated by the artist
31640

Natalie Dower
Square Root Two Spirals Nine
Moves
2015
Oil on linen
60 x 85 cm
Donated by the artist
31639

John Ernest (1922–1994)
Relief: Triangular Motif II
1959
Formica, aluminium, wood and
hardboard
42 x 45 x 7.5 cm
Donated by Joyce and Michael Morris
31573

John Ernest
Linear Relief II
1964
Wood, aluminium and Perspex
76 x 60.7 x 4.2 cm
Donated by Joyce and Michael Morris
31543

John Ernest
Mosaic Relief III
1964
Aluminium and Formica on
cellulose-sprayed board
100.5 x 111 x 10 cm
Donated by Joyce and Michael Morris
31547

John Ernest
Sketch for Mosaic Relief IV
c.1966
Pencil and ink on paper
25.55 x 35.5 cm
Donated by Joyce and Michael Morris
31625

Matthew Frère-Smith (1923–1999)
Double Khombic
1965
Aluminium
81.5 x 81.5 x 81.5 cm
Purchased 1969
31178

Matthew Frère-Smith
Octahedron
1965
Ink on paper
25 x 25 cm unframed
Purchased 1969
31179

Matthew Frère-Smith
Maquette for Tenso Structure
1966
Aluminium and steel wire
66 x 58 x 58 cm
Purchased 1970
31181B

Stephen Gilbert (1910–2007)
Construction
1954
Painted aluminium
91.3 x 31 x 45.8 cm
Purchased 1972
31183

Stephen Gilbert
House model 'Néovision'
1955
Aluminium, steel and paint
16 x 36.4 x 38 cm
Purchased 1982
31271

Stephen Gilbert and Peter Stead
(1922–1999)
House Néovision
c.1955
Ink on paper
56 x 76 cm
Gift from a private donor
31329C

Stephen Gilbert
Structure 12 B
1961
Aluminium
34 x 65 x 35 cm
Donated by Joyce and Michael Morris
31158

Adrian Heath (1920–1992)
Growth of Forms
1951
Oil on canvas
1125 x 50.9 cm
Gift of Grace Barratt, through the Alumni
Association
31337

Adrian Heath
Composition: Red and Black
1954–55
Oil on canvas
86 x 61 cm
Purchased with support from the V&A
Purchase Fund, 1977
31188

Anthony Hill (1930–2020)
Reconstructed by Richard Plank
(b.1951)
1953–54 (1982 reconstruction)
Catenary Rhythms
Paint and ink on board
61.6 x 122.7 cm unframed
Gift from the artist, 1983
31301

Anthony Hill
Progression of Rectangles,
Version II
1954–59
Wood, Perspex and brass
40.5 x 40.5 x 4.5 cm
Donated by Joyce and Michael Morris
31539

Anthony Hill
Relief Construction
1956–60
Perspex, aluminium and plywood
30.5 x 48.5 x 4 cm
Donated by Joyce and Michael Morris
31557

Anthony Hill
Prime Rhythms
1958–62
PVC, wood and Perspex
50 x 50 x 4.5 cm
Donated by Joyce and Michael Morris
31602

Anthony Hill
Five Regions Relief
1960–62
Aluminium, wood and Perspex
61 x 54.9 x 9 cm
Purchased 1975
31193

Anthony Hill
Five Regions Relief
1960–62
Aluminium, wood and Perspex
65 x 63.5 x 6.5 cm
Donated by Joyce and Michael Morris
31541

Anthony Hill
Co-Structure, Version 3, Hommage
à Roberto Frucht
1970–75
Welded stainless steel
60 x 127 x 100.5 cm
Donated by Joyce and Michael Morris
31599

Anthony Hill
Parity Study No. 2
1970
Photoprint on aluminium
62.5 x 25.5 x 35.5 cm framed
Donated by Joyce and Michael Morris
31578

Anthony Hill
The Nine – Hommage à
Khlebnikov No. 2
1976
Laminated plastic on aluminium
92 x 91.5 x 3 cm
Donated by Joyce and Michael Morris
31540

Malcolm Hughes (1920–1997)
Rational Concepts
1977
Screenprint on paper
59.8 x 59.8 unframed
Donated by Joyce and Michael Morris
31585

Tess Jaray (b.1937)
Tamlin
1971–72
Acrylic on canvas
152.5 x 213 cm
Gift from East England Arts, 2002
31416

Michael Kidner (1917–2009)
Colour and Tone Wave
1967
Acrylic on canvas
102 x 768 cm
Donated by Joyce and Michael Morris
31535

Michael Kidner
Sussex
1967
Lithograph on paper
44.2 x 60.2 cm
Donated by Joyce and Michael Morris
31605

Michael Kidner
Intersection
1992
Fibreglass, rubber, paint, metal,
elastic and wood
152 x 152 x 43 cm
Purchased with support from the V&A
Purchase Fund, 1993
31321

John Law (b.1941)
Square Root of 2 Construction
1983
Steel, MDF, Formica and paint
80 x 80 cm
Gift from the Contemporary Art Society,
1986
31293

Richard Paul Lohse (1902–1988)
Four coloured groups
c.1952–66
Silkscreen on paper
45 x 45.2 cm unframed
Given by the artist, 1969
31205

Richard Paul Lohse
Movement of four contrasting
groups to one centre
c.1952–65
Silkscreen on paper
48 x 45 cm unframed
Given by the artist, 1969
31204

Richard Paul Lohse
Six systematic colour movements
from yellow to yellow
1955–56
Oil on linen
180 x 30 cm
Purchased 1969
31202

Peter Lowe (b.1938)
Relief, Series A, No. 10
1974
MDF, paint and melamine
50.8 x 50.8 x 8 cm
Purchased with support from the V&A
Purchase Fund, 1976
31206

Kenneth Martin (1905–1984)
Screw Mobile
1953
Brass and mild steel
83.5 x 18 x 18 cm
Donated by Joyce and Michael Morris
31560

Kenneth Martin
Mobile Reflector, Elliptic Motif
1955
Steel, duralumin and aluminium
70 x 96 x 75 cm
Donated by Joyce and Michael Morris
31571

Kenneth Martin
Variable Screw
1967
Brass
33 x 34.5 x 34.5 cm
Purchased 1968
31208

Kenneth Martin
Black Sixes
1967–68
Oil on canvas
140 x 152.5 cm
Purchased 1968
31207

Kenneth Martin
Chance and Order III
1972
Screenprint on paper
68.8 x 68.7 cm
Donated by Joyce and Michael Morris
31567

Kenneth Martin
Chance, Order, Change
1981
Ink, pencil and gouache on paper
42.2 x 30 cm unframed
Donated by Joyce and Michael Morris
31609

Kenneth Martin
Chance, Order, Change –
Sheaves: Commences, Becomes
1982
Ink, pencil and gouache on paper
42.3 x 30.2 cm unframed
Donated by Joyce and Michael Morris
31601

Kenneth Martin
Chance, Order, Change: Time
Sequence 1, 10 Days in June
1983
Ink, pencil and gouache on paper
31 x 43 cm unframed
Donated by Joyce and Michael Morris
31608

Mary Martin (1907–1969)
Climbing Form
1957
Plywood, Perspex and steel
36 x 7 x 7 cm
Donated by Joyce and Michael Morris
31631

Mary Martin
Pierced Relief
1959
Wood and Perspex
30 x 39.5 x 8 cm
Donated by Joyce and Michael Morris
31562

Mary Martin
White-Faced Relief
1959
Wood, plywood, paint, plastic and
white PMMA
64 x 94.5 x 11.5 cm
Purchased 1968
31209

Mary Martin
Rotation
1968
Polystyrene and mirror glass
13 x 13 x 9 cm
Donated by Joyce and Michael Morris
31589

Vera Molnár (b.1924)
Twenty-five Squares
1989
Ink on paper
50 x 50 cm unframed
Purchased with support from the V&A
Purchase Fund, 1991
31319A

Vera Molnár
Twenty-five Squares
1989
Ink on paper
50 x 50 cm unframed
Purchased with support from the V&A
Purchase Fund, 1991
31319B

Vera Molnár
Twenty-five Squares
1989
Ink on paper
50 x 50 cm unframed
Purchased with support from the V&A
Purchase Fund, 1991
31319C

Vera Molnár
Twenty-five Squares
1989
Ink on paper
50 x 50 cm unframed
Purchased with support from the V&A
Purchase Fund, 1991
31319D

François Morellet (1926–2016)
Sphère-trame
1962
Stainless steel
45 x 45 x 45 cm
Purchased with support from the V&A
Purchase Fund, 1981
31268

Simon Nicholson (1934–1990)
Sculpture No. 6902
c.1960–70s
Plastic and polystyrene balls
185.5 x 71 x 71 cm
Bequest, 1990
31339

Simon Nicholson
6303
1963
Acrylic and rubber on paper
14 x 9.8 x 2 cm unframed
Bequest from Lady Sainsbury, 2014
L55

Victor Pasmore (1908–1998)
Transparent Relief Construction in
Black, White and Ochre
1956–57
Plywood, paint and PMMA
68.5 x 79 x 17.5 cm
Purchased with support from the V&A
Purchase Fund, 1988
31296

Ernest Race (1913–1964)
Antelope Chair
1951
Steel rod, aluminium, plywood
and paint
81 x 54 x 46 cm
Anonymous gift, 1985
31303

Ernest Race
Springbok Chair
1951
Stove enamelled mild steel rod
with aluminium and PVC
Diameter 79 x width 55.5 x
circumference 64 cm
On loan from a private collection

Merete Rasmussen (b.1974)
Form
2011
Stoneware with blue slip
26 x 36 x 42 cm
Accepted under the Cultural Gifts Scheme
by HM Government from Leslie Birks Hay
and allocated to the Sainsbury Centre,
2016
50765

Eric Snell (b.1953)
Cuneiform III
1978
Aluminium, paint, PVC, resin,
electrical motor and components
236 x 236 x 15 cm
Purchased 1982
31270

Jesús Rafael Soto (1923–2005)
Kinetic Construction
1965
Painted wood and nylon thread
47 x 29 x 13.4 cm
Purchased 1968
31225

Jean Spencer (1942–1998)
Square Relief 4
1968
Wood with PVA
61 x 61 cm
Purchased with support from MLA/V&A
Purchase Grant Fund, 2008
31429

Jean Spencer
Untitled (Green and Blue)
1990
Pastel on paper
71.5 x 71.5 cm framed
Purchased with support from MLA/V&A
Purchase Grant Fund, 2008
31430

Jeffrey Steele (1931–2021)
Syntagma Sg III 104
1992
Oil on linen
61 x 61 cm
Loan from the estate of Jeffrey Steele

Peter Stroud (1921–2012)
Relief
1957
Metal and Perspex
60.8 x 61 x 4.8 cm
Donated by Joyce and Michael Morris
31704

Peter Stroud (1921–2012)
Transparent Relief
1958
Copper, plastic, canvas board and
Perspex
48.5 x 61 x 5 cm
Donated by Joyce and Michael Morris
31706

Trevor Sutton (b.1948)
Painting A
1980
Oil and acrylic on canvas
95 x 171 cm
Gift from the Contemporary Art Society,
1983
31274

Takis (1925–2019)
Signals Series II
1968
Steel, tubular chrome-plated steel,
acrylic, electrical components and
glass
202 x 25 x 25 cm
Purchased 1968
31234

Jean Tinguely (1925–1991)
For Statics
1959
Ink on paper
16.5 x 21.5 cm unframed
Donated by Joyce and Michael Morris
31628

Michael Tyzack (1933–2007)
Nickel Yard
1967
Acrylic on canvas
122 x 64.5 cm
Donated by Joyce and Michael Morris
31570

Victor Vasarely (1906–1997)
Tlinco
1956
Screenprint on paper
66 x 50.5 cm unframed
Purchased 1968
31238

Victor Vasarely
Planetary Folklore Participants
No. 1
1969
Polystyrene, metal and magnets
52.8 x 52.8 x 2.5 cm
Purchased 1970
31237

Mary Webb (b.1939)
Circle Line Series: The Isle of
Manhattan 9
1983
Screenprint on paper
30.5 x 30.5 cm
Donated by Mary Webb, 2012
50510

Mary Webb
Circle Line Series: The Isle of
Manhattan 2
1984
Screenprint on paper
30.5 x 30.5 cm
Donated by Mary Webb, 2012
50509

Mary Webb
Fritton
1971
Oil on canvas
152.5 x 152.5 cm
Gift from East England Arts, 2002
31417

Stephen Willats (b.1943)
Visual Automatic No. 1
1964–65
Wood, paint, Perspex, electrical
components and mixed media
219 x 219 x 26.5 cm
Loan courtesy the artist and Victoria Miro

Gillian Wise (1936–2020)
Black and White Relief with Prisms
1961
Perspex, glass and Formica
38 x 66 x 7 cm
Donated by Joyce and Michael Morris
31592

Gillian Wise
Relief: Sixfold progression on two
planes
1968–69
Perspex, elastic, metal pegs and
hardboard
61 x 91 x 7.2 cm
Purchased 1969
31243

Gillian Wise
Net 1, Peano closed
1975
Screenprint on paper
32 x 32 cm unframed
Donated by Joyce and Michael Morris
31614

Gillian Wise
Net 2, Peano open
1975
Screenprint on paper
32 x 32 cm unframed
Donated by Joyce and Michael Morris
31617

Gillian Wise
Net 3, Tiré à
1975
Screenprint on paper
32 x 32 cm unframed
Donated by Joyce and Michael Morris
31615

Gillian Wise
Quatre Épingles
1975
Screenprint on paper
32 x 32 cm unframed
Donated by Joyce and Michael Morris
31616

Gillian Wise
Textum Ars
1991
Digital drawings
Dimensions variable
Given by the artist, 1991
31320A

Gillian Wise
Textum Ars
1991
Digital drawings
Dimensions variable
Given by the artist, 1991
31320B

Li Yuan-Chia (1929–1994)
Cosmic Point Multiple
1968
Steel, styrofoam, cellulose paint
and barrium ferrite
91 x 91 x 2 cm
Purchased 1968
31245

Li Yuan-Chia
Double-Sided Black and White
Magnetic Relief
1969
Steel, wood, magnets and paint
61 x 91.5 x 5 cm
Purchased 1969
31244

Signals Newsbulletin
Volume 1: Number 8, June–July
1965
Donated by Joyce and Michael Morris

**Soundings Three at Signals
London**
Signals Gallery, 1966
Invitation card
Donated by Joyce and Michael Morris

Construction England
Arts Council, 1963
Exhibition leaflet
Donated by Joyce and Michael Morris

Structures Vivantes
Redfern Gallery, 1964
Invitation card
Donated by Joyce and Michael Morris

**Construction: England: 1950–
1960**
Drian Galleries, 1961
Exhibition leaflet
Donated by Joyce and Michael Morris

Denise René in London
Redfern Gallery, 1968
Exhibition catalogue
Donated by Joyce and Michael Morris

THIS BOOK CELEBRATES the planned bequest (1984) of over 200 works from Joyce and Michael Morris. The bequest was honoured after the passing of Joyce Morris in 2015 at the age of 93 after Michael Morris' death in 2009. David Ellis, Director of Development at UEA, was instrumental in honouring the wishes of Joyce and Michael Morris along with his colleague Joyce Griffin (Development and Legacy Manager). Our former colleagues Alastair Grieve and Veronica Sekules were both key agents in securing the bequest and for developing the collection of abstract and constructed art since its inception in 1968. The driving forces behind the formation of the abstract art collection were Willi Guttsman (University Librarian) and Peter Lasko (Professor in the school of the History of Art). We now have a wonderful collection and a legacy of research from which to draw at UEA, plus the research happening elsewhere that is included in this publication. Thank you to Jon Wood and Andrew Bick for contributing such wonderful essays.

We are grateful to Andrew Johnson for his beautiful book design and the exhibition graphic design. Hannah Wooller and Daniel Swift Gibbs of Hudson Architects conceived a dramatic exhibition design. New photography was undertaken by Denisa Ilie. The book was expertly copyedited and indexed by Brenda Stones.

Exhibitions and publications like these can only be achieved through the help and support of a wide range of people. We would like to thank personally those artists included in the show that are still creating work, many of whom have shared their own knowledge in the area with us. These are Yaacov Agam, Rana Begum, Richard Bell, Dominic Boreham, Nicole Charlett, Lubna Chowdhary, Norman Dilworth, Natalie Dower, Tess Jaray, John Law, Peter Lowe, Vera Molnár, Merete Rasmussen, Eric Snell, Trevor Sutton, Mary Webb and Stephen Willats. We are grateful to Rob Airey and the Barns-Graham Charitable Trust who agreed to donate an important painting by Wilhelmina Barns-Graham to the collection, which is illustrated in this publication, and to Victoria Miro Gallery for facilitating the inclusion of work by Stephen Willats. Paul Martin, the son of Kenneth and Mary Martin, has been as supportive as ever.

A number of our colleagues have worked on preparing the works for exhibition and publication. Over the last year, we undertook a conservation project concerning the Morris Bequest, led by Conservator Maria Ledinskaya. This conservation was generously funded by the Pilgrim Trust, the Henry Moore Foundation and the Gabo Trust. Lisa Newby was the Project Curator on the exhibition and supported our research into the Morris archive. Further thanks go to Conservation Technician Laura Robinson and Paper Conservator Rebecca Hawthorne. Thom Haley facilitated new photography. Thanks also to Executive Director Paul Greenhalgh and Acting Director Ghislaine Wood for their support and commenting on early versions of essays.

As ever, we would like to acknowledge the support of David Sainsbury, Baron Sainsbury of Turville, the son of our founding benefactors, Robert and Lisa Sainsbury, for his continued support. We would also like to thank the Sainsbury Centre Board, Pro Vice Chancellor Sarah Barrow and the Vice Chancellor, Professor David Richardson. □
Tania Moore and Calvin Winner

acknowledgements

ANDREW BICK is an artist, curator and writer who researches Systems and Constructionism. Recent solo exhibitions include Museum Haus Konstruktiv (2017), Hales Gallery (2018) and Galerie von Bartha (2019). A monograph on his work was published by Hatje Canz Verlag/Haus Konstruktiv (December 2020).

TANIA MOORE is the Joyce and Michael Morris Chief Curator at the Sainsbury Centre and curator of *Rhythm and Geometry: Constructivist art in Britain since 1951*. She has published on artists including Leiko Ikemura, Elisabeth Frink, Magdalene Odundo and Henry Moore. In 2018 she received the Art Fund New Collecting Award to acquire sculptors' drawings by contemporary women artists for the Sainsbury Centre collection.

CALVIN WINNER is Head of Collections at the Sainsbury Centre. He has a specialist interest in twentieth-century and contemporary art. He has written about, curated and co-curated exhibitions concerning Bill Viola, Thomas Houseago, John Hedgecoe, Francis Bacon, Alberto Giacometti, Antony Gormley, Rana Begum, Elisabeth Frink and the writer W.G. Sebald. In recent times, he has led on creating a Sculpture Park for the Sainsbury Centre across the campus of the University of East Anglia.

DR JON WOOD is an art historian and curator, specialising in modern and contemporary sculpture. He worked for many years for the Henry Moore Foundation and as an editor of the *Sculpture Journal*. He has published widely on the European avant-garde and edited collections including *Contemporary Sculpture: Artists' Writings and Interviews* (2020) and *Modern Sculpture Reader* (2012). His published work on Constructivism includes essays on the work of Mary Martin and Stephen Gilbert and long interviews with Gillian Wise and Norman Dilworth.

author biographies

Titles below are listed in sequence of date.

Naum Gabo and Antoine Pevsner, 'The Realistic Manifesto', 1920, published in Charles Harrison and Paul Wood, *Art in Theory 1900–2000: An Anthology of Changing Ideas* (Oxford, Malden and Carlton: Blackwell Publishing, new edn 8, 2007)

Naum Gabo, Ben Nicholson and Leslie Martin (eds), *Circle: International Survey of Constructive Art* (London: Faber and Faber, 1937)

Charles Biederman, *Art as the Evolution of Visual Knowledge* (Minnesota: self-published, 1948)

Adrian Heath, *Abstract Painting: Its Origins and Meaning* (London: Alec Tiranti, 1953)

Lawrence Alloway, *Nine Abstract Artists: Their Work and Theory* (London: Alec Tiranti, 1954)

Lawrence Alloway, Reyner Banham and David Lewis, *This is Tomorrow* (London: Whitechapel Art Gallery, 1956)

Alan Bowness, *Construction England* (London: Arts Council of Great Britain, 1963)

William Seitz, *The Responsive Eye* (New York: MoMA, 1965)

Alastair Grieve, *Art and the Machine* (Norwich: University of East Anglia, 1968)

Anthony Hill (ed.), *Directions in Art, Theory and Aesthetics: An anthology* (London: Faber and Faber, 1968)

George Rickey, *Constructivism: Origins and Evolution* (London: Studio Vista, 1968)

Stephen Bann, *Experimental Painting: construction, abstraction, destruction, reduction* (London: Studio Vista, 1970)

Norbert Lynton and Stephen Bann, *Systems* (London: Arts Council of Great Britain, 1972)

Stephen Bann (ed.), *The Tradition of Constructivism* (London: Thames & Hudson, 1974)

Stephen Bann, *Constructive Context* (London: Arts Council of Great Britain, 1978)

Gerhard von Graevenitz, *Pier + Ocean: Construction in the Art of the Seventies* (London: Arts Council of Great Britain, 1980)

Alastair Grieve, *Anthony Hill* (London: Arts Council, 1983)

Joanna Drew and Ann Jones, *The Non-Objective World* (London: South Bank Centre, 1992)

Tam Giles et al., *Countervail* (Sheffield: Mappin Art Gallery, 1992)

Alastair Grieve, *The Sculpture of Robert Adams* (London: Lund Humphries, 1992)

Veronica Sekules (ed.), *The University of East Anglia Collection of Abstract and Constructivist Art, Architecture and Design* (Norwich: University of East Anglia, 1994)

Margaret Garlake, *New Art New World: British art in postwar society* (New Haven and London: Yale University Press, 1998)

Alan Fowler and Brandon Taylor, *Elements of Abstraction: space, line and interval in modern British art* (Southampton: Southampton City Art Gallery, 2005)

Alastair Grieve, *Constructed Abstract Art in England: A Neglected Avant-Garde* (New Haven and London: Yale University Press, 2005)

Celia Davies and Sarah Martin, *Kenneth Martin and Mary Martin: Constructed Works* (London: Camden Arts Centre, 2007)

Alan Fowler, *A Rational Aesthetic: the Systems Group and associated artists* (Southampton: Southampton City Art Gallery, 2008)

Gladys Fabre and Doris Wintgens Hötte (eds), *Van Doesburg and the International Avant-garde* (London: Tate Publishing, 2009)

Alastair Grieve (ed.), *Victor Pasmore: Writings and Interviews* (London: Tate Publishing, 2010)

Concrete Parallels/Concretos Paralelos: British Constructivism and Brazilian Concrete and Neo-Concrete Art (São Paulo: Cultura Inglese, 2012)

Brandon Taylor, *After Constructivism* (London and New Haven: Yale University Press, 2014)

Neil Walker (ed.), *Victor Pasmore: Towards a New Reality* (London and Nottingham: Lund Humphries in association with Djanogly Gallery, Nottingham Lakeside Arts, 2016)

Sam Cornish, *Kaleidoscope: Colour and Sequence in 1960s British Art* (London: Hayward Publishing, 2017)

Laurent Delaye, *British Constructivism: The Catherine Petitgas Collection* (Chichester: Pallant House, 2017)

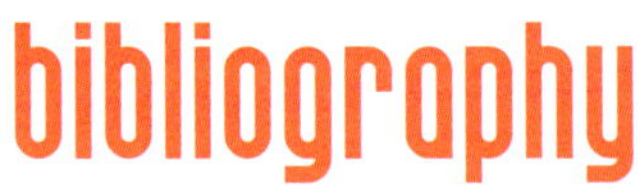

Every effort has been made to seek permission to reproduce the images in this book. We are grateful to the individuals and institutions who have assisted us in this task. Any omissions are unintentional.

Unless otherwise stated, all images are courtesy Sainsbury Centre.

© 1990 Richard Bell: 80

Architectural Press Archive / RIBA Collections: 22, 105

Courtesy Wilhelmina Barns-Graham Trust: 12

DACS 2021: 2, 16, 26, 41, 42, 44, 45, 46 (top), 49 (right), 54, 55, 69, 90, 93, 115, 116, 129, 136–137, 152

DACS 2021. Photo Denisa Ilie: 1, 8, 21, 24, 27, 38 (top and bottom), 40, 66 (bottom), 67, 103, 107, 108, 124 (top and bottom)

© Estate of Jeffrey Steele. Photo Ben Deakin: 135

© Estate of Kenneth and Mary Martin: 35, 75, 76, 97 (top)

© Estate of Kenneth and Mary Martin. Photo Denisa Ilie: 11, 17, 19, 25, 62–63, 64, 97 (bottom), 98, 100, 101

© Estate of Lynn Chadwick: 23

© Estate of Michael Kidner: 49 (left), 119

© Estate of the artist: 29, 36, 72, 84, 126 (top and bottom), 127, 128

© Estate of the artist. Photo Denisa Ilie: 14–15, 28, 56, 66 (top), 102, 117, 132

© Gilbert Weikert Family: 39, 65, 70, 71, 74 (top and bottom)

© Gilbert Weikert Family. Photo Denisa Ilie: 37

John Maltby / RIBA Collections: 86–87, 89, 95

Martin Charles / RIBA Collections: 122

© Merete Rasmussen: 60

© Natalie Dower. Courtesy of Eagle Gallery / EMH Arts, London: 51, 52, 112–113, 118

© Nicole Charlett: 53

© Lubna Chowdhary. Courtesy the artist and Jhaveri Contemporary: 58

Photographer unknown: 10, 20, 33

© Rana Begum and Marina Tabassum. Photo Brotherton-Lock: 110

© Rana Begum. Photo Thierry Bal: 131

RIBA Collections: 91

© Stephen Willats. Courtesy the artist and Victoria Miro: 32

© Takis Foundation: 47

© the artist: cover, inside gatefold, 6, 30, 31, 34, 43, 57, 81, 82, 130

© the artist. Photo Denisa Ilie: 120

© The World of Lygia Clark Cultural Association: inside covers, 46 (bottom)

photographic credits

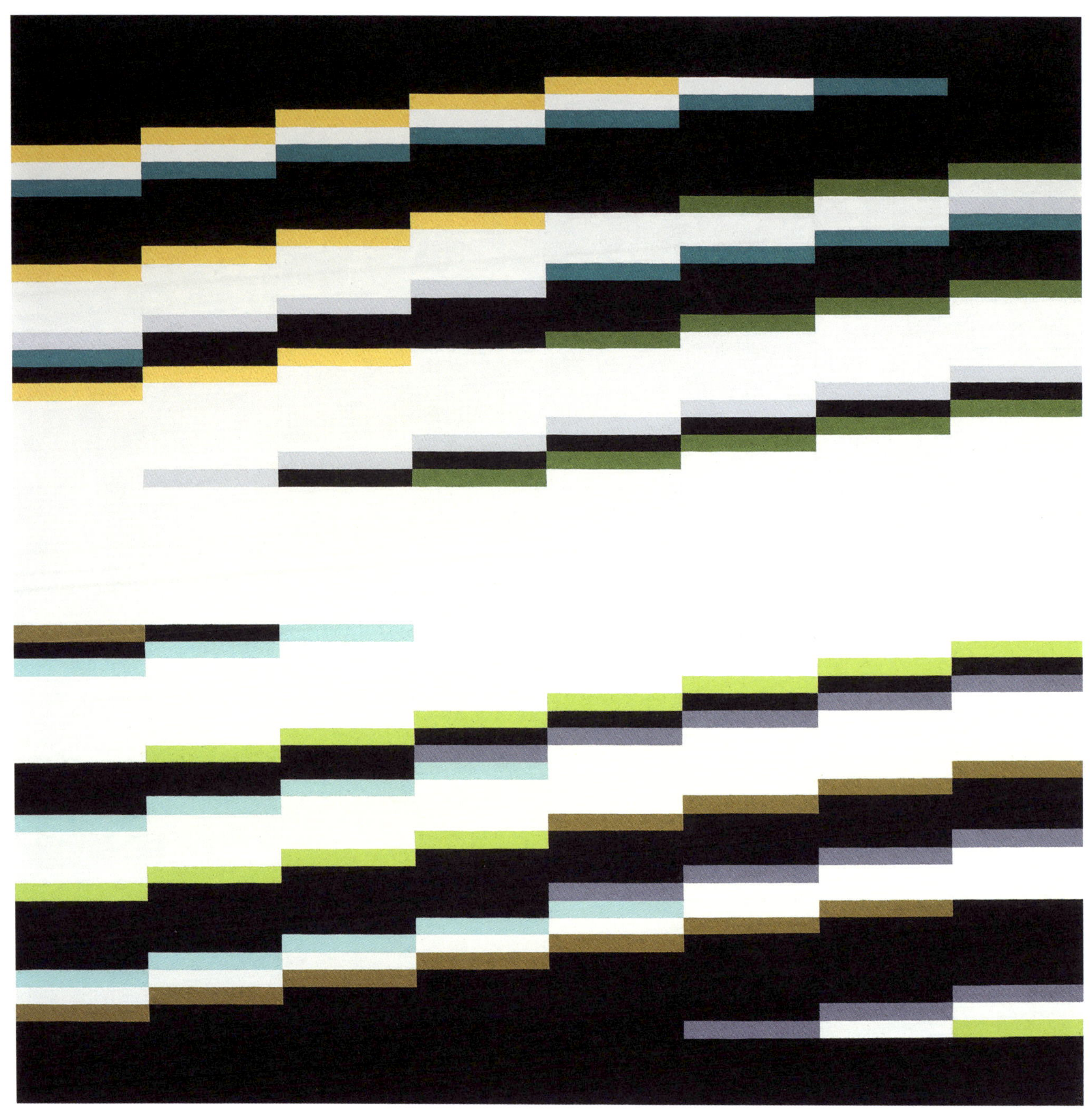

↑ Jeffrey Steele
Syntagma Sg III 104
1992
Oil on linen
Loan from the estate of
Jeffrey Steele

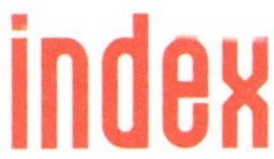

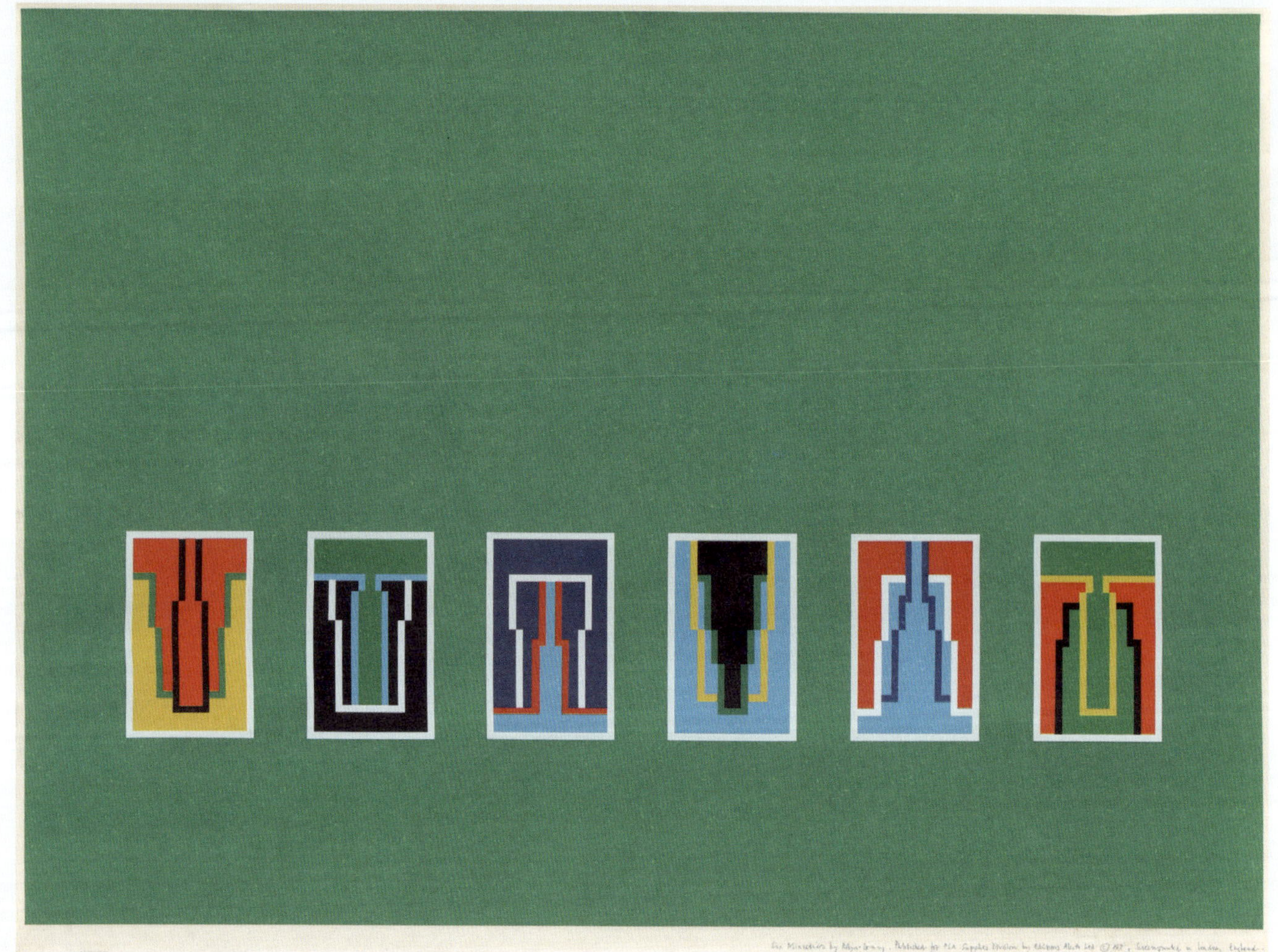

↑ Robyn Denny
Six Miniatures III (Green)
1975
Screenprint on paper
Sainsbury Centre